## The Novels of Thomas Bernhard

Thomas Bernhard (1931–1989) is one of the most important writers of the postwar period, not only in his native Austria, but throughout Europe. Almost all his works have been translated into English, and his novels, plays, and non-fiction works have won international acclaim. The present study provides an accessible introduction to Bernhard's novels for an English-speaking readership, and also makes an original contribution to the ongoing debate on this fascinating author. The book's primary emphasis is on Bernhard's later fiction, but it also explicates the early texts of the 1960s and 1970s. The book makes use of insights from recent approaches to fiction that pay attention to what can be termed "narrative dynamics." Earlier studies of Bernhard have tended to remain within the descriptive framework established in narrative studies of the 1950s and 1960s; this book views Bernhard's prose works from a more nuanced vantage point.

Jonathan Long is lecturer in German at the University of Durham, UK.

*Studies in German Literature, Linguistics, and Culture*

Edited by James Hardin
(*South Carolina*)

# THE NOVELS OF THOMAS BERNHARD

---

## FORM AND ITS FUNCTION

### J. J. LONG

CAMDEN HOUSE

First published 2001
by Camden House

Camden House is an imprint of Boydell & Brewer Inc.
PO Box 41026, Rochester, NY 14604–4126 USA
and of Boydell & Brewer Limited
PO Box 9, Woodbridge, Suffolk IP12 3DF, UK

ISBN: 1–57113–224–4

Library of Congress Cataloging-in-Publication Data

Long, J. J. (Jonathan James), 1969–
    The novels of Thomas Bernhard: form and its function / J. J. Long.
       p. cm. – (Studies in German literature, linguistics, and culture)
    Includes bibliographical references and index.
    ISBN 1–57113–224–4 (alk. paper)
    1. Bernhard, Thomas — Criticism and interpretation. I. Title. II. Series.

PT2662.E7 Z772 2001
833'.914—dc21
                                                        2001023092

A catalogue record for this title is available from the British Library.

This publication is printed on acid-free paper.
Printed in the United States of America

# Contents

# Acknowledgements

M UCH OF THE initial work on this book was undertaken during a period of doctoral research at the University of Nottingham. My first debt of thanks is to my supervisor, Professor J. H. Reid, for giving unstintingly of his time, expertise, and advice throughout my postgraduate studies. Thanks are also due to all the teachers, friends, and colleagues whose contribution to this book has been less quantifiable but no less valuable. In particular, I would like to acknowledge the help of Elizabeth Boa, Steve Giles, Peter Knight, Greg Bond, Herwig Engelmann and Alexander Irmer. I am also indebted to two anonymous readers at Camden House for their careful reading of the draft MS.

Visits abroad were facilitated by research grants from the British Academy, the Renate Gunn Travel Scholarship of the University of Nottingham, the DAAD, and the University of Durham. This book has been published with the generous assistance of the University of Durham.

Parts of chapters 2 and 3 of this study first appeared in *Seminar*, vol. 37, number 1, February 2001, pages 33–52. I am grateful to the editor of that periodical for permission to reprint the material here.

For her love and her continuing role in the plot, I would like to say a big thank you to Marita. Finally, thanks are due to my parents, whose love and support represent a debt that I can never truly repay. It is to them that I wish to dedicate this book.

Jonathan J. Long
Durham, 2000

# Introduction

## Thomas Bernhard: A Destroyer of Stories?

I N THE TWENTY-FIVE YEARS between the publication of his first novel, *Frost* (1963), and the performance of his last stage play, *Heldenplatz* (1988), Thomas Bernhard came to be acknowledged as one of Austria's most important postwar writers. He was honored with numerous literary prizes, both within the German-speaking world and across Europe: the Georg-Büchner-Preis and Bremer Literaturpreis in Germany, the Premio Prato and Premio Mondello in Italy, the Prix Séguier and Prix Medici in France, and a host of other, minor prizes. In his native Austria he was awarded the Kleiner Österreichischer Staatspreis für Literatur, the Anton-Wildgans-Preis, the Franz-Theodor-Csokor-Preis, and — the award most valued by Bernhard himself — the Grillparzer-Preis. His untimely death in February 1989, at the age of fifty-eight, cut short a career that had also been extraordinarily productive: eighteen full-length plays, two volumes of one-acters, five volumes of autobiography, several collections of stories, and sixteen longer stories and novels.

Despite this vast creative output, however, Bernhard was strangely reticent about making programmatic statements on aesthetics. Unlike his compatriot Peter Handke, he did not carry out overt polemical attacks on the literary establishment in order to justify his own artistic practice, nor did he accept a university post as writer in residence. He also never delivered the prestigious "Frankfurter Poetik-Vorlesungen." Bernhard's most significant comments on poetics can be found in the short text "Drei Tage." In June 1970, the Austrian director Ferry Radax shot a film called *Der Italiener,* whose screenplay had been adapted by Bernhard from his own short story of the same name.[1] In lieu of the interview that Radax requested but Bernhard refused to give, the author was filmed sitting on a park bench in Hamburg, delivering a monologue in which he expounded his thoughts on narrative, the business of literary creation, and his "Selbstverständnis" as a writer. The shooting took three days (hence the title), and the transcript of the monologues was published as a kind of appendix to *Der Italiener* in 1971.

One famous and oft-quoted statement from "Drei Tage" concerns Bernhard's relationship to traditional modes of storytelling:

> Andererseits bin ich natürlich auch kein heiterer Autor, kein Geschichtenerzähler, Geschichten hasse ich im Grunde. Ich bin ein *Geschichtenzerstörer, ich bin der typische Geschichtenzerstörer*. In meiner Arbeit, wenn sich irgendwo Anzeichen einer Geschichte bilden, oder wenn ich nur in der Ferne irgendwo hinter einem Prosahügel die Andeutung einer Geschichte auftauchen sehe, schieße ich sie ab. (It 88)

Critics have repeatedly turned to this statement, convinced that it offers an adequate description or explanation of Bernhard's narrative techniques, and glossing it according to their own interpretative priorities.[2] The most sophisticated literary interpretation of the term "Geschichtenzerstörung" is provided by Hermann Helms-Derfert, for whom it refers to Bernhard's emancipation from any form of artistic and social prescription. He also claims, however, that the most advanced modernist writers had already abandoned the "organic" work of art "als sie sich von den Fesseln der traditionellen Erzählkunst endgültig befreiten" (1). He goes on to propose that "Geschichtenzerstörung" refers to narrative form as well as other aspects of Bernhard's texts: "Die monologische, dissoziierte Rede des dezentrierten Subjekts, das musikanaloge Sprechen, das die Wörter in Töne zu verwandeln scheint, die Aufhebung traditioneller Gattungsbegriffe oder schließlich die paradoxe Handlungsverläufe, die der Logik der Wirklichkeit widersprechen" (3).

Helms-Derfert's grappling with "Geschichtenzerstörung" is interesting because it illustrates some of the problems that the term entails. As a literary-historical concept, it is inadequate because it does not allow Bernhard's texts to be differentiated from those of authors writing in the earlier part of the twentieth century. Applying "Geschichtenzerstörung" to questions of content and thematics involves turning it into a synonym for antirealism — there is, after all, no reason why nontraditional genre categories or contradictory, nonmimetic action sequences should militate against storytelling as such. When used to characterize the formal properties of Bernhard's texts, on the other hand, it functions only at the most generalized level, which renders it of limited value as an analytical concept. Discussing Bernhard's work in terms of "Geschichtenzerstörung" runs the risk of reducing diverse narrative techniques to a single principle. This, in turn, is problematic because it is extremely imprecise, and because it tends surreptitiously to reinforce the notion of Bernhard's work as a "monolithischen Block" — a notion of which Helms-Derfert is highly critical.

The point is that "Drei Tage" dates from 1970, at a time when Bernhard's major publications consisted of just three novels and the "Erzählungen" *Amras* and *Ungenach*. These latter are the most fragmentary of Bernhard's texts, and the notion of "Geschichtenzerstörung" is more applicable to his early work than to the later fiction. The chapter on *Frost* and *Verstörung* investigates those features of Bernhard's texts which threaten to disintegrate the narrative fabric. Nevertheless, to regard "Geschichtenzerstörung" as an aesthetic *prescription* rather than a mere *description* of Bernhard's previous narrative practice places it under untenable strain, for the later fiction is characterized by considerably less radical narrative fragmentation, and "Geschichtenzerstörung" ceases to function as an adequate descriptive label.

This point was apparently recognized by Ingeborg Hoesterey when she pointed out, in 1988, that Bernhard's subtle and varied narrative techniques had hitherto received little critical attention (117). Although some critics have turned their attention to formal issues in the intervening dozen years,[3] a detailed analysis of Bernhard's narrative strategies remains a significant gap in the existing secondary literature. This book undertakes that analysis. Using narrative theories of primarily French and American provenance, I offer narratological readings of what I perceive to be Bernhard's most interesting and significant fictions. The quantitative emphasis falls on the late (post-1975) work, because it is here that Bernhard demonstrates the greatest skill and subtlety in the manipulation of narrative strategies. Critical attention is devoted to the *functioning* of form within the economy of each individual text.

The book thus represents an endeavor to go "beyond formalism" in the study of narrative. First, it attempts to restore to textual analysis a sense of narrative dynamics, of the way in which formal design guides the forward reading of the text in time. Second, it seeks to clarify the relationship between thematic and formal concerns in narrative texts. Third, it examines the way in which texts themselves problematize questions of narrative representation and narrative transmission. The strategies adopted by Bernhard's narrators either *mirror* or *resolve* the representational or existential problems raised explicitly at the level of the represented world. In other words, narrative turns out to be related to thematics in terms of either *analogue* or *response*. And rather than being a "Geschichtenzerstörer," Thomas Bernhard emerges as a skilled and highly self-aware story*teller*.

## Bernhard and the Critics

Bernhard's commercial success and official recognition by prize-giving juries have gone hand in hand with an intense interest in his work on the part of academic critics. The quantity of secondary literature on his prose alone is so vast that a comprehensive overview would demand a book-length study of its own. For practical reasons, then, I address studies that represent the key strands in Bernhard criticism, subjecting each approach to a critique from the point of view of narrative studies. The urgent necessity for a differentiated appraisal of Bernhard's narrative techniques will emerge as a result.

### Intertextuality

Bernhard's works — prose and drama alike — are saturated with references to other writers and thinkers, to an extent that invites an exploration of these "intertextual" connections. Julia Kristeva is usually accredited with formulating the concept of intertextuality, and her definition has been adopted or adapted by numerous poststructuralist critics. Intertextuality is seen as the general discursive space that makes literary texts intelligible. In other words, it is a set of pre-existent signifying practices that form the context necessary for any "poetic" utterance to be understood (Culler, *Structuralist Poetics* 139–40). Roland Barthes's *S/Z*, a good example of this approach, expounds a theory of the text in which a given work is a tissue of anonymous discourses, including literary conventions as well as stereotypical assumptions, clichés, and descriptive systems of a culture that result from the repetition of connections and associations in and between texts.

Because the quotations of which the text is constituted are anonymous, however, they evade the individual's capacity to grasp them or trace their origins. This highlights the problem of applying the poststructuralist notion of intertextuality to the concrete study of texts. On the one hand, as Jonathan Culler has shown, critics who espouse a general theory of intertextuality as an anonymous discursive space often resort in their critical practice to a more or less traditional form of "Quellenforschung" (*Pursuit of Signs* 100–110). On the other hand, the same theory can be enlisted to justify the arbitrary listing of associations, parallels, and the like. Of the various studies of Bernhard that rely on some concept of intertextuality, Joachim Hoell's study of Bernhard's *Auslöschung* adopts the first approach, while Gernot Weiß's *Auslöschung der Philosophie* provides an example of the second.

Hoell explicitly rejects a poststructuralist concept of intertextuality on the grounds that an intertextual study must not be allowed to become a "Freibrief für beliebige Assoziationen des Rezipienten." Instead, he defines "text" as "literary text" and limits his discussion to those authors and works that are mentioned within the pages of *Auslöschung* (27). The reason for this, he claims, is that these writers were the most important for the real Bernhard, as well as being the authors whose works constitute the pretexts of the fictional Murau's "Auslöschung" (10). In those instances where a writer is mentioned without a specific work being thematized, the intertextual reference is a "Systemreferenz." So, for example, the French Enlightenment thinkers and nineteenth-century Russian writers mentioned by Murau are significant "denn inhaltlich bestimmte Erfahrungen und Erkenntnisse der Zeit der Aufklärung wie poetologische Verfahren der Romankunst des 19. Jahrhunderts werden mit Murau's Innen- und Außenleben verknüpft und konfrontiert" (29). Whenever specific texts are mentioned, however, an intertextual reading addresses the work in detail in order to broaden the meaning of certain thematic areas within *Auslöschung* (29). In the body of his text, Hoell draws numerous thematic parallels between the texts listed by Murau and the text of *Auslöschung* itself.

Hoell's use of intertextuality is problematic both at a general level and at the level of individual analyses. His decision to limit his analysis to those texts explicitly listed by Murau is undermined by his tendency to augment the texts under direct discussion with a plethora of other sources. In the chapter on *Der Prozeß* (108–25), he enlists other works by Kafka and Bernhard, theoretical treatises on bureaucracy and totalitarianism, and secondary sources in a way that implies precisely the type of "poststructuralist" intertextuality he rejects. *Auslöschung* emerges as a text that is caught up in a set of signifying systems and practices that far exceed the limited corpus of texts named by Murau and could potentially proliferate infinitely. Hoell seems to acknowledge this in his choice of epigraph from *Verstörung*: "Aber wir sind eingeschlossen in eine fortwährend alles zitierende Welt, in ein fortwährendes Zitieren, das die Welt ist" (9). Furthermore, his claim that the authors mentioned in *Auslöschung* were the ones most highly regarded by Bernhard is unverifiable and relies on a naive conflation of narrator and author. This conflation can be witnessed in the biographical parallels he draws between Bernhard's life and the biographies of other authors (212), and in the decision to treat Maria in *Auslöschung* as though she were the real Ingeborg Bachmann rather than a fictional character within a novel.

Hoell's treatment of Maria points to the most significant problem with his approach, namely a general failure to address the role played by the various textual elements within the narrative economy of both *Auslöschung* and its putative "source" texts. The technique of positing thematic parallels ignores the mediating function of narrative form. Because Hoell lacks a theory of narrative, he does not explore Murau's exploitation of intertextual references for other, nonthematic purposes such as the creation of narrative authority, nor does he consider ways in which Murau's critiques of, for example, Thomas Mann, might serve covertly to ironize the narrator. As a result, his study merely shows that certain topoi in *Auslöschung* can also be found in texts by the myriad authors whom Murau cites.

Gernot Weiß's study operates with a theory of intertextuality that is diametrically opposed to that of Hoell. Following Derrida, he begins by dismantling the hierarchical distinction between literature and philosophy in which the latter had traditionally been seen as the privileged term (11–15). He goes on to deconstruct the opposition between "original" and "quotation" and the related pair, "serious" and "unserious" statements (17–20). In doing this, Weiß seeks to prevent the "philosophische Rede" in Bernhard's texts from being dismissed as merely "hohl und nichtig" or "unserious" (20). This in turn justifies the practice of a reading narrative as a vehicle for philosophical discourse. The goal of Weiß's analysis is to investigate the "*Stimmigkeit philosophischer Begriffe im literarischen Text,*" and the "Philosophiekritik" of his title is made visible by "*Brüche, begriffliche Verzerrungen,*" which mark "*die Punkte, an denen Bernhards Texte sich kritisch gegen die philosophischen Konstruktionen wenden, die ihnen eingeschrieben werden*" (21).

Weiß's introduction performs, in reverse, the classic tactic of deconstruction. Whereas Derrida's readings of philosophical works treat them as texts and elevate to a central position the question of language that philosophy had traditionally dismissed as contingent, Weiß reestablishes the hierarchy he wished to deconstruct, privileging philosophy as the prior term that is then "inscribed" in literature. Weiß sees "conceptual distortions" as providing a critical perspective on philosophy, signaling that his concerns are, precisely, conceptual. In the main chapters of his book he undertakes a mammoth process of allegorization, translating decontextualized aspects of Bernhard's texts into philosophical terms and then showing how they correspond or, occasionally, fail to correspond to the thought of an eclectic range of thinkers. In a chapter on *Das Kalkwerk*, for example, the problems of "Geist," resignation, and marriage are discussed with reference to Kierkegaard (46–57), Konrad's retreat into the lime works is equated with a Heideggerian "Transzendenz des In-der-Welt-Seins" (57–64), and the technique of embedded quotation read as an illustration of Heidegger's critique of language as "Gerede" (68–9). Konrad conforms to Novalis's concept of the genius (71), but the fact that *every-thing* distracts him from his study is explained with reference to Pascal, for whom distraction allows us to live with the knowledge of our own "Nichtigkeit" (65–7). Konrad's study is then shown to be impossible according to the terms of Wittgenstein's philosophy of language (72–7).

The question that ultimately presents itself is this: what has all this got to do with Thomas Bernhard? Even if we accept that the philosophical discourses Weiß isolates are indeed "inscribed" in Bernhard's texts (and not randomly imposed upon them by the critic), Weiß fails to explore the ways in which the philosophemes are mediated by the novels' form. How, for example, are five such diverse thinkers as Kierkegaard, Heidegger, Pascal, Wittgenstein, and Novalis integrated within the narrative fabric? Does the text as a *narrative*, rather than as a set of propositional statements, contribute to "Philosophiekritik"? What shifts in meaning do the philosophemes undergo by being placed in a new — narrative — context? Weiß's virtuosic display of style and erudition leaves these central questions unanswered, producing a reading that bypasses the most interesting and significant property of Bernhard's novels: they *tell stories*.[4]

## Historical Allegory

Few European countries have been as profoundly changed in the course of the twentieth century as Austria, and like many postwar Austrian writers, Bernhard repeatedly turned his attention to the question of Austrian history. Two major studies of his novels analyze this "Geschichtsproblematik" from different standpoints.

Andreas Gößling's monumental study, *Thomas Bernhards frühe Prosakunst* mobilizes the weighty terminological, conceptual, and stylistic apparatus of Hegelian aesthetics, Freudian psychoanalysis, and the Marxism of the Frankfurt School in order to establish several sets of binary oppositions that embody two antithetical historical world-views. On one side of the opposition stand Christianity, philosophical idealism, feudalism, stasis, and "Geist," while on the other side stand rationality, science, modernity, flux, and "Verstand." Gößling traces the tension between these two competing world views as it is manifested both in the antinomical narrator-protagonist pairings of the three novels in question, and in the physical spaces (landscape, buildings) in which the novels are set. At the same time, landscape also functions as a "Bewußtseinslandschaft," a "Traum- oder Wunschumwelt" (11), symbolizing the psychic struggles of the narrators and protagonists to come to terms with the irrevocable loss of the "unified subject."

The striking thing about Gößling's study is its combination of exhaustiveness and reductiveness. He accounts for a staggering quantity of textual detail, but manages to bring almost everything under the umbrella of the feudalism-modernity opposition. This has a leveling effect: all textual elements appear to be of equal value, and there is no sense of their relative significance within the narrative economy. Furthermore, Gößling's approach, for all its concern with the thematics of history, imposes a radically synchronic schema on Bernhard's texts, as shown by his extensive use of geological metaphors. As a result, the novels' status as narratives possessing an inescapably temporal dimension is never explored. That the chosen narrative mode is central to the "meaning" of any text claiming to represent history, however, has been shown, in differing ways, by cultural critics such as Hayden White and Dominick LaCapra.[5] To omit a discussion of narrative form as a temporal construct ultimately reduces *Frost*, *Verstörung*, and *Korrektur* to static illustrations of the "Geschichtsphilosophie" that precedes them.

Hermann Helms-Derfert recently proposed a considerably more differentiated approach to the question of history. He addresses the historical position of the narrators as inhabitants of the Second Austrian Republic who attempt to constitute themselves as autonomous subjects, but are repeatedly faced with the fact that the social institutions of family, state, religion and culture have left ineradicable traces in their subjectivity. The consequence of this is a perception of history as a burden:

> Der soziale, politische und kulturelle Konsens- und Identifikations-druck wird um so leidvoller als drückende Fessel empfunden, als die in der Elternwelt mikrokosmisch abgebildete Zweite Republik sich gegen alle Neuerungen sperrt und in blinder Traditionsgläubigkeit das alt-österreichische Erbe pflegt, ohne aus dieser Erbschaft allerdings noch schöpferisch Kapital schlagen zu wollen und zu können. (4)

Helms-Derfert's method resembles that of Gößling, in that he reads individual novels as allegories of Austrian history. Whereas the fundamental conflict in Gößling's study is an abstract one of competing world views, however, Helms-Derfert turns his attention to the ways in which the central figures in Bernhard's novels embody both the cultural legacy of the Habsburg monarchy (which is hence omnipresent as a critical foil to the Second Republic), and the attempt to deal with it in the postwar period.

*Die Last der Geschichte* is one of the most sophisticated and interesting books on Bernhard, but, like any allegorical reading, it entails a thoroughgoing symbolic interpretation according to which all textual details "actually" signify something else. In Helms-Derfert's approach, many of his chapters contain the word "als" to imply the equivalence of two disparate entities: "Altösterreich als implizite Kritikfolie für den bürgerlichen Kapitalismus" (41), "Der Kegelbau als politische Restauration" (117), "Das Jägerhaus als Sinnbild der Moderne" (223), etc. Helms-Derfert does not explicitly address, however, the features of the narrative that invite, encourage, or legitimize such an allegorical reading. In addition, he propounds an eschatological conception of history as progressive disintegration in which any attempt at restoration is doomed to failure, but like Gößling he does not consider how Bernhard's narrative techniques might mirror, relativize, or represent a response to this view of the historical process.

## Feminism

Despite the misogyny demonstrated by many of Bernhard's protagonists, his work has given rise to relatively few feminist readings. These nevertheless deserve discussion because they represent the only approaches to Bernhard's work whose agenda is overtly political, and show with particular clarity the problems of such an approach when it fails to take narrative form into account.[6]

Bernhard's best-known feminist critic is Ria Endres, whose 1980 dissertation *Am Ende angekommen* caused a minor furor within German studies. "Ich werde nicht interpretieren," she declares, "sondern die Zersetzung eines männlichen Diskurses betreiben, der so dunkel in Ästhetik verpackt ist" (7). Her slim book is a sustained attack on Bernhard, whose work she reads at the level of both syntax and thematics as symptomatic of patriarchy in its death-throes. The historical stagnation of patriarchy is manifested in the repetitive, "static" structure of Bernhard's sentences: "Die Struktur der Gegenwart ist die Struktur der Sprache, in der die mächtigen Fragmente der Vergangenheit hängen, nämlich als Klischees" (25). Bernhard's characters both act and speak in order to compensate for a lack of fecundity or potency (50–7 and *passim*), and their excessive intellectualism is an attempt to repress or spiritualize Eros (45–6), which is characterized by Endres in terms of the body, the libido, and nature, and equated with the feminine. The repressed returns, of course, but as a destructive force (67–8, 80–1). Women, meanwhile, are virtually absent from Bernhard's fictional worlds, and when they are present, they function merely as male projections (98–100).

*Am Ende angekommen* is dominated by Endres's avowed personal antipathy towards "dem Dichter Bernhard" (7). There is thus a certain irony in the fact that her aggressive rhetoric of pure statement (rather than argument) resembles so closely that of Bernhard's protagonists. More importantly, the negative affect permeating Endres's text is never

justified or problematized with reference to Bernhard's novels themselves. She relies instead on the assumption that Bernhard's fictional
creations are mere mouthpieces of the author. Once the author-
narrator identification is dismantled, it becomes possible to make the
same points as Endres but to evaluate Bernhard's achievement differently, lauding his outstanding diagnosis of the impasse of late twentieth-century patriarchy. In addition, Endres's dual focus on syntax and
content means that she ignores the crucial question of narrative transmission. The gender politics of narrative is not merely a question of the
represented world; structures of narrative perspective encourage the
reader to identify with that world or to distance herself from it. This
varies from text to text, and is not adequately addressed by Endres's
stance of universal condemnation.

Andrea Reiter offers what she conceives as a corrective to Endres's
negative and blinkered appraisal of Bernhard's female characters. Taking many of her examples from Bernhard's post-1980 output (which
Endres could not have known), she seeks out positive as well as negative representations of women, listing wives, lovers, landladies, mothers,
"Lebensmenschen," and sisters to demonstrate the diversity and increasing individuality of Bernhard's women figures. Although she
points out that Endres takes no account of narrative form, however
("Die Bachmann" 171), she commits the same lapse, with the result
that her discussion is purely content based. This leads to a naive reading
of gender relationships in Bernhard that takes the narrators' words at
face value and ignores formal issues. Discussing the violent treatment of
women in *Das Kalkwerk*, *Korrektur*, *Ja*, and *Holzfällen*, for instance,
Reiter claims: "One must not, however, overlook the fact that the men
who act in such ways do so in utter desperation, a point Endres disre-
gards" (170). This justification of the male protagonists shows the extent to which Reiter has adopted the value systems of the texts she
analyzes, a consequence of failing to consider the textual strategies that
encourage this very process. Because she never analyzes narrative technique, her discussion of Bernhard and gender ultimately functions as an
apologia and tends to affirm rather than call into question the patriarchal ideology of the texts under discussion.

A similar problem infects Mireille Tabah's two articles on the representation of women in *Auslöschung*.[7] Taking as her starting point the
thesis that "das männliche Subjekt sich über die Ausgrenzung und
Unterwerfung jenes 'Anderen' konstituiert, das im patriarchalischen
Bild der Frau festgeschrieben ist" ("Misogynie" 77), Tabah examines
the way in which Bernhard's images of women replicate the stereotypical fantasies of femininity characteristic of patriarchy. Murau's mother is

a representative of nature, sexuality, anti-intellectualism, opportunism, and hypocrisy, to the extent that she becomes "das Symbol der Übel, die Österreich und die Welt bedrohen" ("Dämonisierung" 151). The poet Maria, on the other hand, represents "den Inbegriff des selbständigen, unbestechlichen, gelassenen Geistes" ("Dämonisierung" 154) while also being childlike ("Dämonisierung" 156). She is ultimately an androgynous, desexualized woman, a "Projektionsobjekt und Spiegelbild des Mannes, der sie zu seiner eigenen Selbstverwirklichung benutzt" ("Dämonisierung" 156).

Making the binary opposition of demonization-transfiguration the basis of a critical reading of *Auslöschung* is problematic on several counts. First, such a strategy runs the risk of reproducing rather than undermining the binary thinking of patriarchal discourse. Second, Tabah's approach becomes all the more questionable once we realize that she can construct the opposition only by ignoring significant elements of the text, such as the obvious eroticism of Murau's relationship with Maria. Finally, a more detailed study of Murau's textual practice would reveal that he actually problematizes the oppositions in the very act of constituting them. His mobilization of binary oppositions is so crass and so explicit that they function as caricatures of patriarchal fantasies and invite the critic to examine those moments of the text which appear to subvert them. Tabah, however, does not do this.

As I will argue in chapters 2 and 3, an adequate understanding of gender politics in Bernhard's texts cannot be gained by analyses that concentrate on content and "images of women" at the expense of rhetoric.[8]

## "Musical" Prose

The role of music in Bernhard's life is well documented in his autobiographical pentalogy: the solitary violin playing in the boarding school shoe-cupboard (*Die Ursache*), the lessons in singing and music theory with Maria Kehldorfer and Theodor Werner (*Der Keller*), and the beneficial effect of singing on the patient's lungs (*Die Kälte*) mark the salient points in Bernhard's use of music to construct his personal myth.[9] Music is of central thematic importance in many of Bernhard's novels and dramas: primarily *Die Macht der Gewohnheit, Der Ignorant und der Wahnsinnige, Der Untergeher, Holzfällen*, but also, to a lesser extent, *Ja, Beton*, and *Korrektur*. Bernhard himself alluded on several occasions to the act of writing as a "musical process": "Ich würde sagen, es ist eine Frage des Rhythmus und hat viel mit Musik zu tun. Ja, was ich schreibe, kann man nur verstehen, wenn man sich klarmacht, daß zuallererst die musikalische Komponente zählt und daß erst an zweiter Stelle das kommt, was ich erzähle" (*Von einer Katasrophe* 109).[10] Numerous critics have attempted to analyze Bernhard's texts in terms of musical structures, with varying degrees of competence and success.

One of the earliest articles on Bernhard to employ musical terminology extensively is Manfred Jurgensen's "Die Sprachpartituren des Thomas Bernhard." Jurgensen is concerned with the status of language in Bernhard's writings. His argument seems to be that rather than expressing or mediating ideational content, Bernhard's language merely "performs itself," thereby offering a formal analogue of what Jurgensen calls the "Tautologie der Gedankensprache" (100). The meaning of Bernhard's works thus *is* their style (101). Jurgensen's analysis is hampered, however, by a conceptual and linguistic obscurity, a problem exacerbated by the deployment of musical metaphors whose actual reference is difficult to ascertain. In the following examples, musical terminology is bandied about with no attempt to relate it in a systematic or meaningful way to the texts under discussion:

> Bernhard schreibt Arien in verschiedenen Denkarten, so wie ein Komponist in unterschiedlichen, jedoch aufeinander bezogenen Tonarten komponiert. Es sind gedankliche Kompositionen, in denen er Bezugsverhältnisse sprachformal ästhetisiert. (101)

> Die völlig durchkomponierte ("verrückte") Korrelation der Begriffe "Schauspiel" und "Hochwasser" [in *Verstörung*] z.B. läßt sich als musikalischer Satz, gleichsam als Fuge bis in alle Einzelheiten erkennen. (111)

Throughout the article, any genuine comparability that might exist between the two media remains unexplored. Musical concepts are used indiscriminately and impressionistically, and tend to turn Jurgensen's article into the same kind of self-referential linguistic construct that Jurgensen perceives Bernhard's novels to be. As a critical tool, the musical model tells us remarkably little about the texts it is supposed to elucidate.[11]

Andrea Reiter's 1989 essay, "Thomas Bernhard's 'Musical Prose,'" has been described by Anton Krättli as belonging "zum besten [. . .], was über den Schriftsteller geschrieben worden ist" (qtd. in Kuhn 34). Such lavish praise, however, can be made only by ignoring the serious problems raised by the article. In a withering critique of Reiter, Gudrun Kuhn points out that the analogies she posits between a section of *Alte Meister* and a double fugue rely on incorrect application of musical terminology, a faulty *syntactic* analysis of Bernhard's prose, a confusion of syntactic and semantic categories, and an arbitrary selection of a passage of text which structurally and thematically exceeds the bounds that Reiter's analysis presupposes (Kuhn 34–8). There is no need to rehearse Kuhn's rigorous and highly technical arguments in detail here. Reiter's article raises more immediate questions concerning the application of musical terminology to verbal texts.

She criticizes Jurgensen for remaining "entangled in musical metaphor," and rightly points out that Bernhard's own comments on the musicality of his prose do not mean that his work is "sufficiently characterized as musical by virtue of an interpretation which applies musical metaphors: that would merely be a mannerism of the interpreter" (193). Yet her entire analysis is crammed with musical terminology whose function is strictly metaphorical. The decision to describe the rhetorical devices of chiasmus and oxymoron in terms of "Schoenberg's mirror principle in serialism" (197), or to regard Reger's anti-Heidegger tirades as a series of modulations (199), or to see in the repetition of certain sentences "a kind of refrain" typical of the rondo (200): these are all metaphors, but their status as such is never acknowledged, nor are the limits to their applicability ever explored. Furthermore, Reiter's attempts to explain Bernhard's work in terms of motivic sequence are hedged by the admission that the passage she selects from *Alte Meister* deviates from its putative musical model. This calls the analytic usefulness of the model into question, and indeed, Reiter's metaphors eventually cease to be musical and become spatial: expansion-contraction, up-down (194). Any link with music is so attenuated as to render it valueless as a critical concept.

The final major problem with Reiter's analysis is its inability to account for textual macrostructures. She sees "musical prose" as something totally divorced from wider questions of narrative structure and narrative meaning. Instead, she atomizes the novel in question (*Alte Meister*) into a set of randomly isolated passages and subjects them to a "musical" analysis, which, even if it worked, would tell us nothing about the function of "musical" structures within a *narrative* text.

In *Thomas Bernhards Trilogie der Künste: "Der Untergeher," "Holz-fällen," "Alte Meister"* (1999), Gregor Hens suggests some ways in which musical analysis can be made productive for a discussion of narrative form and narrative thematics. Hens's overall thesis is that the novels *Der Untergeher, Holzfällen,* and *Alte Meister* form a trilogy linked not only by their thematic concerns with art, but by the fact that they each undertake a literary transposition or "Verarbeitung" of structural devices derived from, respectively, music, drama, and visual art. Like Reiter, he stresses: "Es genügt nicht, sich in musikalischen Metaphern zu ergehen, oder mögliche musikalisch-kompositorische Strukturen (wie z.B. motivverdächtige Wiederholungen und Variationen) aufzuführen" (30). The key words here are "ergehen" and "aufzuführen." Hens's analyses are no less reliant on metaphor than Reiter's, but the terminology is instrumentalized in a more effective way.

It is in a discussion of *Der Untergeher* that Hens's use of musical concepts is developed most extensively. The text, he claims, is

> eine einzigartige Komposition, bestehend aus drei Stimmen, die jeweils von einer der Figuren repräsentiert werden. Die Lebenswege der drei Freunde laufen eine Zeitlang parallel, sie überlappen sich, sie verzweigen sich und folgen einander, sie werden variiert, kopiert und umgekehrt, d.h. sie bedingen sich gegenseitig, zumindest aus der Sicht des zugegebenermaßen voreingenommenen Erzählers. (33)

It is the metaphor of the three "voices" and the "contrapuntal" structure of the relationship between the three friends that proves most analytically productive for Hens at both the microtextual (36–44) and macrotextual (56–79) levels, "polyphony" also being used to describe those passages in which the narrator simultaneously thinks one thing and says the opposite (70–1).

Hens's use of musical terminology is different from that of other critics in that he does not fetishize or absolutize it. Rather, he emphasizes the functioning of musical structures within the overall narrative schema of *Der Untergeher*. The narrator's use of musical structuration, he argues, ultimately generates events at the level of action that are implausible or otherwise inexplicable. In other words, the "surface structure" of counterpoint and voice-leading determines the "deep structure" of the action. The narrator uses contrapuntal techniques because he not only sees the world as a manifestation of aesthetic structures but is "die Personifizierung dieser strukturellen Anforderungen" (74). The text dramatizes the failure of aesthetics to come to terms with a reality principle that asserts itself forcefully at the end of the text in the form of the Holocaust and Wertheimer's Jewishness.

No critical discourse is free from metaphor. Indeed, much poststructuralist theory delights in metaphorical exuberance. The effectiveness of such metaphors, however, depends on their ability to throw light on the primary texts under discussion. In this respect, much music-oriented criticism of Bernhard is found wanting: the metaphorical status of the discourse is not explored, terminology is applied imprecisely or even arbitrarily, music proves incapable of accounting for macrotextual structures, and the demonstration of Bernhard's "musical" techniques too often becomes an end in itself. It is easy to agree with Irmgard Scheitler's suspicion that critics' use of musical terminology betrays a "Bedürfnis, interpretatorische Ratlosigkit angesichts unkonventioneller Texte überdecken zu wollen" (Scheitler 83–4). Hens, whose book avoids most of these pitfalls, points out that musical mod-

els are not universally applicable to all of Bernhard's works (49). Any
interpretative approach that attempts such a blanket application of musical terminology runs the risk of failing to address both the specificity
of each text and its status as narrative.

## Narrative Form and Bernhard's "Gesamtwerk"

In the years immediately following Bernhard's death, the most urgent
task facing Bernhard criticism was the assessment of his output as a
completed body of work. Around 1990 a spate of books appeared that
tried to work out the central principles, constants, and developmental
trends in a body of work now regarded as closed. Studies by Willi
Huntemann, Eva Marquardt and Oliver Jahraus represent three different approaches to this problem. Although all of them devote some attention to questions of narrative form, the fact that formal analyses take
place within the context of larger arguments means that they do not
engage with the functioning of narrative form within individual texts.

Huntemann's discussion of Bernhard's prose is structured around
two pairs of oppositions. His two categories of narrative mode are "der
für die Prosa der 60er Jahre charakteristische Typ der 'authentischen
Selbstdarstellung'" (diaries, notes, letters) and "der 'Erzählerbericht als
memoria mortui'" typical of the later novels. This opposition corresponds to that between the "erlebenden Erzähler" of the early works
and the "zitierenden Erzähler" of the late prose (*Artistik* 113). Using
these two sets of distinctions in order to draw, respectively, the horizontal and vertical axes of a graph, Huntemann constructs a "Raster,
dem die Prosatexte in (annähernd) genetischer Folge einbeschrieben
werden können" (111). By plotting the "coordinates" of each text
within the parameters of the graph, he produces a spiraliform representation of Bernhard's aesthetic development (112). The ultimate
point of the argument is to refute the frequently-made accusation that
Bernhard's work was repetitive to the point of tedious monotony:

> Die für Bernhards Werk so charakteristische Lesehaltung einer ge-
> spannten Erwartung und gleichzeitiger Voraussicht des Altbekannten
> könnte durch bloße, statische Wiederholung (reine Zirkularität) auf
> längere Sicht in ästhetisch befriedigender Weise nicht aktiviert werden.
> In der Wiederholung ist ein *Fortschreiten* auf einen imaginären Punkt
> hin erkennbar, womit sich eben die Form der Spirale in der anschauli-
> chen Darstellung dieser Tendenz ergibt. (115–6)

Although there is no doubting the ingenuity of Huntemann's
schema, the positioning of individual texts on the graph often appears
arbitrary, governed by the need to demonstrate a "genetic" development rather than by the qualities of the text in question. *Holzfällen*, for

example, is deemed be an "Erzählerbericht als memoria mortui" and to have a "zitierenden Erzähler" (112). Yet this novel is unusual precisely for its *lack* of quotation of other characters, and the reasons for its position in Huntemann's scheme are thus highly tenuous. The same applies to the position of Bernhard's other novels of the 1980s from *Der Untergeher* to *Auslöschung*.

This points to a more central problem with Huntemann's analysis, namely his reliance on narratological concepts whose applicability is called into question rather than affirmed by Bernhard's novels. Huntemann stresses that the positions of the various texts in the scheme are relative rather than absolute, and his distinction between "experiencing narrators" and "quoting narrators" is presumably also relative. The problem is that Bernhard's narrators — with the exclusive exception of the narrator of *Das Kalkwerk* — systematically subvert the distinction. It is not only that they all both quote *and* experience; it is also that the act of quotation is often simultaneously the representation of an experience of *listening*. Furthermore, Huntemann never makes explicit the criteria he uses to decide whether a narrator is "erlebend" or "zitierend." How, for example, is the "Famulant" in *Frost* any more an "erlebender Erzähler" than Murau in *Auslöschung*? It appears that Huntemann's scheme of Bernhard's development rests on a view of narrative form as a set of variables that can be applied across the board, without taking into account the peculiarities of individual narratives or the way in which the texts in question undermine the conceptual framework within which his discussion moves. I wish in no way to detract either from Huntemann's insightful comments on specific texts or from the intrinsic interest of his attempt to describe "Das System Thomas Bernhard." I merely point out that a totalizing analysis of narrative form is necessarily limited in its relevance for a discussion of individual works.

In two monographs, Oliver Jahraus sets out to demonstrate that intratextual and intertextual repetition is the essential constitutive feature of Bernhard's prose. "Das Invariante," he writes, "ist grundlegend, das Variante ein aus dem Invarianten ableitbares Epiphänomen" (*Wiederholung* 32). Jahraus's critical method is to isolate the thematic, contextual, lexical, syntactic and narrative-structural constants in Bernhard's prose. Throughout the chapter on narrative form, he repeatedly shows that the structures of narrative embedding characteristic of Bernhard's texts are both a cause and an effect of the impossibility of referential authenticity. The situation of narration, he argues, is always one of repetition (45). The narrative transmission between text and reader reproduces acts of narrative mediation that have already taken place within the represented world of the text: "Das Erzählte [wird] von [dem Erzähler] nicht als Erlebnis, sondern nur als bereits vollzogene Wiedergabe wiedergegeben" (37–8). Such a reading rephrases in broadly poststructuralist terms the argument, familiar to us from the discussion of Jurgensen above, that Bernhard's prose is self-referential and has little (if any) connection to extratextual reality.

It is clear from this sketch of Jahraus's argument that the desire to subsume all of Bernhard's novels beneath a single overarching framework can be achieved only by reducing a variety of narrative techniques to the principle of "Wiederholung der Wiederholung" (38 and *passim*). The role of narrative embedding within individual works is never addressed, even though such considerations would appear urgently necessary when analyzing texts such as *Frost*, *Das Kalkwerk*, and *Auslöschung*, in which the embedded perspectives differ widely in terms of structure and function.

One critic whose approach to Bernhard's "development" entails analyses of individual texts is Eva Marquardt. Marquardt plots the "Weg des Erzählers von der Peripherie ins Zentrum" as it is manifested in *Frost*, *Das Kalkwerk*, *Korrektur*, *Der Untergeher*, and *Auslöschung* (20–67). A reading of Bernhard's novels that fails to take into account narrative structures, she argues, would create the impression that the texts are characterized by increasing "Welthaftigkeit": the world appears more accessible as the narrators come to occupy an increasingly central role. At the same time, however, this impression is problematized by increasing self-reflexivity. So, for example, the "reality" of the represented world is undermined by the abandonment of any fixed text in *Korrektur*, by the contradictions in the discourse that betray the unreliability of the narrator in *Der Untergeher*, and by Murau's implicitly dismantling the fictional illusion in *Auslöschung* (180–2).

In terms of narrative analysis, Marquardt's study is more adequate than those of Huntemann and Jahraus. Her focus remains rather narrow, however, concentrating on questions of narratorial unreliability and epistemology. These questions are fundamental, but they exhaust neither the function of narrative form nor the possibilities of narratology. Narratorial unreliability, for instance, can have other functions within a text beyond signalling epistemological uncertainty. Marquardt fails to explain why the narrators tell stories at all if their texts simply illustrate the unreliability or inaccessibility of the stories they tell.

## Narrative Theory

Narratology facilitates foremost an understanding of *how texts work*: how is our perception of the represented world determined by the nar-

rator and structures of focalization, and to what end? How is our reading of the text guided by sequences of enigma and resolution? What is
the role of the ending in the narrative economy? And what are the assumptions necessary for the understanding of narrative texts — even
when individual narratives deviate from or subvert these assumptions?
These are not contingent or peripheral questions; they are, on the contrary, central to the meaning, point, and purpose of storytelling.

One possible reason for the relative neglect of narrative analysis in
the critical literature on Bernhard is the marginal position of narrative
studies within the German critical tradition. The most influential narrative theorists writing either in German or within Germanic studies are
Käte Hamburger, Dorrit Cohn, Franz Stanzel, and Eberhard Lämmert.
None of these, however, is centrally relevant to the reading of Bernhard's writings offered here. The sections on prose narrative in Hamburger's *Die Logik der Dichtung* (1957) ultimately constitute a theory
of fictionality, issues that are peripheral to the current discussion.[12]
Cohn's *Transparent Minds* bears the descriptive subtitle *Narrative
Modes for Presenting Consciousness in Fiction*. Although chapter 4 of her
study contains concepts of undoubted applicability to Bernhard's work,
her focus on the representation of consciousness is too narrow to serve
as the basis of a more general reading of narrative technique.

More relevant is Franz Stanzel's 1979 treatise, *Theorie des Erzählens*,
a theoretical account of narration in prose fiction. Stanzel establishes a
circular typology (the "Typenkreis") of narrative forms, and distinguishes three "Erzählsituationen" typical of the novel: the "auktoriale
Erzählsituation" (third-person omniscient narrator), "personale Erzählsituation" (third person narrator, but the narrative world filtered
through the consciousness of a single figure), and "Ich-Erzählsituation"
(first-person narrator). Since Bernhard's novels are exclusively first-
person, it is the latter category that is of particular interest to us.

Within the "Ich-Erzählsituation," Stanzel distinguishes various positions depending on the role of the narrator in the text:

> Als Unterscheidungskriterium bietet sich das Verhältnis des erzählen-
> den zum erlebenden Ich an. Auf unserem Weg entlang des Typenkrei-
> ses begegnen wir zuerst einem Ich-Erzähler, dessen erzählendes Ich
> sich sehr ausführlich als Erzähler kundgibt (Tristram Shandy, Siggi
> Jepsen in Siegfried Lenz' Roman *Deutschstunde*), dann dem klassi-
> schen Ich-Erzähler, bei dem das Verhältnis zwischen erzählendem und
> erlebendem Ich zwar nicht quantitativ aber doch der Bedeutung nach
> ausgewogen ist (David Copperfield, Felix Krull), und schließlich jener
> Ich-Erzählung, in der das erlebende das erzählende Ich fast ganz aus
> dem Blickfeld des Lesers verdrängt (Huckleberry Finn). (258)

In addition to these categories, Stanzel also introduces the notion of the "Erzähler als Augenzeuge auf dem Schauplatz des Geschehens, als Beobachter, als Zeitgenosse der Hauptfigur, als dessen Biograph, u.s.w." (263).

From this summary of Stanzel's *Theorie des Erzählens*, we see that its applicability to Bernhard's texts is severely limited. One problem with a typological theory of narrative is its inability to account for any novels that elude the taxonomical slots into which they are supposed to fit. Despite its proliferation of categories, the "Typenkreis" cannot cope very well with novels whose narrators occupy several positions, either simultaneously or sequentially. In applying Stanzel's categorical distinctions to *Frost*, for example, we find a narrator who is simultaneously an "erlebendes Ich," an "erzählendes Ich," and an "Ich als Augenzeuge." This means that the novel would occupy three positions on Stanzel's circle, thereby undermining the entire purpose of a typology.[13] Furthermore, Stanzel's theory never addresses the problem of framed narrative. As we shall see in the chapter on *Korrektur*, this has led to some bizarre attempts to describe a relatively straightforward case of narrative embedding in terms of three different types of novel within *Korrektur*, a statement that is clearly meaningless. Rather than increasing the number of taxonomical subdivisions within the typology, it makes more sense to seek a more flexible critical vocabulary for the analysis of Bernhard's novels.

Although Eberhard Lämmert's theory has largely been superseded by the greater sophistication of "structuralist" narratology, it has the merit of plainly stating the key conceptual dichotomy underlying the dominant tradition of twentieth-century narrative theory. Lämmert makes a distinction between the chronological series of actions, and the way these actions are represented in the text (25). The assumption that a narrative is the portrayal of a set of events that are deemed to precede representation is shared by those theorists who have sought to establish a narrative *grammar* and those who have expounded a descriptive narrative *poetics*.

"Narrative grammar" seeks to lay bare the fundamental deep structures underlying all individual surface manifestations of narrative. Vladimir Propp's pioneering study *Morphologie du conte* (first published in Russian in 1928) involved the analysis of a corpus of 200 Russian folk tales in order to abstract the constant elements from the variables. The result was a set of thirty-one functions, where a function is the "*l'action d'un personnage, définie du point de vue de sa signification dans le déroulement de l'intrigue*" (31). These functions, according to Propp, occur in a fixed order in every text, even though not all thirty-one have to be present in any given tale. Building on and refining Propp's researches, A. J. Greimas proposed a six-figure actantial model, dividing plot structure into three pairs of binary opposites (qtd. in Toolan 93–6):

giver/receiver
subject/object
helper/opponent

Every "plot" can thus in principle be analyzed by attributing either one of Propp's functions or one of Greimas's actantial labels to the characters or other forces within the narrative.

The main weakness of these models is their reductiveness: the critic merely applies a static, invariable model to any narrative in a way that tells us nothing about its circumstances of production, reception, cultural significance, or structural peculiarities. "Flushed with triumph," as Terry Eagleton writes, "the structuralist rearranges his rulers and reaches for the next story" (95). Nevertheless, this so-called "high structuralist" approach contains two implications that were to become of central importance to later theorists. The first is that a story can be distinguished from the mode of its telling. The second is that narratives involve struggle and exchange: although appearing static, Propp's and Greimas's models imply that narrative middles are a site of conflict between elements that are oriented towards the narrative end (helpers, donors), and elements that retard and impede it (opponents). This is a key insight into the functioning of narrative, and one to which we shall return extensively throughout this study.

The so-called "low structuralist" work of the early Roland Barthes, Tzvetan Todorov, and, supremely, Gérard Genette endeavored to provide not a model of the deep structure of all thinkable plots, but a descriptive framework which would account for all the possible features of the *surface structure* of any given narrative text.[14] Corresponding to this shift in emphasis, they reconceptualized the basic configuration of deep and surface structures as the opposition between *story* and *discourse*,[15] the former being a chronological chain of events, and the latter being the representation of these events in a semiotic system, that may be language (as in a novel), pictures (as in a cartoon), a combination of the two (as in film), or another medium such as dance.

The distinction between story and discourse is not only useful but essential to narrative analysis:

> To make narrative an object of study, one must distinguish narratives from nonnarratives, and this invariably involves reference to the fact that narratives report a sequence of events. If narrative is defined as the representation of a series of events, then the analyst must be able to identify these events, and they come to function as a nontextual

given, something which exists prior to and independently of narrative presentation and which the narrative then reports. [...] [N]arratological analysis of a text requires one to treat the discourse as a representation of events which are conceived of as independent of any particular narrative perspective or presentation and which are thought of as having the properties of real events. (Culler, *Pursuit of Signs* 171)

Separating story and discourse allows the critic to turn his or her attention to questions of time structure, narration, focalization, space, characterization, and so on, in order to establish the distinctive features of the narrative discourse and to ascertain what is at stake — psychologically, ideologically, or epistemologically — in the telling of a particular tale in a particular way.

The trouble is that narratives tend to invert the hierarchical story-discourse relationship and thereby question the premises of the theory designed to account for them.[16] This tendency can be witnessed in all narratives, but is foregrounded to a high degree in Bernhard's novels. The fact that the story is an abstraction inferred from the discourse assumes stable relationships between the narrative levels, but as we shall see in relation to *Der Untergeher*, these relationships can become fluid or even reversible. Likewise, both *Der Untergeher* and *Das Kalkwerk* thwart the reconstruction of a definitive story from the information provided at the level of discourse.[17] This foregrounds the primacy of the discourse, and any interpretation of these novels has to account for the functioning of a discourse whose effect is to cast radical doubt on the constitution of the fictional world. This does not, however, invalidate the story-discourse dichotomy, for if we did not read the novels of Thomas Bernhard with the assumption that a sequence of events will be related to us, there would be nothing at all problematic or disorientating about a narrative that prevented us from ascertaining exactly what that sequence is. Contradictory representations of events would be interpretable simply as a set of unrelated scenarios. The refusal to provide definitive information about the represented world is disorientating precisely because we expect to be able to reconstruct a story from the discourse. The story-discourse opposition thus not only establishes the norm, but renders visible the exceptions for which analysis has to account.

For all its merits, classic structural analysis neglects one crucial feature of all storytelling, namely the temporal aspect of its reception. In his seminal study *S/Z*, Roland Barthes introduced an approach to narratives that facilitated analysis of their dynamic quality: written stories are read over time. The theoretical apparatus of *S/Z* was developed in response to one particular text, Balzac's *Sarrasine*, and is self-confessedly improvizational and provisional. Nevertheless, several of Barthes's key concepts are significant for the understanding of narratives in general, particularly the insight that the forward reading of the narrative text relies on the creation of suspense. Suspense is, of course, a psychological category rather than a formal property of narrative. Barthes, however, replaces the notion of suspense with what he terms the "hermeneutic code," a concept which is not free from psychological assumptions but which allows the reading process to be linked more clearly to textual form. Narrative texts, Barthes argues, typically pose an enigma at the beginning and resolve it at the end. The narrative middle, or "dilatory space," is expanded by keeping alive the reader's desire for resolution, and this is achieved through the use of "hermeneutic morphemes," which may take the form of partial responses, decoy responses ("leurres"), false responses, equivocation, and such like (215–6). The hermeneutic code thus plays a vital role in narrative dynamics, guiding the forward reading of the text in time by simultaneously promising and delaying the desired end.

Barthes terms the hermeneutic code the "voix de la vérité," and in the Balzac novella he analyzes, the resolution of the enigma does indeed reveal the truth that la Zambinella, object of the protagonist's desire and fantasy, is in reality a castrato. In reading Bernhard's novels, however, we are faced with texts that subvert the assumptions subtending the hermeneutic structure of narrative. In *Frost* and *Verstörung*, for instance, hermeneutic structuration is greatly attenuated. Not only is it unclear from the outset which "enigma" is supposed to be solved, but the ending results in no great revelation and the narrative fabric threatens to disintegrate into mere chronicle. *Das Kalkwerk* and *Der Untergeher* are examples of texts that fail to fulfill the promise of a revelation: the enigmas are left unresolved, and the hermeneutic code ceases to function as a vehicle for narrative truth. *Holzfällen, Alte Meister,* and the first section of *Korrektur*, on the other hand, are structured according to hermeneutic principles, but when the enigmas are resolved they turn out to be of staggering banality, and the "voix de la vérité" appears in a heavily ironic light. The aspect of irony also governs the use of the hermeneutic code in *Auslöschung*, where the narrator's disingenuous protestations that he does not know the outcome of his own tale are unmasked as "Notlügen" whose function is to facilitate the construction of the narrative.

Because so many of Bernhard's texts call into question narratological categories, the use of narratology in this study is not a question of mere "application," but a question of dialogue. By providing a flexible set of analytic concepts that specify the norms governing the production and reception of narrative texts, narrative theory facilitates an understanding of the deviant and peculiar qualities of Bernhard's prose. In the process, the function of the two central theoretical categories discussed above undergoes reassessment. The story-discourse dichotomy has usually been understood in terms of the representation of a determinate fictional world in a particular way. Barthes's definition of the hermeneutic code sees it as a means of conveying a central truth about the world of the text. On a traditional reading, then, both devices ultimately serve to communicate narrative content. In the novels of Thomas Bernhard, however, they do not always fulfill this function. Story and discourse, and the hermeneutic code, have to be re-read as performative categories. Sequences of enigma and resolution no longer reveal the truth, but merely allow the story to "get told," while the collapse of the story-discourse dichotomy forces a reconceptualization of narrative in terms of "point" rather than representation: for what psychological or ideological reasons do narrators produce a narrative discourse that thwarts rather than facilitates our perception of the story?

The first two chapters of this book discuss Bernhard's four early novels. The analysis of Bernhard's first two novels, *Frost* and *Verstörung* (1967), mobilizes the distinction, borrowed from linguistics, between the syntagmatic and paradigmatic grouping of narrative events. Syntagmatic grouping refers to the "horizontal" distribution of narrative events along a time-line. It is also possible, however, to group events paradigmatically by analyzing the "vertical" resemblance of one narrative event to other events in the same story.[18] The text of *Frost* is the narrator's response to the confrontation between his own "sane" world of medicine and the "mad" world of the painter Strauch, whom he is sent to observe. A formal analogue of this confrontation is provided by the syntagmatic and paradigmatic relationships between episodes — not only within the narrative exchanges between the narrator and Strauch, but also in the structure of the text as a whole. In *Verstörung*, the syntagmatic axis is so weakened that it loses its capacity to organize temporal relations within the text. This shifts interpretative attention to the paradigmatic relations existing between events, which implies a notion of time that is static. This in turn corresponds to the historical stagnation of the Second Austrian Republic, which is repeatedly stated or implied by the text's thematics.

*Das Kalkwerk* (1970) raises problems of a different kind. The analysis centers on questions of embedded narrative perspective, not only to show the difficulties of establishing what the "story" (in the narratological sense) actually is, but also to demonstrate that these seemingly epistemological problems are inextricably tied up with the text's gender politics. The final novel of Bernhard's early phase, *Korrektur* (1975), addresses similar thematic problems to those of *Verstörung*, but also represents a departure in its manipulation of narrative teleology. Narrative ordering relies heavily on the assumed explanatory function of the ending: each event is significant to the extent that it contributes toward the attainment of the narrative end, and from the vantagepoint of the end, the foregoing can be integrated and given meaning. Thus traditional narrative is goal-directed or *teleological*. The first of *Korrektur*'s two chapters is structured around the enigma of how the narrator will order the posthumous papers of his friend, Roithamer. The expected *telos*, however, fails to materialize, and the act of ordering never takes place. The sense of narrative teleology is ironically undermined, which corresponds to the ironizing of Roithamer's own teleological thought at the level of the represented world itself.

Chapters 3 to 5 of this study analyze three texts whose central subject is friendship. Chapter 3 returns to the question of narrative form and gender in Bernhard's fiction, examining it this time in terms of the hermeneutic code: *Ja* ostensibly celebrates the central female character, but this surface discourse is undermined by the exploitation of her death to create the structures of enigma and resolution that make the narrative possible. The discussion of *Wittgensteins Neffe* in chapter 4 juxtaposes Paul Wittgenstein's unsuccessful attempts to narrativize his life with those of the narrator in order to explore the conditions necessary for the production of form and meaning in narrative. Chapter 5 investigates the problem of narrativizing a life from a slightly different angle, as the narrator of *Der Untergeher* is faced with the task of establishing the causes of his friend Wertheimer's suicide. Although the novel appears to be structured like detective fiction, the narrative form calls into question the claim that the hermeneutic code is a vehicle for narrative truth, and forces a re-examination of the function and significance of the end in the narrative economy.

In the final three chapters, attention is turned to Bernhard's last three novels. *Holzfällen* scandalized the Viennese public when it appeared, and chapter 6 examines the narrative techniques that encouraged its reception as a *roman à clef*. On one level, the text can be read as a response and antidote to the charge of artistic stagnation leveled by the narrator at his fellow guests at the "artistic dinner party," but at the same time the novel contains numerous "metafictional" elements that stress its nature as a verbal construct. The "double reading" of *Holzfällen* offered here attempts to negotiate a path between the naive reading to which the novel was initially subjected, and an aestheticizing reading that ignores its referentiality. Chapter 7 shows how the narrative discourse of *Alte Meister* functions as a formal analogue to the technique of fragmentation adopted by the main character Reger to deal with the burden of the Habsburg cultural legacy. The last main chapter investigates the representation of the National Socialist past in Bernhard's monumental final novel *Auslöschung*. Published shortly after the electoral successes of Kurt Waldheim and Jörg Haider in 1986, it is Bernhard's final reckoning with the theme and contains an explicit injunction to keep alive and articulate memories of the National Socialist period and its living victims. Again the problem of ending is paramount, for does not narrative — whose very existence as a mode of historical understanding relies on the organizational function of the end — necessarily entail closure? The function of narrative embedding in *Auslöschung* is explored in the light of this apparent paradox between explicit content and the exigencies of narrative form.

In conclusion, I discuss the issue of Bernhard's "development." His work is seen not in terms of linear progression, but in terms of a series of overlappings, recursions, and leaps, as the author played through a repertory of permutations in the relationship between explicit thematics and formal strategies. Bernhard's relationship with Austria is then addressed from the point of view of Robert Menasse's influential concept of the "sozialpartnerschaftliche Ästhetik."

## Notes

[1] For an account of the filming, see the interview with Ferry Radax in Fialik.

[2] See e.g. Kohlenbach 58–9; Rietra 109; Huntemann, *Artistik* 181–2; and Mariacher, *'Umspringbilder'* 169–75.

[3] See the section on "Narrative Form and Bernhard's 'Gesamtwerk.'"

[4] In this connection, see Huntemann's criticism of Gerald Jurdzinski's *Leiden an der 'Natur': Thomas Bernhards metaphysische Weltdeutung im Spiegel der Philosophie Schopenhauers* (Huntemann, *Artistik* 15–17).

[5] See e.g. White, *Metahistory* and *Tropics of Discourse*; LaCapra, *Representing the Holocaust*.

[6] Although other critics, notably Gößling and Gamper, employ analytic techniques derived from Frankfurt School Marxism, their studies cannot be said to be genuinely materialist.

[7] Both articles rehearse the same arguments, the latter introducing a slight modification in its acknowledgement that Murau is partially aware of his own misogyny.

[8] For a more detailed approach to the same topic, see my article "Resisting Bernhard."

[9] The anonymous friend and teacher in *Die Kälte* was revealed after Bernhard's death to have been the conductor Rudolf Brändle, whose memoir *Zeugenfreundschaft: Erinnerungen an Thomas Bernhard* is one of the more interesting books of the "I knew Thomas Bernhard" variety, and provides an informative companion-piece to *Die Kälte*.

[10] Cf. also: "Das sind die Sätze, Wörter, die man aufbaut. Im Grunde ist es wie ein Spielzeug, man setzt es übereinander, es ist ein musikalischer Vorgang" (It 80).

[11] The same can be witnessed in Huntemann's discussion of "Prosa und 'musikalische' Überstrukturierung" (*Artistik* 179–84), where a few comments on music give way to meditations on linguistic skepticism, style, monotony, and "Geschichtenzerstörung."

[12] We will return to Hamburger's theory in connection with the problem of deixis in *Alte Meister*.

[13] The same applies to most of Bernhard's other novels as well. For a critique of Stanzel in relation to Bernhard's autobiographical texts, see Parth 43–51.

[14] See Barthes, "Introduction"; Todorov, *Introduction* and *Poétique*; and Genette.

[15] Genette and his disciples, notably Shlomith Rimmon-Kenan and Mieke Bal, divide the text into three levels, effectively splitting 'discourse' into 'text' (which involves time structure, focalization, and characterization) and 'narration' (which concerns the act of narrating itself). Patrick O'Neill has pointed out, though, that how narrative texts are divided has less to do with the objective structures of the texts themselves than with the pragmatic concerns of the critic (*Fictions of Discourse* 22). In the present context a division into three is of negligible value for critical practice; I have retained the bipartite terminology favoured by Seymour Chatman in *Story and Discourse*.

[16] For theoretical discussions of this phenomenon, see Culler, *Pursuit of Signs* 172–87, and O'Neill, *Fictions of Discourse* 6–7.

[17] Cf. Hens's analysis of *Der Untergeher*, in which he claims that the discourse is responsible for the structure of the action, and not *vice versa*. Cf. also Marquardt 67.

[18] For an analysis of story in these terms, see Cohan and Shires 54–68.

# I.

# The Early Fiction

# 1: *Frost* and *Verstörung*

## *Frost*

BY 1963, THOMAS BERNHARD had been publishing in anthologies for almost ten years, and was also the author of four slim volumes of poetry and a libretto. But none of these works had attracted significant critical or public attention. In 1962, he also had a volume of short prose pieces, *Ereignisse*, at the proofs stage with the S. Fischer Verlag. These terse and often fantastic pieces of "Kürzestprosa" did not, however, appear until 1969 with the Literarisches Colloquium in Berlin. The main reason for this is suggested by Hans Höller: "Bernhard war von der Idee eingenommen, daß sein erster Prosa-Band unverwechselbar und überwältigend zu sein habe, ein Text, mit dem er die *Welt erobern* müsse."[1] The desire to take the literary world by storm caused Bernhard to withdraw *Ereignisse* so that *Frost* would be his first published volume of prose.

A measure of Bernhard's success in "conquering the world" can be gauged by the numerous positive reviews that the novel received.[2] Even today, the encounter with *Frost* can be an overwhelming experience. The originality of its subject matter, the bleakness and darkness of the world it describes, and the metaphorical density of its language have lost little of their fascination and power in the three and a half decades since the novel's first publication.

The narrator of *Frost* is a "Famulant," a medical student who is doing his clinical training in surgery at a provincial hospital in Schwarzach, under a surgeon named Strauch. As part of his training, he has been charged with the task of secretly observing the surgeon's brother, a painter who has all but withdrawn from human society and now lives in a remote provincial "Gasthaus." To this end, the narrator catches the early train at half past four one winter's morning, and sits in a stuffy compartment filled with exhausted snow shovellers returning from their night-shift. The train makes its way through a steep ravine, bearing the narrator towards Weng, an imaginary village at the head of a mountain valley in Austria's Salzach. The novel consists of a series of diary or notebook entries, recording the twenty-seven days that the narrator spends in Weng. Inserted between the entries for the twenty-sixth and

twenty-seventh days are the six letters that he writes to the surgeon
Strauch in the course of his sojourn.

In the diary entries, the narrator transcribes the confrontation between two distinct worlds. On the one hand is the realm of the empirical: he describes his surroundings and the life of the village, reminisces
about his own past life, and reflects on his future career options. On the
other hand is the potentially insane world of Strauch, whose monologues are addressed to the narrator in the course of daily rambles, and
transcribed by the latter in the notebook that constitutes the text.

This dual aspect of the narrative is figured in an episode where the
narrator finds himself standing on the doorstep of the inn:

> "Hören Sie, die Hunde! Hören Sie nur: das Hundegekläff." Und [der
> Maler] ging hinaus und in sein Zimmer. Als ich ihm folgte, in das
> Vorhaus hinaus, wo ich stehenblieb, hörte ich durch die offene, halb
> eingefrorene Gasthaustür das langgezogene Heulen der Hunde. Und
> das Gebell. Das unendlich langgezogene Heulen, in das das Gebell
> hineinbiß. Vor mir das Bellen und Heulen und hinter mir das Lachen
> und Erbrechen und Kartenschlagen. Vor mir die Hunde, hinter mir
> die Gäste. (Fr 135)

Throughout the text the painter makes the narrator aware of the bark-
ing of dogs, which is always audible even though the creatures themselves remain invisible (Fr 39, 46, 137, 311). In a longer passage, it
becomes apparent that the painter Strauch associates dogs with all
those forces that threaten to overwhelm the individual (Fr 150–2),
culminating in the pronouncement, "das ist das Gekläff des *Weltunter-
gangs*" (Fr 152). Once we realize the howling of dogs is a significant
element in Strauch's cosmology, the above passage begins to signify,
functioning as a metaphor for the situation of the narrator. He simultaneously inhabits the coarse physical world of the inn and the mystical-
apocalyptic mental world of the painter. The threshold of the inn signifies the boundary between sanity and madness.

The function of the narrative is to mediate between these two distinct
spheres of experience. This accounts for the profound schism that lies at
the heart of the text and manifests itself on numerous textual levels.

It is a commonplace in the literature on *Frost* that the narrator's role
is to act as a surrogate for the reader. As Strauch's narratee, the narrator
embodies both the problems of reception that the reader encounters,
and the attitudes that he or she should adopt toward Strauch's monologues.[3] This, however, simplifies the problem. First, the narrator is the
recipient of Strauch's monologues *as well as* those told by other characters in the inn: the engineer, the "Wasenmeister," the "Wirtin," and
the gendarme. Second, the narrator's role is both receptive and pro-

ductive: he is responsible for ordering his observations and representing them to a potential reader. It becomes apparent that he intends for his diary to be *read* in the oft-quoted passage "*Die Felsschlucht,*" where he repeats the opening words of that particular micronarrative, "Um Unklarheiten in diesem 'Fürchterlichen' vorzubeugen, sie einfach nicht zu gestatten, sich und *dem, der das liest,* nicht, ein und für allemal nicht zu gestatten" (Fr 295, my italics).

An analysis of the reader position offered by *Frost,* then, has to take into account the relationship between the narrator and *all* the other storytellers within the text, not merely Strauch. It also has to consider the question of writing: the issue of narrative representation that is frequently thematized in the text.

A large proportion of *Frost* is not told but *re*told: several events are related to the narrator by a third party, then relayed on to the reader.[4] In these acts of storytelling the textual duality first manifests itself, for the narratives of the villagers differ palpably from Strauch's monologues. The narratives are significant in that they appear to be unproblematic examples of narrative transmission, posing no problems of understanding or representation for the narrator. At the same time, however, he attributes no significance to them other than that of the empirical: we learn nothing of his reactions to the various stories. He does not interpret them as conveying figurative or conceptual meaning, nor does he establish a specifically contrastive relationship between these narratives and Strauch's discourse.

Where Strauch's monologues are concerned, the narrator's reaction is primarily one of confusion and incomprehension, and this leads him to muse repeatedly on the problem of writing. The interrelated problems of understanding and representation are directly addressed in one of the most frequently quoted passages of the text:

> Was ist das für eine Sprache, die Sprache Strauchs? Was fange ich mit seinen Gedankenfetzen an? Was mir zuerst zerrissen, zusammenhanglos schien, hat seine "wirklich ungeheuren Zusammenhänge"; das Ganze ist eine alles erschreckende Worttransfusion in die Welt, in die Menschen hinein [. . .]. *Wie* aufschreiben? *Was* für Notizen? Bis wohin denn Schematisches, systematisch? (Fr 137)

The lack of coherence and general fragmentation of Strauch's monologues represent a barrier to understanding: "Auch wenn er sagt: 'Die Wirklichkeit hat niemals ein Mitgefühl,' und es ganz für sich sagt, wie es scheint, ohne Zusammenhang zwischen dem, was er vorher gesagt hat, und dem nachher, verstehe ich eigentlich nicht, was er meint" (Fr 136, cf. also 225, 229, 252). Even a letter to his parents is fraught with the difficulty of constructing something coherent: "Einzelheiten setzten sich in meinem Kopf zusammen. Dann aber, nachdem ich drei, vier Sätze geschrieben hatte, warf ich das Papier in den Ofen" (Fr 90). The narrator is equally incapable of writing to the surgeon, claiming that the very act of committing to paper what he has in mind kills and falsifies it (Fr 229). He ends up calling into question the very writing project on which he is engaged, namely the diary that constitutes the bulk of *Frost*: "Ich weiß nicht, ist alles Unsinn? Unsinn, was ich jetzt schreibe ja tief in die Nacht, in der 'grenzenlosen Unwissenheit der Finsternis'" (Fr 281).

Both narrative situations — unproblematic comprehension and virtual incomprehension — paradoxically appear to produce the same result: the narrator's own discourse tends to reproduce the narrative and syntactic forms used by the characters he quotes. The straightforward stories told by the "Wirtin" and her guests are linear in their progression and contain little metaphorical elaboration, while Strauch's largely circular, static monologues are conveyed in the densely figurative but conceptually vague formulations of the painter himself. The split at the heart of the text between the empirical world of Weng and the mystical-apocalyptic world of Strauch is thus inscribed in the narrator's attempts to transmit the various micronarratives of which his text is composed.

The narrator is, however, incapable of formulating a "metadiscourse" that would allow him and his readers to understand Strauch in terms of a more familiar language. Consequently, he slowly begins (as most commentators on *Frost* have noted) to lose his contours as a separate individual and falls increasingly within Strauch's sphere of influence. Eventually he announces, "Ich bin nicht mehr ich" (Fr 281), and the six letters to the surgeon recapitulate the process in both their explicit content and their form. The narrator is initially certain of his ability to differentiate himself from the painter (Fr 296), then expresses contradictory sentiments in this regard in the second letter (Fr 300–1), and finally admits in the fourth letter: "Tatsache ist, daß ich von den Gedanken Ihres Herrn Bruders durchsetzt bin" (Fr 306). Even in the early letters, the language used by the narrator to present his "findings" is precisely that of Strauch.

Yet to claim that the narrator occupies the reader's position in the text is clearly not the case. While he may fail to integrate into an overarching whole the various micronarratives told to him by the "secondary narrators" within the represented world, the reader *is* in a position to make sense of this failure, which is conditioned by the narrator's status as an inhabitant of two incommensurable worlds, and by his attempts to mediate between them.

The distinction drawn between Strauch's monologues and the stories told by the other characters is a simplification, for the passages that betray a failure of narrative transmission in terms of the narrator's receptive and productive capacities are associated solely with the fragmentary and trope-laden language of Strauch's inner life. Those episodes where Strauch succeeds in putting together a coherent narrative are not affected by the same problems. Therefore, the text's fundamental duality exists not merely in the relationship between Strauch and the other characters in the novel; it is also reproduced within his monologues.

Much of what he says to the narrator is perfectly lucid, and consists of more or less straightforward narratives that give the lie — at least in part — to the narrator's claim: "Die Erzählkunst ist anderen Charaktern vorbehalten, nicht ihm" (Fr 74). Strauch's narratives fall into three main groups. The first group is concerned with his previous (damaged) life. We learn, for example, about his childhood; his relationship with his parents, grandparents, and siblings; and his general loneliness (Fr 31–3). We are told of his housekeeper (Fr 66–7), his early encounters with death (Fr 70–71), his experiences as a supply teacher (Fr 170–5, 198–9), his sister's rape (Fr 197–8), and his career as an artist (Fr 204–5). The second group of Strauch's narratives helps to fill in background information about the "Wirtin" and her husband (Fr 109–10), her rapacious sexuality (Fr 21–3, 166), the local priest (Fr 143–4), the morbidity of the local population (Fr 152), and the building of the inn (Fr 168). Third, he reports coherently on events that happen to him at Weng when he is not in the company of the narrator: his visit to the "Armenhaus," during which he has a conversation with the "Oberin" but fails to notice that there's a man dying in the same room (Fr 103–8); his being the last person to speak to the "Holzzieher" before the latter is crushed beneath the tracks of his sleigh (Fr 226–8); and his discovery of the gruesome aftermath of the cattle theft, where he finds the river running red with the blood of slaughtered cows (Fr 272–9).

Yet the narratives belonging to this third group are already explicitly signaled by the painter as belonging to an order of meaning beyond that of the merely empirical. When he finally notices the man in the "Armenhaus," he assumes that he is already dead, then realizes that he is alive, until he falls, dead, from the bench on which he has been lying (Fr 105–7). It remains unclear whether the man was ever alive in the first place, or whether Strauch had hallucinated his movements. There is also a hint that Strauch's assumption that he was dead has somehow *caused* the death.[5] Furthermore, the repetition of the words "wie ein Hund" is an allusion to Josef K.'s last words in Kafka's *Der Proceß*. Intertextual references of this kind are usually interpretative hints to the reader, providing a literary context against which the present work might be read. In *Frost*, however, not only are the links between Bernhard's and Kafka's texts decidedly unclear, but Josef K.'s last words, "wie ein Hund," in *Der Proceß* are themselves open to multiple interpretations. Meaning is both hinted at and withheld.

In the *"Geschichte mit dem toten Holzzieher,"* Strauch is disconcerted by the presence of two strangers, whom he sees shortly before the accident and again, in exactly the same place, four hours later, as though they had been waiting for him (Fr 226, 228). After the "Holzzieher's" funeral he remarks, "'Merkwürdig, ich war der, der mit dem Holzzieher das letzte Wort gesprochen hat. Kein Mensch weiß das,'" a comment that sends shivers down the narrator's spine (Fr 262).

In the episode entitled *"Das Viehdiebsgesindel,"* not only does the river of blood have heavily Biblical connotations, but Strauch finds a headscarf that he describes as a "'fürchterliches Indiz [. . .] nicht wahr, man könnte sich ohne weiteres vorstellen, daß es sich bei den Opfern um Menschen handelt [. . .]'" (Fr 278). Thus, even in these three episodes, the empirical threatens to flip over into the parabolic or allegorical without the "hidden meaning" being clearly specifiable.[6] Once we get to the *"Geschichte mit dem Landstreicher,"* who juggles with his own legs and makes his head disappear (Fr 234–40), any attempt to read events as representations of an empirical world is thwarted.

These episodes reveal intimations of hidden meanings behind events firmly rooted in Strauch's everyday experience. In this sense they are symptomatic of many of his monologues, which are dominated by the "master trope" of pan-signification, namely the tendency for everything to signify something else.[7] At several points this is explicitly signaled. On one occasion the painter says: "Von jedem Gegenstand, von allem kann man auf alles kommen" (Fr 119), and in the following lengthy passage, the narrator discusses the way in which this occurs through a process of metaphorical identifications:

> Wie er das Gasthaus mit einem Kärntner Gebirgsdorf und mit einer Tänzerin, die nur ein einziges Mal in der Oper aufgetreten ist und die er als "ein Naturtalent, aber sehr gefährlich" bezeichnet, in Zusammenhang bringt, das ist aufschlußreich. Einen Gemüsehändler, der ihm einmal auf den Kopf geschlagen hat in der Meinung, er sei ein Paradeiserdieb, mit Napoleon dem Dritten. (Fr 112)

A further passage shows pan-signification operating through metonymy, as objects are linked to one another by contiguity (nearness): "ein Tisch ist auch ein Fenster, und ein Fenster ist auch die Frau, die am Fenster steht, ein Bachbett zugleich das Gebirge, das sich im Bachbett spiegelt, eine Stadt auch die Luft über dieser Stadt" (Fr 217).[8]

Pan-signification reaches its probable extreme when the narrator realizes that Strauch's way of using words detaches them from their conventional meaning and fills them with random semantic content in a way that draws attention to what structural linguists have called the "arbitrary nature of the signifier": "Das Wort 'Kornähre' hat unter Umständen die Bedeutung 'unsere ganze Wohlstandsgeschichte'" (Fr 231); and "'[. . .] Frost zum Beispiel' sagte der Maler, 'bedeutet bei dem einen die Frostbeule, die er hat, bei dem andern ein Sommerstädtchen . . . Schließlich kann Frost auch *Untergang eines Weltreichs* bedeuten, wie wir wissen'" (Fr 259). These examples undermine the assumption of a stable relationship between words and the concepts to which they refer (their referents). In principle, any verbal sign could signify *anything*.[9]

Pan-signification also manifests itself in Strauch's use of the abstract as a trope for the concrete and vice versa, and in his tendency to interpret natural objects as ciphers for something else: "'Hier ist jeder Stein für mich eine Menschengeschichte', sagt der Maler. 'Sie müssen wissen, ich bin diesem Ort verfallen. Alles, jeder Geruch, ist hier an ein Verbrechen gekettet, an eine Mißhandlung, an den Krieg, an irgendeinem infamen Zugriff . . .'" (Fr 53). *Pace* Schmidt-Dengler, this latter example does not fall under the rubric of the concrete being seen in terms of the abstract; it is not that "die Geschichte in die Natur eingegangen [ist]" ("Zurück zum Text" 213). Rather, the natural world is linked metonymically — "gekettet" is clearly a relation of contiguity, not similarity — to history by being the *site* of war, crime, violation.

If pan-signification exists in nature, then the related concept of pan-causality governs the individual body:

> "Es besteht wahrscheinlich ein geheimer Zusammenhang zwischen meinem Kopfschmerz und diesen Fußschmerzen," sagte er. [. . .] Die Schmerzen, die er im Fuß hat und die in der Frühe plötzlich da waren, seien mit den Schmerzen in seinem Kopf verwandt. "Mir scheint, es sind dieselben Schmerzen." Man könne an zwei verschiedenen, weit auseinander liegenden Körperteilen die gleichen Schmerzen haben, "ein und denselben Schmerz." (Fr 48)

The narrator contrasts this "holistic" view of the body with the medical-scientific view of disease, claiming that Strauch's ailment is nothing more than a harmless boil caused by his march through the "Hohlweg" on the previous day, and has nothing to do with his aching brain (Fr 49). But the painter perseveres in the belief that there is an occult link between the boil on his foot and his headaches (Fr 82, 84–5), both being governed by the same absent but omnipresent cause.

These examples demonstrate Strauch's method of analogical thought ("Analogiedenken"), which Hermann Helms-Derfert has linked to the writings of the Romantic poet Novalis (17–18), and which the narrator of *Frost* himself adopts when he claims, in his first letter to the surgeon, to have discovered "*einen* Weg der Entdeckungen, einen solchen der *neben*einander-*in*einander-*unter*einander verlaufenden, *mit*einander korrespondierenden Anschauungsmöglichkeiten, der, wie ich hoffe, brauchbare Ergebnisse zeitigen wird" (Fr 297).

Although pan-causality and pan-signification imply a world in which everything is interlinked there is also a sense in which they ultimately entail a breakdown of connections. So, for example, exposing the arbitrariness of signs results in a collapse of signification. Employing the abstract as a trope for the concrete and vice versa subverts the distinction between the two, resulting simultaneously in a "stets zurückgenomme-ne[r] Realismus" and a "stets zurückgenommene Symbolik" (Schmidt-Dengler, "Zurück zum Text" 213). Seeing the natural world as a sign of the events that have taken place in it undermines the distinction between matter and history, and categories of time and space. Furthermore, Strauch's holistic view of the body collapses the mind-body duality upon which the tradition of Western philosophy and medical science depend, and his tendency to interpret the world solely in relation to the self results in a blurring of the boundaries between inner and outer, self and world. At one level Strauch construes everything as an analogue of something else, involving, at another level, a dissolution of conceptual thought, the "Auflösen ohne Ende aller Begriffe" (Fr 43). "Der Maler Strauch," writes the narrator, "gehört zu denen, die alles flüssig machen. Was sie anrühren, schmilzt" (Fr 111). The "begriffslos[e] Begriffswelt" (Fr 305) that Strauch inhabits is a world of pure identity, devoid of difference, where two opposite concepts can be used at the same time and without contradiction: "Ein Gesetz, daß alles sich wiederholt, gleichzeitig unwiederholbar ist"; "'ich bin ein Opfer meiner Theorien, gleichzeitig ihr Beherrscher'" (Fr 43).

Our capacity for thinking in analogies is in principle unrestricted: to the mind, anything can be perceived as resembling anything else. Nevertheless, in the foregoing I have implied a contrast between "plausible" and "random" similarities. The ability to make such distinctions is based on the assumption that two things can be legitimately compared only if the comparison remains within certain socially sanctioned conceptions of similitude.[10] The boundaries of metaphor are "policed" by convention, and once the perception of resemblances begins to exceed these implicit norms, the suspicion of madness is aroused. Foucault defines the madman as "celui qui s'est *aliéné* dans l'*analogie* [. . .], il n'est le Différent que dans la mesure où il ne connaît pas la Différence; il ne voit partout que ressemblances et signes de la ressemblance" (Foucault 63). This corresponds precisely to Strauch's habit of mind: everything is seen in terms of its resemblance to something else. In this sense, he speaks the language of madness, and the narrator, as his surreptitious amanuensis, transcribes the content and syntax of Strauch's monologues in a way that blurs the boundaries between Strauch and his own sense of selfhood, even as it reinforces the split between Strauch and the external world.

There is a second fundamental difference between Strauch's monologues and the words of the other characters concerning their status as narrative. Much of what Strauch says is not open to analysis in strictly narrative terms because it lacks the criteria by which narrative is usually defined.[11] There is thus a further conflict at the heart of the text between the coherently linear stories told by other characters and the static outpourings of Strauch.

Several critics have drawn attention to the symptoms of schizophrenia manifested by some of Bernhard's characters. Jürgen Petersen points out that both Strauch and Saurau are schizophrenics ("Beschreibung" 145), while Renate Fueß analyzes several of Bernhard's prose and dramatic works in terms of the "double bind," a psychological dilemma particularly associated with schizophrenia. Bernhard Sorg analyzes Saurau's language in *Verstörung*, claiming that his thought processes are characterized by abrupt jumps from one "Empfindlichkeitswort" to another, a feature typical of the speech of schizophrenics (*Thomas Bernhard* 76). From the point of view of narrative analysis, however, the most useful discussion of schizophrenia is provided by Fredric Jameson. Drawing on Lacanian psychoanalysis, Jameson proposes a link between linguistic malfunction and the psyche of the schizophrenic. Personal identity, he claims, is the effect of a temporal unification of the past and future with one's present, and this unification is a function of language, "or better still the sentence as it moves along its hermeneutic circle through time. If we are unable to unify the past, present, and future of the sentence, then we are similarly unable to unify the past, present, and future of our own biographical experience or psychic life" (*Postmodernism* 26–7). When the signifying chain breaks down and the ability to formulate complete sentences collapses, psychic experience is reduced to a series of unrelated present moments in time.

This clearly corresponds to the properties of Strauch's monologues: his sentences follow one another without any specifiable coordinating or subordinating relations between them, each one existing as though in an atemporal void. As Jameson writes: "a primacy of the present sentence in time ruthlessly disintegrates the narrative fabric that attempts to reform around it."[12] In the following passage, for example, the narrator relays one of Strauch's monologues in the third person:

> Die Morgen kommen über ein Kornfeld herauf. Über den See. Über den Fluß. Über den Wald. Vom Hügel herüber. Im frischen Wind Vogelstimmen. Abende, die in Schilfrohr und Schweigen untergehen, in das er seine ersten Gebete hineinspricht. Pferdewiehern zerreißt die Finsternis. Säufer, Fuhrwerker, Fledermäuse erschrecken ihn. Drei tote Mitschüler auf der Straße. Ein gekentertes Boot, das ein Ertrunkener nicht mehr erreichen konnte. Hilferufe. Riesige Käselaibe haben die Kraft, ihn zu erdrücken. Versteckt in einem Bräuhauskeller, fürchtet er sich. Zwischen Grabsteinen wird ein Spiel gespielt, in dem Zahlen von einem zum anderen geworfen werden. Totenschädel blinken in der Sonne. Türen gehen auf und zu. In Pfarrhäusern wird gegessen. In Küchen gekocht. In Schlachthäusern geschlachtet. In Bäckereien gebacken. In Schusterwerkstätten geschustert. In Schulen unterrichtet: bei offenen Fenstern, so daß einem angst und bang wird. Umzüge zeigen bunte Gesichter. Täuflinge schauen schwachsinnig. Ein Bischof läßt alle in Hochrufe ausbrechen. (Fr 71)

Every time a stable story or scenario begins to form, it is interrupted by a non sequitur, which thwarts any attempt to establish narrative coherence and compels the reader to devote attention to each individual sentence. This characteristic of *Frost* makes certain passages almost unreadable. More importantly, however, it allows a diagnosis of Strauch's "madness" in linguistic terms and enables us to conceptualize the correlation between temporality, sanity, and narrative on the one hand, and stasis, insanity, and "schizophrenic" writing on the other. The former are characteristic of the stories told by the "Wirtin" and her guests, while the latter are attributes of Strauch's outpourings.

This distinction applies, *mutatis mutandis*, to the structure of the novel as a whole. Bernhard's choice of diary form in *Frost* is of crucial significance but has hitherto received rather scanty attention from critics. It is a mode of writing that goes back to the beginning of the novel's dominance as a cultural form, even if it has lately been largely displaced into more popular genres (George and Weedon Grossmith's *The Diary of a Nobody*, Helen Fielding's *Bridget Jones's Diary*, and so on). Consisting of a series of dates, the diary form implies a notion of linear temporality. Furthermore, the dating of entries signals the way in which the novel is to be read by creating in the reader certain expectations of genre.[13] Our "intertextual" acquaintance with other diary novels leads us to expect a "teleological" narrative in which individual details can be integrated and given meaning from the perspective of the end.

Nevertheless, the diary form is in principle (if not often in practice) considerably more complex than this. The typical mode of narration in the novel is "ulterior," the events having notionally already happened before the narrative begins, whereas diary novels involve what is known as "intercalated narration": each individual episode is recorded retrospectively but without the writer's knowledge of the events that are going to follow it. The diary form is thus potentially endless and therefore also potentially meaningless. The function of the editor, with which many traditional diary (and epistolary) fictions begin, is to guarantee meaningfulness: we are going to be presented with a set of events whose significance may not have been immediately apparent to the person or persons writing, but which in fact possesses the shape and attributes of the well-formed plot.

Thomas Bernhard's diary novel, however, not only dispenses with an editor, but cannot be understood in terms of teleology. Although the opening of the novel implies that it will lead to a diagnosis of Strauch, such a diagnosis depends on the narrator's ability to occupy the position of a medical or scientific observer. As the narrator slowly abandons this position, the reader is forced to abandon any expectation of a resolution. In its open-endedness, *Frost* robs the reader of a stable moment of closure from which to gauge the ultimate significance or "point" of the narrative. The "Famulant" returns to the hospital in Schwarzach and then resumes his studies in Vienna, but he proffers no answers to the questions he has raised about his own future (Fr 160–1). He learns from the newspaper that Strauch has gone missing in the snow (Fr 316), but any definitive knowledge of Strauch's death is withheld. At the end of the text the narrator, like his counterpart in another Austrian text dealing with the search for a missing person in the snow, remains "ein Chronist, dem der Trost des Endes fehlt" (Ransmayr 275).

The result of this technique is that *Frost* resists interpretation in terms of the "hermeneutic circle" to which Jameson refers. The hermeneutic circle is the process of reading a text in which the parts are comprehensible only in terms of the whole, which is itself comprehensible only in terms of the parts. A provisional conception of the whole guides our interpretation of individual details, while simultaneously being corrected and modified by them. *Frost*, however, can clearly not be read in this way. *Frost* is such a challenging reading experience because it is almost impossible to posit a provisional whole toward which individual narrative episodes could be seen as contributing. Conversely, the whole does not amount to a "plot" within which the individual episodes can be retrospectively integrated. Instead, the narrator merely accumulates narrative fragments, an aspect of the text to which an early reviewer alluded when he commented that Bernhard had failed to produce a readable and comprehensible narrative, but that some "geschlossene Prosastücke" could be isolated from the context of the novel and lead an independent existence (Jokostra).

Peter Bürger has addressed the problems posed by this kind of accumulative text in a discussion of André Breton's surrealist novel *Nadja*:

> Zwar besteht zwischen [den einzelnen Ereignissen] kein narrativer Zusammenhang, so daß die letzte Begebenheit die voraufgegangenen erzähllogisch voraussetzte; wohl aber besteht ein Zusammenhang anderer Art zwischen den Ereignissen: Sie folgen alle dem gleichen Strukturmuster. In Begriffen des Strukturalismus formuliert: Der Zusammenhang ist paradigmatischer, nicht syntagmatischer Natur. (P. Bürger 107)

Bürger's categories are to be understood as relative rather than absolute, for it is possible to analyze any narrative in terms of both the syntagmatic and paradigmatic relations existing between the events it portrays. Syntagmatically, events are ordered sequentially by means of enchainment or embedding. Paradigmatic groupings of events, on the other hand, "are based on *type*, events of one kind as opposed to another; or on *location*, events occurring at one setting as opposed to another; or on *actors*, events involving one set of characters as opposed to another" (Cohan and Shires 67).

Although the use of the term "paradigm" here involves a metaphorical extension beyond its meaning in structural linguistics, it is clearly useful as a tool in narrative analysis. All three of Cohan and Shires's criteria for the paradigmatic grouping of narrative events are simultaneously present in *Frost*. In terms of type, most of the twenty-seven days rehearse the confrontation between the two worlds in a series of communal mealtime scenes at the "Gasthaus," and the narrator's walks through the snowbound landscape with the painter. Similarly, the limited spatial setting and small cast of characters mean that events lend themselves to paradigmatic grouping according to location and actors.

Conventional, unproblematically "hermeneutic" narratives continuously generate the question "what happened next?" and thus tend to foreground the sequential ordering of events. In *Frost*, however, hermeneutic structuration is problematized: there is a discrepancy between the questions the text raises and the answers it provides, and the end loses its capacity to guarantee narrative meaning. The function of the narrative syntagma in *Frost*, then, is paradoxically to encourage a shift of interpretative attention towards the paradigmatic relationships between the fragments: they are seen in a relation of resemblance. In other words, the various episodes are connected *analogically*, which in turn introduces a moment of stasis into the progression implied by the diary entries.

Furthermore, the twenty-seven-day period spent by the narrator in Weng appears to exist in what Robert Menasse terms "eine enthistorisierte Meta-Zeit." Menasse attributes this to the "Abfolge nicht näher datierter Tage," in which historically unspecifiable events take place (*Überbau* 97). But it is also due to the narrator's failure to provide genuinely narrative links between the period at Weng and the biographical events that precede and follow it. The events in Weng exist in no clear causal or even temporal relationship to the remainder of the narrator's life. It is as though they were removed from time.

We have seen that *Frost* involves a collision, in the form of syntax and content, between the "sane" narrative world of Weng and its inhabitants on the one hand, and the "mad" discursive world of Strauch on the other. This same conflict is also inscribed in the text's narrative structure: there is a profound diremption between the narrative linearity promised by the diary form and the narrative stasis created both by the paradigmatic relations between individual fragments, and by the fact that the narrator's sojourn in Weng remains an isolated episode, severed from its consequences for his future experience. The tension between linear narrative sequences and analogically related episodes reproduces at the level of narrative form the confrontation of sanity and madness that forms the thematic nexus of the text. The interpenetration of the two forms — the syntagmatic and the analogical — thus replays the blurring of boundaries between sanity and insanity that occurs at the thematic and syntactic level in the narrator's steadily succumbing to the pull of Strauch's monologues.

## *Verstörung*

On the opening page of Bernhard's autobiographical memoir *Wittgensteins Neffe*, we learn that *Verstörung* was written in 1966 in Brussels (WN 7). It was published in 1967, four years after *Frost*, and was Bernhard's second novel. In the interim he had published various pieces of short fiction, the most notable being the novella-length text *Amras*. *Amras* is a highly fragmentary narrative telling the story of two brothers, Karl and Walter, the survivors of a fourfold suicide attempt that claimed the lives of their parents. As the text's epigraph, "Das Wesen der Krankheit ist so dunkel als das Wesen des Lebens," makes clear,

*Amras* moves within the same orbit of madness, morbidity, and mortality as *Frost* had done.

Bernhard continues his exploration of these thematic issues in *Verstörung*. The novel's narrator is the son of a country doctor, who accompanies his father on his rounds one late-September Saturday. The text is divided into two long sections. The first, untitled, narrates a series of visits to patients who are all more or less chronically, if not terminally, ill. The second section, which accounts for roughly two thirds of the novel, takes place at Schloß Hochgobernitz and is entitled "Der Fürst." The eponymous prince bears the name Saurau, and the remainder of the text consists primarily of a transcription of his extended monologue. The first section of *Verstörung*, then, sees the narrator and the doctor driving steadily further into a ravine, but in the second section they climb up to the lofty Hochgobernitz with its panoramic views. Critics are largely in agreement about the meaning of spatial symbolism in *Verstörung*. In terms of pathology, the movement from "low" to "high" represents a shift from physical to mental disease; historically speaking, the topography of the text symbolizes the contrast between the Second Austrian Republic and the Habsburg Monarchy; while politically it is informed by the opposition between the bourgeoisie or proletariat, and the feudal aristocracy (Helms-Derfert 41; Donnenberg, "Gehirnfähigkeit" 32, 34).

*Verstörung* is not an intricately plotted novel. The events are related temporally but not causally or logically, and mere chronological succession is the principle governing the organization of the narrative syntagma. As Josef Donnenberg points out, the linear narrative of the doctor's visits is a device that links the individual narrative episodes "externally," while the fact that they are all pathological case histories relates them "internally" ("Gehirnfähigkeit" 31). The way in which Donnenberg elaborates this thesis makes it clear that his terms correspond closely to the syntagma-paradigm opposition used to characterize the narrative of *Frost*:

> Die einzelnen Berichtsabschnitte sind nicht einfach additiv gereiht, wie etwa beim Stationenroman, sondern korrelativ gruppiert, d.h. wechselseitig aufeinander bezogen, in Analogien einander entsprechend. Sie sind thematisch analog (Krankheitsfälle bestimmter Art) und sie sind analog in der Konfiguration der betroffenen Personen. ("Gehirnfähigkeit" 32)

Donnenberg effectively argues that the lack of causal connections between events is counterbalanced by the paradigmatic relations existing between them: they are linked by means of their structural and thematic similarity. The question is this: what is the function of these aspects of narrative structure in *Verstörung*? The answer lies not only in the thematics of disease, but in a more compelling similarity between the diverse episodes in *Verstörung*: the almost obsessive concern with transgenerational relationships.

Questions of parents and children — particularly fathers and sons — occupy a privileged position in *Verstörung* because they inform the novel's two major character configurations: the narrator accompanying his father on his rounds provides the motivation for the text; and Saurau's monologue persistently returns to thoughts about his dead father and his absent son. The other episodes in the text likewise rehearse a repertoire of relationships between parents and their offspring. Underlying these relationships is a sense that transmission from generation to generation — in terms of heredity, cultural values, and property — has become problematic or disrupted. Rather then being purely personal, this disruption is symptomatic of the wider problem of Austrian history. This is hinted at in several episodes in the first section, and becomes explicit in Saurau's monologues. As we shall see, the Prince's concerns with his own family situation are inextricably linked to more general questions of Austria's cultural, political, and economic past, and the relationship between Habsburg absolutism and the capitalist democracy of the Second Republic.[14] The narrative form of *Verstörung* thus has to be understood in the light of the problems of both personal and historical transmission.

In the narrative of the teacher with whose death the novel opens, questions of transmission are limited to the issue of "Erziehung." The doctor tells the teacher's story as he and the narrator are having lunch in a "Wirtshaus." We learn that he was a pederast whose "mehrmalige[r] Umgang mit einem *nervösen Knaben*" caused him initially to flee to the Tyrol, then to Italy and Slovenia for two years, after which he gave himself up and spent four years in custody (V 51–2). The sexual assault of a child is an example of a problematic relationship between generations. The teacher-pupil relationship based on the passing on of knowledge is displaced into deviant sexuality that collapses generational difference, and the resultant death sees the teacher's parents burying their child.[15]

During the doctor's visit to Frau Ebenhöh, we learn that her son suffers from an inexplicable mental disability. Both her own family and that of her husband, we are told, contain nothing but "feinnervige, ordentliche Menschen," whereas her son is an "Ungestüm" (V 33) who thus represents an anomaly in terms of genetic transmission.[16] Furthermore, he plunges his father into severe depression and causes him to be plagued by "Erziehungszweifeln" — a failure to transmit knowledge

and cultural values (V 32). Genetic and cultural transmission are aug-
mented in this case by questions of property. Frau Ebenhöh has already
bequeathed her house to her son, despite her conviction that as soon as
she is dead he will sell it and squander the money "in der kürzesten
Zeit" (V 34), an anxiety that pre-empts on a small scale Saurau's decision to make his son the only heir of Hochgobernitz, despite his profound fear that his son will liquidate the estate. The son of the
Ebenhöh family represents a rupture in the continuity of the family line
in terms of genetic material, cultural values, and property.

In the story of the young Krainer, this thematic constellation is repeated in transposed form. The disability this time is both mental and
physical, but fulfills the same function in that it betokens the end of the
family line. Krainer also represents a discontinuity in the transmission of
cultural values. In the days before the onset of his mental illness he had
been a gifted cellist, oboist, and pianist, until he had suddenly assaulted
his teacher with a violin bow (V 73). His sister tells the narrator that
the teacher stopped visiting, and her brother's condition worsened until he became pathologically violent. He is now not only bedridden, but
sometimes has to be restrained by a cage-like apparatus placed over his
bed. "Jetzt sei es ihm nicht mehr möglich, gleich welche Musikstücke
im Kopf zu harmonisieren," his sister adds. "Seine Musik sei *entsetzlich*" (V 74). Having once been a vehicle for the preservation of the
music of the past, Krainer now merely distorts it, and this is exemplified
in his defacing the engravings of great composers that adorn his room.
It is notable that most of the composers were born within the territo-
ries of the old Habsburg empire: Bartók, Beethoven, Mozart, Haydn,
Schubert, Gluck, and Bruckner (V 75–6): Krainer's illness impedes
transmission of a *specifically Austrian* musical tradition.

There is thus a historical dimension contained within Krainer's narrative, and this dimension becomes more prominent in the story of the
Fochler family, owners of a mill that had been given to them in the last
century by a member of the Saurau family as the result of a bet (V 63).
This fact can be read as a microcosmic representation of the shifts in
the distribution of property between the nineteenth century and the
present: rather than existing as subjects of the Saurau family within a
feudal structure, the Fochlers are now producers within market capitalism. Illustrative of this historical change is their acquisition of a Turkish
"Gastarbeiter": there are no longer limits to the mobility of labor,
which can now be exported and imported just as goods can.

As the narrator strolls around the grounds of the mill, he comes
across a large aviary in which the birds appear desperately agitated (V
58–9). The younger of the two Fochler sons then takes him into a shed

where he sees forty-two dead exotic birds, about the same number as are still in the cage. They had been strangled by the Fochlers and the Turk, and the three men plan to kill the remaining birds that evening (V 60). The birds were bequeathed to them by a recently deceased uncle, and the reason for killing them is that since his death three weeks previously there has been no letup in their "fürchterliches Geschrei" (V 60–1). The birds, says the miller's son, had been strangled in a way that preserved their plumage:

> Auf diese Weise müßten sie sich von den Vögeln nicht trennen [. . .]. Sie wollten sie selber präparieren und ausstopfen und ein ganzes Zimmer, das Zimmer des verstorbenen Bruders des Mühlenbesitzers, mit ihnen anfüllen; er, sagte der Müllerssohn, habe die Idee gehabt, ein Vogelmuseum in der Fochlermühle einzurichten. (V 61)

Even on a literal level, this passage addresses the problems of property transfer: how to deal with a bequest that is experienced as a burden. Andreas Gößling interprets this passage as an example of what he calls the "restaurativer Code," namely the desire, shared by several of Bernhard's protagonists, to reconstruct a vanished or destroyed past by means of mere façade (*Thomas Bernhards frühe Prosakunst* 221). It is possible, however, to propose a more specific metaphorical reading of this episode, for the conservative, restorative tendencies demonstrated by some of Bernhard's protagonists are rooted in postwar Austrian cultural and political life.[17] Robert Menasse has suggested that the attempt to create an Austrian national identity by stressing the continuity of the Habsburg past into the Second Republic resulted in cultural policies whose ultimate effect was to turn Austria into a museum: "Hauptaufgabe des nun so kleinen und schwachen Österreich — so hieß es — könne es nur sein, sein großes kulturelles Erbe aus stolzer Zeit zu pflegen und zu erhalten — mit anderen Worten, man beschloß ein republikanisches Museum der Habsburgermonarchie zu sein" (*Überbau* 171). In light of this, the "Fochlermühle" incident can be read as a literalization of the metaphors that Menasse and others have used to characterize Austria's postwar cultural "Selbstverständnis": the impossibility of maintaining a *living* tradition, the notion of *preserving* a *dead* past, the sense that Austria is a *museum*. To see the "Fochlermühle" narrative as a figure for — or, more modestly, an echo of — the situation of the Second Republic would indeed seem far-fetched, were it not that the thematics of tradition and its relation to the present is germane to the entire text and also finds itself embodied, as we have seen, in the family history of the Fochlers.

The narratives of the Krainer and Fochler families demonstrate that problems of transmission from one generation to the next possess a historical significance that transcends the immediate family context. In Saurau's disturbed relationship with his son, the question of history is foregrounded to an even greater extent.

The son is absent. He lives in London and is writing a dissertation on Karl Marx's own doctoral dissertation on the philosophy of Democritus and Epicurus (V 126). The key to their relationship, as most critics of *Verstörung* have noted, is Saurau's minutely detailed premonitory dream (V 118–32). The subject of the dream is a piece of writing composed by the son eight months after Saurau's projected suicide (V 118). In the document, Saurau's son sets forth his plans to liquidate the entirety of Hochgobernitz: "Diese glänzende Wirtschaft habe *ich* ruiniert! Diesen ungeheuren Land- und Forstwirtschafts*anachronismus!*" (V 119). He decrees that absolutely nothing useful should be done anywhere on the estate (V 122), and revels in the fact that, to exact revenge on his father, he now uses the latter's office as a reading room for the study of left-wing political theory (V 123–4).

The son writes about the arrival in Hochgobernitz of the "Gemeindesekretär" Moser, a representative of the state, who tries to persuade him to allow local people to harvest the crops before they rot in the ground (V 128). His response is:

> Aber auch Moser weiß, daß es kein Gesetz gibt, das mir Vorschriften in bezug auf die arrondierten Hochgobernitzschen Gründe machen könnte! Abernten!! Wieder höre ich, was ich schon oft gehört habe, von Gemeindenot, Volksnot, Menschennot, Armut, Gemeinschaft, *Volks*gemeinschaft, Schädlingsbekämpfung usf., schreibt mein Sohn. Aber wie wagt es dieser Mensch, schreibt er, immer wieder aufzutauchen in einer Sache, die erledigt ist, *Hochgobernitz ist erledigt.* (V 128)

There is a profound diremption here between the son's interest in proletarian revolution at a theoretical level and his failure to turn it into meaningful social praxis: the destruction of Hochgobernitz is divorced from social aims and becomes an end in itself. The encounter with Moser shows that Saurau's son's motivation in liquidating the estate is conceived less in terms of social justice and the redistribution of wealth than in the proprietorial rights of the landed aristocracy to act independently of the state. In fact, however, they betray a fear of powerlessness, as the exercise of feudal autonomy is reduced to pointless devastation.[18]

The son's narrative remains at the level of fantasy. There is no indication in the text that he genuinely does intend to dissolve the estate; the destructivity evinced in the dream is attributable solely to Saurau himself. It signifies his awareness of a fundamental disruption of patrilinear succession and the concomitant transmission of property and title. The word "anachronism," which occurs in Saurau's dream, is of key significance. Josef König points out that Saurau is suffering from an "Identitätskrise der Tradition" that springs from the contradiction between the attempt to continue leading a feudal lifestyle and the simultaneous acknowledgement that such a mode of existence is devoid of all meaning in contemporary Austria (König, *Totenmaskenball* 60, 64). Helms-Derfert discerns further traces of this "identity conflict" in the conflict between Saurau's "Selbstverständnis" as a feudal Prince and the modern business techniques he uses to expand and manage his estate (57).

Saurau actually draws attention to this conflict himself: "'Die Modernität *in* einem Gehirn erfrischt mich, *die innere Modernität,*' sagte er, *'die äußere* stößt mich ab'" (V 147). This view precipitates itself in his discourse in the discrepancy between the mechanistic or industrial metaphors he uses for the human mind,[19] and the organic material on which that mind acts in the form of forestry and agriculture. The Prince's fears that his son will destroy Hochgobernitz, then, are the issue of a conflict between the old, feudal Austria and the forces of modernity represented by democracy as a political system, and market capitalism as a mode of economic organization. Taking the representative status of Saurau to an allegorical extreme, Helms-Derfert even suggests that the Prince's madness caricatures the "schizophrenia" of the Second Austrian Republic, "wo — in der Metaphorik des Romans gesprochen — kleinbürgerlicher Geschäftssinn Leichenschändung am toten Erbe der Geschichte treibt" (65).

This calling into question of historical continuity is seemingly belied by the repetition that governs the lives of generation upon generation of Sauraus:

> An seinem Vater könne der Sohn sein zukünftiges Leben studieren, meinte er. Die Zwecke, für die der Vater gelebt hat, seien, in jedem Fall, auch die Sohneszwecke, die Vatervergnügen auch die Sohnesvergnügen, der Vaterekel an der Welt auch der Sohnesekel an der Welt. (V 132)

This repetition becomes even more explicit when Saurau imagines his son walking through Hyde Park wearing the same suit, thinking the same thoughts, and sitting on the same park benches as he had done as a young man (V 145). Furthermore, Saurau now finds himself repeating his own father's existence: "'Mich beunruhigt die Entdeckung,' sagte der Fürst, 'daß ich in der Bibliothek immer mehr Bücher aus den regalen herausziehe, die *auch mein Vater* gelesen hat. Jetzt werden viele Eigenschaften meines Vaters in mir lebendig'" (V 160).

Dorothy Dinnerstein points out that fathers, because of their lack of direct physical connection with babies, have a powerful urge to assert a relation. This can take the form of giving the child a name to establish a genealogical link, for example, and manifests itself in men's concern for immortality through the production of an heir. Men's "impulse to affirm and tighten by cultural inventions their unsatisfactorily loose mammalian connections with children" leads them to place high value on cultural inventions of a symbolic nature (80–1). In the absence of the metonymic biological connection that exists between mother and child, patrilineage has always depended on men's ability (and need) to establish metaphorical links between themselves and their offspring, passing on property to the replica of the self that bears the same name: the son. The sense that children are replicas of their fathers is thus inherent in the transmission of property and aristocratic titles, and as such it represents familial and historical continuity.

At the same time, terms such as "family line" and "lineage" demonstrate that the metaphorical similarity between fathers and sons is subsumed beneath a notion of progress or progression. The ideology of inheritance thus replicates the structure of narrative, and it is no coincidence that the thematics of the family saga, allied to a basically linear mode of narration, characterize so many nineteenth-century novels. In the case of the Sauraus, however, each generation repeats the last, even down to the most trivial details. This foregrounds the "paradigmatic" links between family members at the expense of any sense of progression; the transfer of property and title ceases to imply continuity and becomes instead a symptom of historical and temporal stagnation. In the absence of genuine historical significance or power, the Sauraus merely go through the motions, acting out the role of aristocrats. The heavily foregrounded theatrical metaphors in *Verstörung* can be understood in this light, as life is reduced to "eine perfekt gespielte, aber doch unerträgliche Komödie" (V 177). The Prince generalizes this insight, applying it to the whole of humanity as a quasi-metaphysical principle: "'Die Menschen nichts als Schauspieler, die uns etwas vormachen, das uns bekannt ist. Rollenlerner,' sagte der Fürst" (V 136). Like many of Bernhard's protagonists, though, he generalizes in an attempt to obscure the historically determined nature of his own situation as, precisely, an anachronism.

This sense that the historical past, as represented by the Sauraus, has come to a standstill can be seen in the formal aspects of the text. Hans Höller has pointed to Saurau's tendency to transpose temporal categories into spatial ones at the level of both imagery and grammar (*Kritik* 63). Höller gives few examples of Saurau's imagery, but spatial metaphors for temporal processes abound. The following examples illustrate the point: *Life* is a *school* for death *inhabited by* millions upon millions of teachers and pupils (V 137), and people *go into* business as though they were *slipping into a garment* which they then wear throughout their lives (V 148). The syntax of the monologue is characterized by neologistic composite nouns that paralyze the verbal parts of speech: "die Überfülle der 'phantastischen Gegenstände' erdrückt die Entfaltungsmöglichkeit des Zeit- bzw. Tätigkeitswortes, das in Sätzen wie 'Es gibt . . .,' 'Es ist . . .,' 'Es sind . . .,' 'Es herrscht . . .' usf. auf bloß konstatierende Funktionen eingeschränkt wird" (Höller, *Kritik* 65). A sense of historical stagnation thus permeates the very fabric of Saurau's monologue.

The stories of the teacher, Frau Ebenhöh, the Krainers, the Fochler family, and Saurau himself stress, in different ways, problems of transgenerational transmission. They are all governed by an awareness of a break in continuity, be it a disruption of the family line, a disturbance of adult-child relationships, or a rupture with tradition. This pervasive impression of historical schism is duplicated in the prominent theme of communication in *Verstörung*, which we will now examine.

The conjunction of problematic relationships between parents and their offspring on the one hand, and a concomitant failure of communication — narrative or otherwise — on the other, recurs in most of the character groupings in *Verstörung*. The framing narrative is dominated by a strained relationship between the narrator and his father. Just after the doctor has finished talking about the final phases of his wife's life and about her funeral, the narrator remarks,

> Jetzt fiel mir der Brief ein, den ich vor ein paar Tagen meinem Vater geschrieben hatte und in welchem ich mich in der Beschreibung des unguten Verhältnisses zwischen uns dreien, zwischen ihm und mir und zwischen ihm und meiner Schwester und zwischen mir und meiner Schwester, bemüht habe. Ich hatte ihm in dem Wahn geschrieben, darauf eine Antwort zu bekommen, und wie deutlich sah ich jetzt, daß ich eine solche Antwort niemals bekommen kann.
>
> Meine in dem Brief gestellten Fragen wird mein Vater nie beantworten können. (V 20–1)

The narrator goes on to summarize the content of the letter. The significant question is this: "wen [treffe] die Schuld an dem jüngsten Selbstmordversuch meiner Schwester oder an dem frühen Tod meiner Mutter" (V 21). Although this does not necessarily imply that the narrator blames his father for this catastrophe, the fact that he is at pains not to offend his father, his apprehension about bringing to light thoughts that have hitherto remained unspoken, and his reluctance to dredge up "längst vergessenes Material" in order to justify his own diagnosis of the situation, certainly suggest that the letter was tantamount to an accusation.

Helms-Derfert reads the doctor's decision to take his son on his
rounds as an implicit answer to the questions raised in the letter: the
doctor wishes to persuade his son that the omnipresence of sickness
and disease in the world precludes moral questions of guilt and responsibility, but this argument merely conceals his fear of an uncontrollable
nature that eludes the power of medicine (44). These may be the ultimate implications of *Verstörung* as a whole, but there is nothing within
the text to suggest that such an intention can be attributed to the
doctor. Rather, the episode of the unanswered letter reveals that the
transgenerational problem is intimately linked with questions of narrative transmission. As Peter Brooks has suggested, narrative frequently
involves bringing to light that which has remained hidden, buried, or
repressed (221). That is precisely the purpose of the narrator's letter to
his father, yet the doctor makes no mention of the letter in the course
of the novel. "Schon am Dienstagmorgen mußte ihn mein Vater be-
kommen haben" (V 22), writes the narrator, thereby implying that the
letter has arrived but has failed to produce the intended effect.

This kind of communicative failure emerges at other points, too.
The narrator and his father plan to take a walk by the river and use the
opportunity for an intensive conversation about, as the narrator sur-
mises, his life as a student of mining in Leoben. But the projected discussion is interrupted by the arrival of the "Gastwirt," whose wife is
lying unconscious (V 8). This situation mirrors the narrator's intention
of spending the day with his sister (V 69), an encounter that is postponed (V 189) when the opportunity of accompanying his father presents itself. The two acts that inaugurate the plot, then, involve a change
in narrative intention; the narrator's discussions with his father and sister are blocked by unexpected turns of events and deferred beyond the
time frame of the novel. The intended acts of communication do not
take place.

A more obvious example of failed narrative transmission occurs
when the narrator admits that he has consistently and deliberately given
his father the impression that he has no personal difficulties, and adds:
"Mir leuchtete jetzt nicht ein, *warum.* 'Ich habe immer ein großes
Vergnügen daran gehabt,' sagte ich, 'mit meinen eigenen Schwierig-
keiten fertig zu werden.' Hatte ich *zuviel* gesagt? Mein Vater hörte gar
nicht zu" (V 69). The narrator's speech act is not even received by its
intended recipient, resulting in the momentary comedy of a character
fretting about the potential effects of a comment that goes unheard.

A similarly comical moment occurs later during the visit to the
schoolteacher's widow, Frau Ebenhöh. After hearing the story of
Ebenhöh's son, the doctor tells her about his own family, sketching his

son's situation but concentrating primarily on his psychologically un-stable daughter who, he claims, causes him "ununterbrochene Angst" (V 37). Significantly, the doctor draws attention to the family's com-munication difficulties: "Wir leben so lange zusammen und kennen uns nicht" (V 38). "Mein Vater sprach sehr liebevoll über uns," writes the narrator, "die Ebenhöh schien ihm aufmerksam zuzuhören" (V 36). But as the doctor's speech draws to a close, he notices that she has fallen asleep. He stands up and checks that the narrator is still there. "Es war ihm peinlich," we are told, "daß ich ihm zugehört hatte" (V 39). Narrative transmission between one generation and the next oc-curs in this episode by default. The doctor's speech is aimed at Frau Ebenhöh but fails to produce the intended effect because she falls asleep. At the same time, the narrator functions as the unintended re-cipient of the discourse, but this merely causes embarrassment rather than the resumption of cordial relations.

If the relationship between the narrator and his father is character-ized by a disturbance in passing the message from addresser to recipi-ent, then the problem affects Saurau all the more acutely. As we have seen, his position in history means that he upholds the empty traditions of an Austria that no longer exists, in a desperate attempt to resist the encroachment of modernity. This results in a language that implies sta-sis. The problems Saurau experiences in passing down property from generation to generation find their linguistic analogue in the abundant examples of failed communication scattered throughout the text.

In some of these, the problem lies in the very nature of language it-self: everybody, remarks the Prince, speaks a language that they do not understand (V 139), and even in those moments where language is in principle comprehensible, paradoxically nobody understands it: "'In den besten Augenblicken sprichst du eine Sprache,' sagte der Fürst, 'die jeder versteht, aber es versteht dich niemand'" (V 174). The Prince com-ments: "'Das ganze Wortinstrumentarium, das wir gebrauchen, existiert gar nicht mehr. Aber es ist auch nicht möglich, vollständig zu verstum-men. Nein,' sagte er" (V 146). Just as life at Hochgobernitz consists of the inescapable rehearsal of empty traditions, so Saurau feels compelled to speak a language whose communicative function has been lost.

The more important instances of communicational breakdown, however, concern Saurau's interaction with his son, with whom he has never been able to hold a conversation (V 193). This is illustrated when he invites his son to Hochgobernitz with the express intention of ex-plaining his plans for the simultaneous expansion of Hochgobernitz and simplification of its management, but the son's visit passes quickly without the relevant discussion taking place (V 133–4). On another occasion, Saurau imagines that a conversation occurs but leads to no mutual understanding: "gleich, wovon wir gesprochen haben, gleich, woran wir gedacht haben, wir verstehen uns nicht" (V 163). Elsewhere, the Prince's efforts to establish communication are characterized by a failure of "perlocution" as his words do not create the desired effect. For example, he tells his son about the constant noises in his head and mentions that he is "todkrank," but when he tries to elicit a response by asking "ist das nicht traurig, mein Lieber?" his son remains silent (V 135). Furthermore, his extensive letters to his son receive, after a long period of no communication at all, merely the briefest of replies, leaving the Prince's questions unanswered and consisting instead of "*Verbotstafeln* [. . .], die mein Sohn rund um sich aufstellt, wie: *Eingang verboten!*" (V 171).

For Saurau, then, the problem of passing down title and property is accompanied by a malfunction in the sending of linguistic messages. This problem does not infect merely the framed exchanges between Saurau and his son; it is also inherent in the structure of narrative transmission between Saurau and his present listeners, namely the doctor and the narrator, who are situated at the end of a long line of people to whom Saurau has tried to make himself understood:

> solange ich lebe ist es nichts anderes als ein Michverständlichmachen, das mich auffrißt. Zuerst habe ich angefangen, mich meinen Eltern verständlich zu machen, meinen Geschwistern, meinen Kindern, allen Leuten habe ich mich verständlich machen wollen. Jetzt versuche ich, mich *Ihnen* verständlich zu machen, Ihrem Sohn. (V 185)

The issue of generations is once again present in the shift from parents to siblings to children, but more importantly, this passage betrays Saurau's solipsism: his urge to *be understood* is outwardly directed and is not accompanied by a parallel desire to *understand*. This becomes apparent when the Prince addresses a list of questions to the doctor, but continues without awaiting an answer (V 159). The structure of his consciousness is monological, which is why he is the only significant speaker in the entire Hochgobernitz section.

The role of the recipient of the narrative, therefore, is greatly restricted; the narrator and his father are reduced to the status of passive listeners, whose "thralldom" to Saurau is a narrative correlative of the master-slave relationship characteristic of the Prince's "feudal" ideology:

> An diesem Tag wollte mein Vater am frühen Abend zu Hause sein, er hatte Patienten bestellt, die wahrscheinlich, dachte ich, schon die längste Zeit in der Ordination warten. Der Fürst hielt uns aber fest. Es war meinem Vater unmöglich, wegzugehen. Ich selbst hatte aber auch das größte Interesse an dem, was der Fürst sagte. (V 166)

Hajo Steinert has suggested that like the narrator of *Frost*, the doctor and his son stand, in *Verstörung*, "als Modell für den Leser, der — wie sie — die vorgeführte Welt zunächst durch Anschauung erfassen soll, die dann [. . .] in Faszination übergehen kann" (68). Although we have seen in the chapter on *Frost* that the reader's position cannot be equated with that of the narrator, Steinert's comment nevertheless rightly implies that the only response open to Saurau's addressees *within* the text is passive acceptance and captivation.

In the 1980s and 1990s, theorists of narrative repeatedly pointed out that storytelling is a fundamentally dynamic enterprise whose main characteristic is exchange: narrators tell their tales in exchange for the attention of the listener or reader.[20] Recipients of both oral and written narrative, however, are free to withdraw their attention at any time, and so the telling of tales can be seen as a constant transaction between the teller's wish to narrate and the listener's simultaneous desire to both hear and resist the message. Rather than being informed by this dynamic relationship, however, the narrative encounter between Saurau and the narrator fails to materialize *as exchange*. Instead, it exhausts itself in a relationship of mere thralldom that results in slavish repetition of the Prince's discourse: "Ich zitiere den Fürsten beinahe wörtlich!" exclaims the narrator at one point (V 80).

Repetition without difference, as we have noted, is one of those features that signals stagnation at both a familial and, by implication, a historical level. That this applies to language as well as life becomes clear when the Prince announces: "'wir sind eingeschlossen in eine fortwährend zitierende Welt, in ein fortwährendes Zitieren, das die Welt *ist*, Doktor'" (V 140). As though to confirm and illustrate that quotation, the narrator functions merely to reproduce a discourse whose primary characteristic is stasis. This in turn indicates his inability to make narrative sense of his experience by forging causal or logical links between the Prince's monologue and the experiences that preceded it, and between the events dealt with in the novel and his wider biographical experience. It is here that the narrator of *Verstörung* manifests his kinship with the narrator of *Frost*.

Viewing the novel in this way provides a different perspective on the much-discussed question of "Geschichtenzerstörung." Because the syntagmatic links between events are so weak, the paradigmatic similarity between them is foregrounded as the dominant structural principle of the text. Indeed, this analysis, which shows that the major episodes in the text are in some sense analogous to one another, is predicated on the primacy of paradigmatic grouping. Therefore, the capacity of the linear narrative syntagma to establish and organize temporal relations is subordinated to the "vertical" perception of likeness between events. Such a conception of narrative calls into question the possibility not only of telling *stories* but also of constructing an adequate narrative *history*. To a greater extent even than *Frost*, *Verstörung* takes place in an "enthistorisierte Meta-Zeit" in which every event merely replicates, through metaphorical similarity, another event. The temporal stasis that this ultimately implies is the historical stasis of the Second Austrian Republic, of which *Verstörung* can be seen — quite literally — as the paradigmatic novel.

# Notes

1 Höller, *Thomas Bernhard* 69. Höller is paraphrasing Schmied 320.

2 The most famous review is that by Zuckmayer. For a selection of reviews, see Dittmar, *Werkgeschichte* 52–5.

3 See e.g. Huntemann, *Artistik* 100; Marquardt 35; Höller, *Kritik* 99–100; Damerau 104.

4 See e.g the stories told by the "Wirtin" (Fr 139–40, 219–22, 245–6, 260–1), the "Wasenmeister" (Fr 46–8, 59–62, 97–8, 182–4, 219–22), the Gendarm (Fr 55–6, 231–4), and the engineer (Fr 26, 124–5).

5 This ties in with numerous other fantasies of omnipotence in which Strauch indulges. See Mittermayer, "Strauch im Winter" 8.

6 Petrasch (60–6) attempts to fix the figurative meaning of these episodes, but as with much of the secondary literature on Bernhard, her interpretations say more about her own concerns than about Bernhard's novel.

7 Several commentators make this point in passing, without analyzing it in any detail. See e.g. Sorg, *Thomas Bernhard* 43; Meyerhofer 27.

8 Hermann Helms-Derfert writes of this passage and the following "Kornähre" quotation: "Solche eher zitathafte Anverwandlung mythischen Gedankenguts kann allerdings kaum überzeugen, zumal der Maler anderenorts den 'Blutgeruch' als 'das *einzig Identische*' bezeichnet" (36). Such a statement, however, assumes that Strauch's discourse is informed by a coherent and consistent conceptual framework; this, as we shall see, is untenable.

9 When Manfred Mixner remarks that Bernhard frees language from the reality to which it refers and develops instead an "über die Rationalität begrifflicher Regelsysteme hinausgehendes poetisches Zeichensystem," he is conflating Bernhard with Strauch and ignoring the role played by the dissolution of concepts within the economy of *Frost* as a whole ("Wie das Gehirn" 50).

10 These assumptions are confirmed with particular clarity in the aesthetics of so-called "metaphysical" poetry. Many of these poems draw their intellectual

energy from the device of the "conceit": through a process of persuasion, the poems set out to show that two seemingly unlike entities are in fact similar.

[11] The issue of what constitutes "minimal narrative" is a vexed one, and there is no room to explore it with any theoretical rigour here. A reasonably uncontentious and broad definition would be "at least two events linked chronologically and logically." The three criteria of event, causality, and temporality are all absent from many of Strauch's monologues.

[12] *Postmodernism* 28. Jameson is referring to *Watt* by Samuel Beckett — an author to whom Bernhard is frequently compared.

[13] Jonathan Culler terms this function of literary texts "pragmatic presupposition" (*Pursuit of Signs* 114–8).

[14] The most extensive analysis of this aspect of the text is Helms-Derfert 57–67. See also Höller, *Kritik* 60–79; König, "*Totenmaskenball*" 60–8. A rather more tenuous approach to the theme of generation relationships is provided by Damerau, in whose view the text is concerned with "das Verhältnis des Menschen zum eigenen Körper vor allem in der jüngeren Generation" (145).

[15] As an example of relations of similarity existing between narrative episodes in *Verstörung*, the story of the teacher is mirrored in the situation of Zehetmeyer, one of the applicants whom Saurau interviews for the post of estate manager. He, too, was a teacher and imprisoned for sexual offences, though in this case, he claims that he did not commit them (V 84).

[16] The potential for genetic malfunction is also inherent in the endogamous relationship between the Hauenstein industrialist and his half-sister who live together "wie Mann und Frau" (V 43).

[17] These tendencies are well-documented and need not be expounded in any detail here. See for example Amann and Mitchell.

[18] See also V 146–7, 162, and 192–3 for manifestations of Saurau's obsessive fantasy that his son will destroy Hochgobernitz.

[19] E.g. "Geistesmechanik" (V 102); "Das Gehirn als Kraftwerk" (V 143); "Gehirnmechanismus" (V 146), "Rechenmaschinen, nichts weiter sind die Menschen" (V 161); "Ich bin ein nicht mehr funktionierendes Barometer" (V 183).

[20] The first critic to theorize this view of narrative was Roland Barthes, whose *S/Z* has been highly influential for later studies by theorists such as Chambers, Maclean, and Reid.

# 2: *Das Kalkwerk* and *Korrektur*

## *Das Kalkwerk*

LOOKING AT *VERSTÖRUNG* with the benefit of hindsight, the text seems to contain, in embryonic form, several of the thematic obsessions that were to dominate Bernhard's later work. The difficulty of coming to terms with history and tradition, as objectified in a large ancestral estate, forms the thematic core of the 1968 prose text, *Ungenach*. *Ungenach* resembles *Amras* in its fragmentary collage-like structure, but the salient theme of the text is the decision by the main protagonist, Robert Zoiss, to dispose of the family estate that has come down to him through the deaths of his parents and half-brother. By dividing the entire property between several benefactors (Ug 35–6), he actualizes that which is present in *Verstörung* only as potentiality: the dissolution of "spatialized history."[1] Bernhard was to develop the motif of "Abschenkung" in his major novels *Korrektur* and *Auslöschung*, and we shall return to these texts below.

The industrialist in *Verstörung* is also the earliest of Bernhard's characters to shut himself away in almost total isolation, devoting himself to a massive intellectual project that will in all probability never come to fruition. He is the first in a long line of figures who are engaged in such an academic pursuit: Roithamer in *Korrektur*, Koller in *Die Billigesser*, Rudolf in *Beton*, and the narrators of *Ja* and *Der Untergeher*. Furthermore, his situation preempts in many of its details the central character configuration of *Das Kalkwerk*. *Das Kalkwerk* begins with the murder, by Konrad, of his wife, who is also his half-sister and is known exclusively as "die Konrad" throughout the text. The killing, it transpires, was the last of many acts of violence that Konrad had perpetrated against her. Although it had been the industrialist's habit to practice shooting at two wooden targets attached to tree trunks behind his hunting lodge (V 45), Konrad actually speaks of shooting "intruders" in the area around the limeworks (Kw 37), and occasionally takes aim with a carbine at the peak of a rocky outcrop (Kw 143). Just as the industrialist's house was completely devoid of furniture and decoration, so Konrad progressively sells the family furniture in order to finance his life as a private scholar.

Konrad takes refuge in the lime works because he deems it the ideal place for the completion of his study, "Das Gehör." In the service of the study he uses his wife as an object of experimentation, carrying out "Hörübungen" supposedly derived from the methods of Viktor Urbantschitsch. As professor of otology at the University of Vienna at the turn of the century, Urbantschitsch developed techniques that were designed to bring about the reintegration of the deaf into society (Mittermayer, *Thomas Bernhard* 64; Sorg, *Thomas Bernhard* 84–5). Konrad, however, perverts Urbantschitsch's method, torturing his wife for hours on end by repeating the same sentences and words to her, and demanding an immediate response as to their effects. Being crippled and wheelchair-bound, she is unable to escape. Konrad eventually shoots her, and is found hiding in a cesspit by members of the Austrian rural police force.

The structure of narrative transmission in *Das Kalkwerk* is highly complex.[2] The actual narrator of the novel can be unproblematically identified as a first-person narrator. Narrative theorist Franz Stanzel uses the criteria of "Identität oder Nichtidentität der Seinsbereiche des Erzählers und der Charaktere in einer fiktionalen Erzählung" (120) to distinguish between first- and third-person narratives, and the narrator of *Das Kalkwerk* is clearly part of the same represented world as the other characters. He is a life insurance agent and frequents the Laska, one of the inns from which conjecture concerning Konrad's murder emanates and which function as sources of information for the narrator's report (Kw 9, 28, 107–8). He has also had a certain amount of contact with Konrad (Kw 54, 70, 77), and has managed to sell insurance policies to his two main sources of information, the property managers Fro and Wieser (Kw 117, 148, 188, 210). Beyond these isolated instances, however, the narrator effaces himself almost totally, and merely collates the various reports he receives from Fro and Wieser concerning their conversations with Konrad, occasionally incorporating the various rumors circulating in the district. The text is narrated mostly in the subjunctive of indirect speech and makes extensive use of modal constructions. The following example is taken at random; similar constructions are to be found on almost every page: "Er habe von Natur aus die schärfsten und die angestrengtesten Augen, soll er zu Wieser gesagt haben" (Kw 94).

The narrator's function within the text, however, exceeds that of a mere conduit of information, for the statements he makes about himself are in part contradictory and therefore draw attention to his unreliability. Initially, for example, he says that he had met Konrad on several occasions and immediately become embroiled in intense conversation.

The concluding words of the relevant paragraph, "darüber später . . ." (Kw 8), promise to provide further details about these conversations, but the reader waits for them in vain; the information never materializes, suggesting that the narrator is not in full control of his own narrative enterprise. At another point the narrator mentions "Fro [. . .], mit dem ich *gestern* die neue Lebensversicherung abgeschlossen habe" (Kw 117, my italics), but later claims: "ich habe nicht den Eindruck, daß Fro mit mir abschließen wird, dazu ist er zu vorsichtig" (Kw 148–9). The matter is clouded further when the narrator writes of "Fro, mit dem ich *heute* die Lebensversicherung habe abschließen können" (Kw 210, my italics). There is an unresolvable contradiction between the claims to have closed the deal both "yesterday" and "today," in that order, and the narrator's assertion that the policy has already been sold is incompatible with his later conviction that Fro will not take out the policy (O'Neill, "Endgame" 237). The words "heute" and "gestern" belong to the group of words known as deictics, a group that consists primarily of those personal pronouns, indicative pronouns and adjectives, and adverbs of time and space, whose semantic meaning is dependent on the spatiotemporal context of their utterance.[3] Proximal deictics ("today," "now," "here") tend, within first-person narrative texts, to signal the "discursive situation," namely the spatiotemporal context in which the act of writing takes place.[4] The contradictory use of deixis in *Das Kalkwerk*, however, means that no stable chronology of the discursive situation can be established. If the narrator is unable to present a logically and chronologically coherent report of his own writing project, then his competence to narrate Konrad's story is called all the more radically into question.

The devices of indirect quotation in the subjunctive and the unreliability of the narrator have focused critical attention on the epistemological implications of narrative technique in *Das Kalkwerk*. In other words: what can the reader *know* about the events that culminate in the murder? The embedded perspectives place the reader at a minimum of two — and sometimes as many as five — removes from Konrad's actions (O'Neill, "Endgame" 236–7). The latter are never represented directly; the reader merely learns what Fro or Wieser has said to the narrator about what Konrad has said to them. Thus the represented world of the text remains in a state of conjecture and supposition. Lindenmayr points out that the juridical process would allow the facts of the murder to be established, and that by refusing to reveal, for example, the actual number of shots used to kill Konrad's wife, Bernhard introduces doubt where clarity would be possible (35). Marquardt, on the other hand, stresses that it is the narrator's nescience that prevents him from evaluating the statements of his "witnesses" (39), whilst O'Neill imports an ethical condemnation of the narrator into his article on *Das Kalkwerk*, proclaiming that the narrator knows *all* the reported facts but does not try to make sense of the contradictions that they contain ("Endgame" 237). What is common in all these critics' readings is the realization that the reader's knowledge of the represented world is dependent on the subjectivity of those doing the reporting, and can in no sense be termed reliable or definitive. In other words, the abstraction of a "story" from the narrative "discourse" is impossible.

Embedded perspectives and the structure of quotation distance the reader from the world of the text. At the same time, however, there are elements that work against this distancing, most notably the frequent verbatim rendering of Konrad's monologues (Marquardt 39–40). This technique has important implications for the question of focalization. With few exceptions, not only is Konrad the ultimate source of everything that gets narrated about him, but his speech determines the verbal surface of the discourse. The world of the text is effectively perceived through his consciousness. By reporting his words without comment, Fro, Wieser and the narrator align themselves with his point of view in a tacit gesture of collusion.[5] In cases of such "character-bound focalization," the reader, as Mieke Bal points out, "watches with the character's eyes and will, in principle, be inclined to accept the vision presented by that character" (104). The textual strategies of *Das Kalkwerk* consequently force the reader into "seeing" the represented world from Konrad's perspective.

Whilst the structure of narrative mediation distances the reader from the represented world, then, the focalization procedures simultaneously encourage a degree of identification with Konrad. This dual and ostensibly paradoxical function of the narrative techniques in *Das Kalkwerk* has been noted in passing but not explained (e.g. Bohnert 23–5; Marquardt 40). One of the key thematic areas that critics of *Das Kalkwerk* have tended to ignore, however, is the issue of violence, examples of which permeate the text. Konrad, as we have seen, frequently practices rifle-shooting (Kw 143), and has fifteen previous convictions, primarily for libel but also "wegen sogenannter leichter und schwerer Körperverletzung" (Kw 8, 96–7). Out of fear of violent crime, Konrad has easily accessible firearms secreted in almost every room of the limeworks, and carries a revolver, which, we are told, he would not hesitate to use (Kw 37). Most obviously, however, Konrad inflicts repeated violence upon his wife in the course of his "scholarly" pursuits.

The structure of violence in *Das Kalkwerk* is a function of the narrative techniques through which it is represented. Because the narrative world of the text is mediated through two or more speakers, the reader is distanced from the violence it represents. At the same time, the text's focalization procedures impel him or her to adopt the subject position of the violator. The narrative techniques of *Das Kalkwerk*, then, are significant both on epistemological grounds, and because they provide a powerful means of naturalizing violence against a female victim.

The narration of the actual murder is analogous in its effects. It represents an exception within the text because it consists of a series of episodes in which not Konrad, but a number of other, more immediate sources are quoted:

> mit dieser Waffe [dem Mannlicher-Karabiner] hat Konrad sie in der Nacht vom vierundzwanzigsten auf den fünfundzwanzigsten mit zwei Schüssen in den Hinterkopf (Fro), mit zwei Schüssen in die Schläfe (Wieser), urplötzlich (Fro), am Ende der konradschen Ehehölle (Wieser), erschossen. (Kw 8)

> Wieser spricht auch vom zertrümmerten Handgelenk der Konrad, Beweis dafür, daß die Konrad die Hände vor dem Gesicht hatte, als der Schuß fiel. Fro gebraucht immer wieder das Wort *Unkenntlichkeit*, ununterbrochen sagt er *blutüberströmt*. (Kw 12)

> Im Gmachl ist gesagt worden, Konrad habe die Frau kaltblütig von hinten erschossen, habe sich überzeugt, ob die Angeschossene auch wirklich tot sei, und habe sich augenblicklich gestellt. Im Laska ist auch gesagt worden, der Kopf der Konrad sei durch einen Schuß in die linke Schläfe zertrümmert worden. Ist von der Schläfe die Rede, heißt es abwechselnd die rechte oder die linke. Im Lanner ist auch gesagt worden, Konrad habe seine Frau mit einer Hacke erschlagen und erst, nachdem er sie schon mit der Hacke erschlagen gehabt hatte, mit dem Mannlicher-Karabiner angeschossen, daraus sehe man, daß es sich bei Konrad um einen Verrückten handle. Im Laska sagten sie, Konrad habe seine Frau den Mannlicher-Karabiner am Hinterkopf angesetzt und erst nach ein oder zwei Minuten abgedrückt, sie habe gewußt, wie sie den Lauf an ihrem Hinterkopf spürte, daß er sie jetzt umbringen werde, und habe sich nicht gewehrt. Wahrscheinlich habe er sie, heißt es im Stiegler, auf ihren eigenen Wunsch erschossen, ihr Leben sei nichts als qualvoll und an jedem Tag eine noch größere Qual als an dem vorangegangenen gewesen [.] (Kw 14)

These passages represent a moment of excess in the portrayal of violence. (Similar examples can be found in Kw 11, 13, 146–7.) There is no direct narration of the crime itself: the act disappears beneath a proliferation of discourse, and it becomes clear that the text is not representing facts, but is rather playing through a repertoire of violent fantasies for which the narrator can disclaim responsibility by attributing them to other sources.[6] Indeed, the accumulation of imaginary conjectures of the murder by (often unnamed) characters in the novel means that the violent act itself becomes all the more visibly absent.[7]

Paradoxically, then, the excess of discourse signals a refusal to "write" the murder. The crime exists only as a gap — an "Unbestimmtheitsstelle," in the language of reception theory — which needs to be filled or "actualized" in the course of the reading process. Although such textual indeterminacy is usually considered in relation to an implied or ideal reader (and by extension to an empirical "real" reader), the gaps in *Das Kalkwerk* are filled by various "readers" within the text: Fro, Wieser, and the guests at the Lanner, Laska, Gmachl, and Stiegler. In effect, they usurp the position of the real reader, who is coerced into participating in the construction of fantasies that are not his or her own. In addition, however, the narrator's refusal to rank the various proffered versions of the murder results in an open text, inviting further speculation on the reader's part concerning Konrad's killing of his wife. Frau Konrad's body is constituted within the text as a blank, a *tabula rasa*, upon which the desires and fantasies of various (male) figures can be inscribed. On the one hand, then, the murder is distanced from the reader by not being directly or definitively represented. On the other hand, the indeterminacy of the text undermines that distance by encouraging the reader's imaginative participation in the violence.

The structure of narrative transmission has further implications. "Toute domination," writes Roland Barthes, "commence par interdire le langage" (*S/Z* 75). At a formal level in *Das Kalkwerk*, this is manifested in the fact that Konrad's wife "speaks" in any significant sense just five times (Kw 133, 146, 151–3, 166, 183): three times her words are reported by Konrad to Fro or Wieser, once she speaks to Fro directly (Kw 133), and once to the "Baurat" (Kw 166). In each case, her words are then relayed to the reader by the narrator. Not only is Frau Konrad's voice systematically suppressed from the text; whenever she does speak, her words have always been appropriated by two, sometimes three, male figures. Furthermore, the language she uses reproduces the structures of power and domination that oppress her in a vain attempt to turn them against themselves: she issues the order "*Most holen!*" (Kw 151–3); reminds Konrad that she used to command him, against his wishes, to take her to balls in Paris and Rome (Kw 183), denigrates the study (Kw 146) and questions her husband's sanity (Kw 166). Her attempts at rebellion, then, are attempts to appropriate the rhetoric of power but in fact merely reinscribe the structure of domination from which she would break out.[8] As a speaking subject, Frau Konrad is excluded from the discourse in a way that reduplicates her physical subjugation at the level of the story, thereby preventing any readerly identification with the perspective of the victim and obscuring the implications of bodily violation, namely pain.

Because Konrad is the main focalizer of *Das Kalkwerk*, he is largely responsible for determining the value system of the text. Here again, strategies of naturalization come into play. The privileged term in relation to which everything else is secondary is the "Studie," and it is used to explain and justify every aspect of Konrad's life: the purchase and conversion of the limeworks, the sale of furniture, the bank loans, and most notably the various forms of violation that he inflicts upon his wife. The extent to which the study is instrumental in rationalizing Konrad's behavior can be seen in a rare instance where the narrator reproduces Wieser's own words directly. Wieser expresses the opinion that Konrad's crime was thoroughly understandable. He goes on: "Konrad hatte ein beinahe erreichtes Ziel vor Augen, so Wieser, sie, seine Frau, hinderte ihn, dieses Lebensziel, das Niederschreiben der Studie, zu erreichen. Er mußte sie umbringen, schließlich mußte er sie umbringen, so Wieser" (Kw 167–8). This represents a wholesale acceptance by Wieser of Konrad's own justifications for the murder.

The key rhetorical move Konrad employs in order to "explain" the relationship between the study and his uxorial violence is the insistence on the scientific nature of his "experiments." This is made explicit toward the end of the text, when Konrad talks of his wife as:

> eine Frau, [. . .] die mich einerseits braucht, haben muß, ohne mich nicht existieren kann, oder wenigstens glaubt, ohne mich nicht existieren zu können, die mir andererseits aber bedingungslos für meine Zwecke, und das heißt, für meine Wissenschaft, zur Verfügung steht, die ich, wenn es sein muß, wenn es, wie Konrad zu Wieser gesagt haben soll, wenn es die wissenschaftlichen Umstände erfordern, mißbrauchen kann. (Kw 208; see also 52, 73, 91, 92)

The "einerseits-andererseits" construction in this extract establishes a false antithesis, designed to mask the fact that it is precisely *because* Konrad's wife is dependent on him that he *can* abuse her in the name of science. More importantly, as Teresa de Lauretis points out, "the association of scientific thought with masculinity and the scientific domain with femininity is a pervasive metaphor in the discourse of science" from Francis Bacon to quantum physics (249–50; cf. Merchant 164–90). Conversely, woman has always been identified with nature. This kind of rhetoric is operative in the following passage from *Das Kalkwerk*: "Dem Manne sei angeboren, was der Frau angelernt werden müsse in mühevoller, oft verzweifelter Lehrmethode, nämlich der Verstand als chirurgisches Instrument gegenüber der sich sonst unweigerlich auflösenden, ja sonst rettungslos zerbröckelnden Geschichts- und Naturmaterie" (Kw 129). Here, oppositions are established between man, reason, and surgical dissection on the one hand, and unreason, matter, and disintegration on the other. Woman appears to occupy a middle zone, beginning on the side of nature but possessing the potential to be "cultivated" by man/reason. Elsewhere, the construction of woman as the other of culture is clearer: she is incapable of all intellectual achievement (Kw 25), lacks understanding (Kw 67), and hinders the path of rational man through a "Welt der Verblödung und des ordinären Halbgeistes" (Kw 130). "In the equation with nature, earth, body," writes Elisabeth Bronfen, "Woman was construed as Other to culture, as object of intense curiosity to be explored, dissected, conquered, domesticated, and, if necessary, eliminated" (66). The discourse of science, then, implies the objectification and attempted domination of woman.

By objectifying Frau Konrad in the name of science, and all but forbidding her access to the discursive order, the text divests her of subjectivity and constitutes her body as a purely physical mechanism. This legitimizes Konrad's use of that body as an object of experimentation, which in turn legitimizes the initial woman-nature identification, and so on: the terms are reciprocal and reversible, and as such are ungrounded. But within *Das Kalkwerk*, they constitute a powerful discursive means of naturalizing the violence that Konrad visits upon his wife. Again, the represented body is there to be molded to the configurations of the violator-scientist's desire.

Feminist critics have not been blind to Bernhard's apparently misogynistic representations of women. As we have seen, the main target of Ria Endres's study is Bernhard's portrayal of men, whose behavior she sees largely as compensation for a lack of sensuality, fertility or sexual potency. Mireille Tabah has written on the images of women in *Auslöschung*, but Bernhard's representation of women is often so crass, and falls so neatly into stereotypical categories, that "images of women" criticism runs the risk of stating what is patently obvious.

As the reading of *Das Kalkwerk* has shown, however, it is not merely the negative representation of women that deserves critical attention, but also the narrative techniques that encourage identification with the violator and/or distance the reader from the represented violence. Teresa de Lauretis has pointed out that in instances of reciprocal violence, such as war or sport, both parties are characterized as masculine. In the case of one-sided violence, on the other hand, the perpetrator is by definition masculine and the victim therefore feminine, no matter what their "actual" sex or gender may be. In Bernhard's texts, this gendering is underscored by the fact that the "masculine" and "feminine" positions in the structure of violence are occupied by biological men and women respectively. Violence in *Das Kalkwerk* is not only present in Konrad's treatment of his wife, but is inscribed in the text's structure. The implications of narrative transmission in *Das Kalkwerk* go beyond the epistemological; through its textual strategies, the novel forces the reader to adopt a "male" position, and this is the violence of narrative form.

## Korrektur

*Korrektur* (1975) represents the final work of Bernhard's "early phase" in its exploitation and refinement of thematic and formal concerns which are already familiar to us from his earlier output. At the same time, certain narrative techniques developed in *Korrektur* point forward, as we shall see, to the structural concerns of his later fiction.

The main figure in the text is Roithamer, the second son of an Austrian landowner and his proletarian wife. Roithamer, an intellectual who holds an academic post in Cambridge, unexpectedly inherits the entirety of his family's ancestral estate, but decides to sell the property, using some of the resultant funds to help released convicts. The topos of liquidation in *Korrektur* is accompanied by a simultaneous work of architectural creation. Indeed, Hans Höller dubs *Korrektur* a "Roman des Bauens" (*Thomas Bernhard* 89) because instead of merely destroying or dissolving the family estate, Roithamer uses the family fortune to construct a "Wohnkegel" for his sister at the precise center of the Kobenaußerwald in Upper Austria. In the wake of his sister's death, he composes a long tract "Über Altensam und alles, was damit zusammenhängt unter besonderer Berücksichtigung des Kegels." He then undertakes a correction of this manuscript, reducing it from eight hundred pages to three hundred, then corrects it again, reducing it to a mere eighty pages (Ko 178). Finally, he undertakes the ultimate "correction" and puts an end to his own life.

The catalyst of the narrative is a note discovered on Roithamer's corpse, specifying that his three manuscripts, together with an extensive collection of posthumous papers, are to be left to the narrator. As in *Frost* and *Verstörung*, the text is based on the relationship between the narrator and the central "Geistesmensch," whose words he is responsible for transmitting. The novel opens with the narrator moving into the attic of his and Roithamer's mutual friend, Höller. It was here that Roithamer had done the bulk of the planning for the conical dwelling, and it is here that the narrator begins to sift through and order his

friend's "Nachlaß." This emphasis on the narrator's structuring procedures foregrounds the problems of narrative representation, yet these
have been inadequately addressed by Bernhard's critics up to this point.[9]

The narrator thematizes the question of writing on the very first page: "ich hatte aufeinmal den Gedanken gehabt, mich nicht nur mit dem
Nachlaß Roithamers zu beschäftigen, sondern auch gleich über diese
Beschäftigung zu schreiben, was hier angefangen ist [. . .]" (Ko 7–8; cf.
12). The narrative discourse of *Korrektur* thus has two functions. The
first is to transmit the content of Roithamer's posthumous papers,
while the second is to tell the story of the process of sifting and ordering — "Sichten und Ordnen" — through which this act of transmission
takes place. This apparent dualism in the narrative structure has led
Gudrun Mauch to examine "Die Spannung zwischen dem erzählenden
und dem erlebenden Erzähler" in *Korrektur*, but a description of the
text's formal features in these terms is ultimately misleading because
there are not two but *three* time levels. The time spent by the narrator
settling into Höller's attic constitutes a framing narrative, from which
he recalls events lying further back in the past. The act of writing responsible for recuperating these two narratives, however, takes place on
a third time level. This moment of writing, or "discursive situation," is
demonstrated in the numerous comments whose tense system and proximal deixis signal that they belong to a period of time postdating that
spent in Höller's house: "erst jetzt sehe ich, daß ich wieder zu eigenem
Denken fähig bin" (Ko 38); "über die Tatsache, daß Roithamer Altensam übernehmen und seine Geschwister hatte auszahlen sollen, wäre
eine eigene Abhandlung zu schreiben" (Ko 43).[10]

This three-part time structure was to become a constant in Bernhard's fiction of the 1980s. It corresponds to a shift in the relationship
between the central "Geistesmensch" and the narrator whose task it is
to represent his words and thoughts. We have seen that the narrators of
*Frost* and *Verstörung* actually *reproduce* the monologues of Strauch and
the Prince. It is the overwhelming presence of the latter characters that
bears much of the narrative interest. In *Korrektur*, by contrast, the
framing narrative tells the story not of what Roithamer *says*, but of what
the narrator *remembers* about Roithamer during the process of install-
ing himself in Höller's attic. The drama of the confrontation between
narrator and protagonist, then, is displaced from the level of action in
the represented world into the narrator's consciousness; *Korrektur*
thematizes both the attempt to recuperate the past through an act of
memory within the framing narrative *and* the subsequent representation of this remembering through the act of writing.

This, however, is only half the story, for like *Verstörung*, *Korrektur* consists of two lengthy chapters, between which exists a radical break. Although the first chapter, "Die Höllersche Dachkammer," is ordered according to the aforementioned three-level time structure, the second chapter, "Sichten und Ordnen," is a confused mass of fragments from Roithamer's posthumous papers. These possess no discernible chronological or logical order; the narrator is reduced to a mere agency of quotation whose structuring role is revealed only in the frequent repetition of the phrase "so Roithamer," and the occasional use of reported speech in the subjunctive. There have been various attempts to explain the relationship between these two elements of the narrative. Josef König compares *Korrektur* to a critical edition of Roithamer's writings, "Sichten und Ordnen" being the primary text, and "Die Höllersche Dachkammer" the editorial interpretation ( *"Totenmaskenball"* 249). If this is the case, then the analogy can only be ironic: there is no sense in which the narrator attempts to establish a definitive text, and his "interpretation" fails to throw any light on his "primary" material. Both Gudrun Mauch and Madeleine Rietra apply Franz Stanzel's typology of narrative and conclude that there are "Verschiedene Romantypen innerhalb der *Korrektur*": Bernhard's text starts out as an "Ich-Erzählung" but turns first into a "personale Erzählung" and, in chapter 2, an "auktoriale Erzählung."[11] This would imply, however, that the first-person narrator disappears in the second chapter, to be replaced by a third-person narrator. This is not the case; both critics apply Stanzel's theory in a highly misleading fashion.

Rietra, however, mentions in passing that the division of the text into two chapters mirrors the "Übereinkommen der Schicksale von Roithamer und dem Erzähler" (113). She does not explore this insight further, but it may provide a clue to the key issues at stake in the narrative form of *Korrektur*. There are numerous passages in the first chapter of the text in which it becomes obvious that the narrator is repeating the life of his friend. The narrator, we learn, has discharged himself from hospital and gone straight to Höller's house "ohne Umweg nach Stocket zu meinen Eltern" (Ko 7), just as Roithamer had, in recent years, frequently gone straight to Höller's house from Cambridge without stopping off to see his parents in Altensam (Ko 9). The narrator relives Roithamer's initial visit to Höller's attic as he had described it to the narrator several years previously (Ko 52–6), and when the latter descends to dine with the Höller family, it emerges that he is playing the role of a substitute Roithamer, occupying a position that became vacant upon the latter's death. Frau Höller bangs on the dining room ceiling to "summon" the narrator, just as she had done with Roithamer (Ko 113–5). The narrator continues,

ich dachte, die Höller verhalten sich mir gegenüber wahrscheinlich jetzt so wie sie sich Roithamer gegenüber verhalten haben, in dem Augenblick, in welchem ich die höllersche Dachkammer bezogen hatte, war ich in dem Mechanismus ihres Verhaltens gegenüber Roithamer eingeschlossen gewesen, wahrscheinlich ist jeder [. . .], der nach Roithamer die höllersche Dachkammer bewohnt, in dem Verhaltensmechanismus eingeschlossen, der in Gang gewesen war, wie Roithamer in der höllerschen Dachkammer gelebt hat. (Ko 115)

More significant than this, however, is the fact that both Roithamer and the narrator are heirs to systems of thought that they find extremely burdensome, and these are symbolized by the bequests of which they are the recipients. Roithamer's writings and cone-building project form part of his ongoing attempts to free himself from the mode of thought imposed upon him by Altensam and all it represents. In an extended meditation on this subject, Roithamer insists on the necessity of rejecting the "prefabricated" world offered by one's parental background: "Wir müssen, schon in den ersten Verstandesanzeichen, den Versuch machen, aus der Elternwelt, in die wir hineingezeugt und hineingeboren worden sind, unsere eigene zu machen" (Ko 238). The difficulty of living up to these self-imposed demands, however, becomes apparent in the patterns of repetition to which Roithamer falls prey. At the level of the represented world, he is incapable of escaping Altensam definitively and feels compelled to return in the hope of a reconciliation with his mother, even though past experience has shown such a reconciliation to be impossible (Ko 293–8). At the level of form, the insistence with which Roithamer's writings return to the problem of Altensam, and the extensive lexical repetition that characterizes his discourse, imply that his childhood was the locus of traumatic experience that has been inadequately worked though.

Furthermore, his parents ensure that their influence over him endures beyond the grave by making him heir of Altensam. The narrator suspects that Roithamer's father did this knowing that his second son would liquidate the estate and destroy himself and his siblings in the process (Ko 43–4, 94), and a passage in Roithamer's "Nachlaß" corroborates that view:

So ist der Umstand, daß mir mein Vater Altensam vererbt hat, so Roithamer, [. . .] nichts anderes, als der Ausdruck des Willens meines Vaters, Altensam durch ein solches allen und alles vor den Kopf stoßendes Testament [. . .] zu vernichten, weil er gewußt und in diesem

Bewußtsein vor allem gefühlt hat, daß er Altensam vernichtet, wenn er
es mir vererbt. (Ko 201–2)

This places Roithamer in something of a double bind: Altensam represents the burden of Austrian tradition and a personal past of which he
wishes to divest himself. At the same time, by liquidating Altensam he
is carrying out an intention that is inherent in his father's act of bequest. Selling Altensam in order to fund the building of the cone (Ko
21–2) and to help "die Ausgestoßensten [sic] der Gesellschaft" (Ko
202) is thus an act of liberation that paradoxically reinscribes the "von
unseren Eltern uns vorgegeben[e] Welt" (Ko 238) that Roithamer
seeks to escape.

The narrator's receipt of Roithamer's "Nachlaß" is described in the
following terms: "es war wohl seine Absicht gewesen, mich durch die
Beschäftigung mit seinem Nachlaß zu vernichten, deshalb hatte ich
fortwährend Angst vor dem Einlassen mit diesem seinem Nachlaß" (Ko
160). The narrator thus imputes to Roithamer the same destructive
intention as Roithamer ascribes to his father. The narrator is aware that
his thought up to this point has been dominated by that of Roithamer:

> Da mein Denken in Wirklichkeit das Denken Roithamers gewesen
> war, war ich in dieser Zeit gar nicht da gewesen, nichts gewesen, ich
> war von dem Denken Roithamers, in das ich, aufeinmal und für Roit-
> hamer selbst unübersehbar, für so lange Zeit einbezogen gewesen war,
> ausgelöscht gewesen. (Ko 38; see also 36–7)

Just as Roithamer's capacity for individual thought was hampered by
Altensam, so that of the narrator is impeded by the dominant figure of
Roithamer. The provision in Roithamer's will for the narrator to inherit
his "Nachlaß" is intended to ensure the continuance of his influence
after death, and as such reproduces Roithamer's father's own testa-
mentary intention. Initially, the narrator claims that entering Höller's
attic and confronting Roithamer's "Nachlaß" has freed him from the
"Gefangenschaft, wenn nicht Kerkerhaft des roithamerschen Gedan-
kengefängnisses" (Ko 38). As Margarete Kohlenbach has demonstrated,
however, the narrator's "Befreiungsthese" exists in stark contrast to what
the text implies "behind his back": "Das Ausmaß der Diskrepanz zwischen der Darstellungsweise und dem Selbstverständnis des Erzählers
bezeichnet den Grad seiner Befangenheit" (23; cf. Mauch, "Die Spannung" 214). Not only is there a logical inconsistency in his assertion to
have escaped Roithamer's influence by entering a room in which, as he
claims elsewhere, it is impossible *not* to think like Roithamer (Ko 23–5),
but the narrator's discourse in the first chapter frequently slips into un-
commented quotation of Roithamer's opinions. At the level of lexis, too,

the narrator weaves into his own speech verbal formulations that originate in Roithamer's "Nachlaß."[12] The narrator's efforts to free himself are as limited in their success as Roithamer's had been.

In order to plan and execute the disposal of their oppressive inheritances, both characters repair to Höller's attic. It is here that Roithamer conceives of and develops the idea of the cone (Ko 16), which represents the destruction of Altensam in both a literal and a figurative sense: he spends his fortune on the construction of the cone, which is conceived as a utopian corrective to or compensation for Altensam: "Die Vollendung des Kegels ist dann gleichzeitig auch die Vernichtung von Altensam" (Ko 225).[13] Likewise, for the narrator, Höller's attic is a place where he contemplates the viewing, ordering, and possible publication of Roithamer's "Nachlaß." The structural break in the text thus represents the step taken by the narrator from conception to execution, providing a formal analogue of Roithamer's progression from the "Idee" to the "Verwirklichung" of his "Wohnkegel."[14]

The most striking irony of *Korrektur*, however, is that the very construction that is supposed to bring about Roithamer's sister's "höchstes Glück" ends up precipitating her death, even if the direct causal relation between viewing the cone and dying is decidedly obscure (Ko 344–8). In like fashion, the title of the second chapter of *Korrektur*, "Sichten und Ordnen," announces the narrator's intention to sift through the "Hunderte und Tausende von Bruchstücken" (Ko 180) that constitute Roithamer's "Nachlaß" and provide it with some kind of structure, but the end product of his editorial labors is nothing more than a fragmentary collection of notes evincing no perceptible ordering principle. Thus the final form of the narrator's *text* replicates the failure of Roithamer's building project (cf. Helms-Derfert 146). Both enterprises produce the opposite effect to the one intended.

The chaotic structuration of part two is rendered ironic by the expectations and suspense generated in the first chapter. Throughout "Die höllersche Dachkammer" the narrator vacillates between assuring the reader of his intentions to order Roithamer's manuscript, and expressing grave doubts about the project. The first assurance occurs on the opening page, where the words "sichten und ordnen" appear for the first time (Ko 7), but the narrator's fear of an overhasty engagement with Roithamer's writing and thought soon emerges: "Die Gefährlichkeit eines vorschnellen Eindringens in den roithamerschen Gedankenzustand war mir bewußt, daß ich nur behutsam und sehr sorgfältig und vor allem immer auf meinen Geisteszustand [. . .] achtzugeben habe, dachte ich [. . .]" (Ko 36). These two passages create what Roland Barthes has termed a "hermeneutic" sequence, producing an enigma that structures the forward reading of the text through time with the expectation that the end of the text (or a given segment of text) will reveal the solution to the mystery. The enigma here is whether the weight of Roithamer's influence — as represented by the rucksack-load of paper that the narrator has hauled with him into Höller's attic — will prove too strong, or whether the narrator will actually undertake his planned confrontation with Roithamer's papers.

The first chapter of *Korrektur* is abundant with passages that either stress his editorial intentions or reinforce his qualms (see e.g. Ko 22–3, 84–5, 158–63, 174–6). There are sections where the fact that the narrator finds Roithamer's bequest oppressive is displaced into ethical pronouncements on the responsibility of the editor not to alter what he finds. He insists, for example, that nobody has the right to "bearbeiten" anything (Ko 175), and comments that editing a text is "immer ein Verbrechen, vielleicht das größte Verbrechen," adding "ich werde den Nachlaß Roithamers niemals bearbeiten, dieses Bearbeitungsverbrechen nicht begehen" (Ko 176).[15] Yet even here he writes "ich werde den Nachlaß Roithamers *ordnen, sichten,* dann möglicherweise [. . .] seinem Verleger zukommen lassen" (Ko 176). The distinction between "ordnen" and "bearbeiten" is not a clear one, and the significance of this passage lies not in its establishing clear-cut editorial ethics, but in its betrayal of the narrator's oscillation between resolve and reluctance to tackle the job of "Nachlaßverwaltung."

As the chapter draws toward its conclusion, and the confrontation with the "Nachlaß" can no longer be postponed, the narrator's attention becomes increasingly fixed on the rucksack. Then, suddenly, he picks it up and tips its contents onto the floor, destroying any coherence they might have had (Ko 181, 183). Like a naughty schoolboy, he covers his mouth with his hand and turns round to check that he has not been discovered "in dieser fürchterlich-komischen Situation" (Ko 182). In a highly symbolic attempt at repression, he stuffs the papers into the drawers of the desk in Höller's attic. But like the dead Roithamer, the hidden paper continues to exert its influence, and the narrator is plagued by guilt as he realizes that his intention to bring order to the chaos of Roithamer's writings has now become impossible (Ko 183). The realization that he has robbed himself of the possibility of ordering the "Nachlaß" is precisely the resolution of the enigma that has structured our forward reading of the text. Although the narrator's plan to order Roithamer's writings is projected as the goal or *telos* of the first chapter, the actual *telos* turns out to be the *disorder* created when the narrator tips the rucksack upside-down. Like Roithamer's "Kegel," the end of the narrator's text fails to fulfill its intended function.

At a formal level, then, there is a contrast between the *telos* that the reader is led to expect (the ordering of Roithamer's manuscript) and the chaos of the eventual end of the first chapter. This corresponds to the text's ironizing of Roithamer's teleological thought. Kohlenbach has devoted considerable space to a critique of Roithamer's teleological mindset, and she reads the "Kegel" as a metaphor for this mode of thought, with all elements leading finally to the same vanishing point (144–53). The implicitly self-critical moment in Roithamer's thought process takes place when his sister dies and he realizes that "die Wirkung der Vollendung des Kegels eine andere ist, als die erwartete" (Ko 142). Instead of creating "höchstes, allerhöchstes Glück" (Ko 331), the sight of the "Kegel" results in his sister's death.

In order to integrate this unexpected death into his teleological scheme, Roithamer then announces, "Aber das Bauwerk als Kunstwerk ist erst vollendet, indem der Tod eingetreten ist dessen, für den es gebaut und vollendet worden ist, so Roithamer" (Ko 345), thereby shifting the *telos* of his cone-building project from mere completion of the building to the death it allegedly causes. When the projected endpoint of Roithamer's enterprise is disconfirmed by events, he has no trouble inventing a new *telos* in order to make sense of what has happened.[16] This is not in any way aberrant; on the contrary, such "indifference to disconfirmation" has been observed in apocalyptic religions and thought-systems for which "disconfirmation [is] quickly followed by the invention of new end-fictions" (Kermode 17). This point is demonstrated by the narrator who, as Helms-Derfert notes, reproduces Roithamer's thought processes by extending the teleological scheme to account for Roithamer's suicide as well as the death of his sister (147):

> In diesem Augenblick der Vollendung des Kegels mußte er selbst sein Leben abbrechen, seine Existenz war mit der Vollendung des Kegels abgeschlossen, das hatte er, Roithamer, gefühlt und deshalb hat er auch seinem Leben ein Ende gemacht, zwei Leben hatten mit der Vollendung des Kegels ihre Berechtigung verloren gehabt, hatten aufhören müssen, sagte ich zu Höller. (Ko 142)

These episodes highlight the discrepancy between the perpetual assertions that Roithamer's whole life is goal directed, and the fragmentary form of the second chapter that actually *impedes* the construction of a linear, teleological narrative. On this reading, the notion of *telos* becomes totally arbitrary, an attempt to impose meaning on a set of meaningless events through an act of will and a linguistic-discursive sleight of hand. Furthermore, several points in the text betray an awareness that the construction of narrative teleologies is ineluctably retrospective. Roithamer alludes to this when he states that he has lived

"Als ob ich vorher, die ganzen Entwicklungsjahre, die nichts als eine Entwicklung auf den Kegel hin gewesen sind, auf dieses Ungeheuerliche hin gelebt, hin existiert hätte" (Ko 273). In other words, meaning can be conferred on previous events only from the vantagepoint of the end, from which the foregoing can be interpreted *as though* it necessarily led up to the end in question.

The narrative structure of chapter 1, then, leads us to believe that the narrator's goal is the sifting and ordering of Roithamer's posthumous papers, but then "disconfirms" that assumption when the narrator deliberately tips Roithamer's writings onto the sofa. If the construction of narrative teleology is primarily a retrospective operation, then chapter 1 clearly possesses an ironic moment. The tripartite time structure of the text makes it clear that the narrator knows what happens in Höller's attic before he begins to write about it. By arousing expectations of a more genuine editorial engagement with Roithamer's writings, even in the knowledge that this engagement is ultimately hampered by his own hand, the narrator exposes himself as a manipulator of textual strategies and demonstrates the capacity of narrative form to endow events with a meaning that they do not possess. In the narrator's case, of course, the implied "meaning" is ultimately withheld in a way that is, as the narrator himself states, both "fürchterlich" and "komisch."

This analysis of teleology and its relationship to narrative form shows that, like most of Bernhard's fiction, *Korrektur* is concerned, on one level at least, with the possibilities of narrative representation. These problems are of a different nature from those faced by Bernhard's earlier narrators. The question of narrative endpoints and teleological constructs becomes increasingly prominent in Bernhard's later fiction, where a proliferation of time levels and highly self-conscious uses of the "hermeneutic code" as a structural device take centerstage. The following chapters of this study comprise readings of Bernhard's major late fiction, developing the methodological approach explored in chapters 1 and 2 to demonstrate the extent to which narrative form increasingly functions as a response to problems raised at the thematic level of the texts.

# Notes

[1] For an analysis of *Ungenach* in these terms, see Kucher 221–30.

[2] The narrative form of the novel has been the subject of extensive critical discussion. See especially Bohnert, Lindenmayr, O'Neill, Rossbacher, Marquardt 36–42.

[3] Examples include "I" and "you" (personal pronouns); "this" and "that" (indicative pronouns/adjectives), "today," "yesterday," "tomorrow," "the day after" (adverbs of time); "here," "there," "in that place" (adverbs of space).

[4] The chapters on Bernhard's late fiction contain a detailed discussion of deictics and the discursive situation.

[5] This collusion is occasionally broken, for example when the narrator writes: "während Fro [...] sich vor allem vor Konrad den Anschein gibt, er nimmt die Studie völlig ernst, spricht er vor mir andauernd nur von der sogenannten Studie und fällt dadurch, wie ich glaube, Konrad im Rücken" (Kw 148). But in general there is no ironic distance between the reporting agencies and Konrad.

[6] It is surely no coincidence that Konrad uses a *Mann*licher carbine to kill his wife,

[7] A similar point is made by Tanner (18) in a discussion of William Faulkner's *Sanctuary*.

[8] Cf. Leventhal, who points out that the sole speech-acts between Konrad and his wife are imperatives (27). In this connection it is difficult to agree with Ria Endres, who sees women's silence as a threat to patriarchy (*Am Ende angekommen* 25).

[9] Marquardt (42) is the only critic to stress the thematization of writing in *Korrektur*.

[10] See also Ko 34, 44, 67, 83, 84, 85, 86, 128, 191.

[11] Mauch, "Die Spannung" 209; Rietra 116. Both articles demonstrate the limitations of Stanzel's typology when faced with a text as complex as *Korrektur*.

[12] As an example, see the transformations of the phrase "über $x$ und alles, was mit $x$ zusammenhängt," Ko 9, 16, 23, 57, 133, 155, 158.

[13] Helms-Derfert sees the cone project as an attempt to "restore" Altensam and the Habsburg monarchy (107–48). There is, however, no compelling reason to interpret the cone project in this light. Indeed, Helms-Derfert's argumentation at the decisive point of his chapter on *Korrektur* involves several

leaps to highly implausible conclusions, and forms the weak point of what is otherwise one of the best books on Bernhard.

[14] The frequency of the word-fields "Idee"/"planen"/"Vorstellung" on the one hand and "Verwirklichung"/"bauen"/"Vollendung" on the other repeatedly emphasize the two phases of Roithamer's building project.

[15] There are clear links here with "Drei Tage," in which Bernhard says: "Es darf nichts Ganzes geben, man muß es zerhauen. Etwas Gelungenes, Schönes wird immer mehr verdächtig [. . .] *der größte* Fehler ist, wenn ein Autor ein Buch zu Ende schreibt" (It 87–8).

[16] Kohlenbach describes Roithamer's equation of happiness with death as "eine bloße Hilfskonstruktion zur Rettung des teleologischen Denkens" (137), but does not address the role of teleology as a narrative device.

# II.

## The Late Fiction (i):
## Portraits of Friendships

# 3: *Ja*

HAVING SHUT HIMSELF AWAY to devote his time exclusively to the study of "antibodies in nature," the narrator of *Ja* becomes increasingly debilitated by his lack of human contact. To gain some relief from this situation he calls, uninvited, on his friend Moritz, a real estate agent, whom he has not seen or spoken to for three months. The narrator tells Moritz everything about his illness and mental state, talking incessantly and compulsively at his friend until he realizes that his behavior is not entirely acceptable. Suddenly, footsteps become audible in the entrance hall downstairs, and Moritz mutters to himself, "Die Schweizer." His wife ushers in a Swiss engineer and his Persian companion, who are clients of Moritz and have recently bought a piece of land from him. The narrator and the Persian strike up an immediate rapport, and the development of their relationship forms the ostensible theme of the text.

*Ja* was the first fictional text published by Thomas Bernhard after *Korrektur* (1975). Between these two came the autobiographical works *Die Ursache: Eine Andeutung, Der Keller*, and *Der Atem: Eine Entscheidung*. Bernhard's two further autobiographical memoirs, *Die Kälte* and *Ein Kind*, appeared in 1981 and 1982 respectively. Due to its position in relation to the autobiographies, *Ja* can, in a sense, be seen as belonging to the same phase of Bernhard's career. Indeed, critics have noticed that autobiographical elements are considerably more prominent here than in the earlier fiction.[1] The relationship between the narrator and the "Realitätenvermittler" Moritz bears an unmistakable similarity to the friendship between Bernhard and Karl Ignaz Hennetmair, a real estate agent in Upper Austria who had sold Bernhard three properties in the 1960s and early 1970s before the friendship was abruptly broken off.[2] Hennetmair is one of several friends and acquaintances to have penned a memoir shortly after Bernhard's death, and is also the only one of Bernhard's correspondents to have brought out a volume of letters to and from the author.[3] Among the many banalities, both these books contain fascinating anecdotal material, and provide biographical information on a writer whose life is notoriously ill-documented.

The correspondence contains references to one Maria Radson, who had planned to settle in Ohlsdorf (the village where Bernhard lived) with her husband. She can be seen as a possible model for the Persian woman of *Ja* (*Briefwechsel* 156). In addition, Manfred Mittermayer suggests that Ingeborg Bachmann might also be a real-life counterpart of the "Perserin" (*Thomas Bernhard* 97). Bachmann was a long-time companion of a Swiss architect — the writer Max Frisch — and had briefly used Hennetmair's services in seeking a property in Upper Austria. The esteem in which Bernhard held Bachmann can be gauged from several of his later writings: *Der Stimmenimitator* contains a story entitled "In Rom" (167–8), which is a thinly veiled comment on Bachmann's premature death by fire in her flat in Rome. In Bernhard's last novel, *Auslöschung*, the narrator is lavish in his praise for a poet called Maria. Despite the changed name, critics concur in reading the character as a literary representation of Bachmann. Indeed, the similarities extend to the point of being able to identify the clothes described in *Auslöschung*: an article by Hans Höller reprints a photograph in which Ingeborg Bachmann is attired in a way that corresponds precisely to descriptions of Bernhard's Maria ("Menschen, Geschichte(n)" 222). Thus, *Ja* provides an ideal starting point for considerations of Bernhard's late fiction because its exploitation of verifiably autobiographical data in the construction of fictional texts represents a departure from both the earlier fictional works and the autobiographies.

*Ja* also differs conspicuously from Bernhard's previous texts in terms of narrative techniques. The four major novels that constitute Bernhard's "early" phase have a narrator whose main function is to reproduce the discourse of another central character. The early texts thus mobilize embedding techniques in which the central character's words are framed and mediated by the narrator's discourse. In *Ja*, the narrator's interest appears once again to be directed toward another character, in this case the Persian companion of the Swiss architect. But unlike Strauch, Saurau, Konrad or Roithamer, her words are not quoted *in extenso*. That is not to say that narrative embedding does not take place in this text, but as we shall see, it is a localized device and does not determine the overall structure of narrative transmission. For the most part, *Ja* forms what Willi Huntemann, in his typology of Bernhard's narratives, calls an "authentische Selbstdarstellung" on the part of the narrator (*Artistik* 99–117).

The third feature of *Ja* that sets it apart from Bernhard's earlier output is its elevation of a sympathetic female character to a central position. As we saw in the discussion of feminist approaches to Bernhard, Ria Endres argues that women in his early work are either not represented at all or else conform to a highly schematic set of male stereotypes (*Am Ende angekommen* 98) — a sentiment recently echoed by

Helms-Derfert (55–6, 128). Against this background, the central female character of *Ja* would seem to invite a more positive interpretation: she is one of the few women to escape denunciation and
character-assassination which fall to women's lot in many of Bernhard's
novels. For this reason, Andrea Reiter enlists *Ja* in her attempt to rescue Bernhard from accusations of misogyny ("Die Bachmann").

Her reading of the relationship between the "Perserin" and the narrator is based solely on the content of the narrative: he describes the
Persian as "einen mich durch und durch regenerierenden [. . .] Geh-,
und Denk- und also Gesprächs- und Philisophierpartner" (Ja 12), and
Reiter reads this as an acknowledgement, on the narrator's part, of intellectual equality (161). Through the meeting with the Persian, the
narrator is vouchsafed a temporary release from his pathological condition. He acquires the "Aufnahme*fähigkeit*" necessary for a renewal of
his acquaintance with Schopenhauer (Ja 65–7) and his appreciation of
Schumann (Ja 126). Their works, we learn, had never before failed to
have a therapeutic effect on the narrator, and their sudden inability to
rescue him from his depression is a symptom of the profundity of the
crisis to which the Persian is the antidote (Ja 124). Meeting her also
enables him to embark on the academic study that he had abandoned a
short time before (Ja 67). Based on this kind of content analysis, *Ja* can
be viewed as representing women in a positive light. Through a critical
engagement with questions of narrative form, however, the treatment
of women in this text emerges as much more complex and ambivalent.

## Narrative and Repetition

The question of repetition in Bernhard's works has been examined at
the levels of lexis, the behavior of the characters, and motivic recur-
rence.[4] One of the most significant elements of Bernhard's writing,
however, is repetitive *narration*, whereby an event that happens only
once in the story is narrated more than once in the discourse. Repetitive narration is a dominant device in Bernhard's late prose, and it fulfills a variety of functions.

In *Ja*, the event to which the text returns with almost obsessive
regularity is the first meeting between the narrator and Moritz's clients,
the engineer and his Persian common-law wife. The first two sentences
of the text are symptomatic of the circularity of the novel as a whole.
The opening clause announces the arrival of the "Schweizer und seine
*Lebensgefährtin*" (Ja 7), but it is immediately followed by a preposter-
ously long subordinate clause in which the narrator explains how he
had gone to Moritz's house that afternoon and poured out everything

that had been oppressing him (Ja 7–9). Two and a half pages later, the second sentence begins, "Auf dem Höhepunkt dieser meiner möglicherweise tatsächlich vollkommen unstatthaften, wenn auch verzweifelten Kopf- und Körperentspannungsversuche waren im moritzschen Hause auf einmal Schritte zu hören" (Ja 9): the arrival of the Swiss couple once again. The meeting is then described in an unproblematically linear fashion, until the narrator launches into an extended flashback or "analepsis," which provides details about his withdrawal from society and his arrival at the crisis point that caused him to seek the company of Moritz, resulting in the meeting with the engineer and the Persian (Ja 14–23).

This pattern, by which an extended analepsis leads back, however circuitously, to the encounter in Moritz's house, is repeated throughout the first half of the text (Ja 23–7, 37, 38–42, 68–76). Repetitive narration in fiction tends to be motivated by one of two things. It can, of course, serve the interests of multiperspectivalism: several narrators report on the same event from different subject positions. But it can also be a manifestation of character psychology: repeatedly narrating an event signals a desire simultaneously to hide and reveal a cause of guilt, and/or an attempt to narrativize a traumatic experience that has been inadequately worked through. It is possible to read *Ja* in the light of the latter explanation: the narrator's experience of a depression from which not even Schopenhauer and Schumann can release him is so traumatic that it would in all probability have driven him to suicide (Ja 23). The form of the narrative thus dramatizes the narrator's attempt to come to terms with this experience through the act of storytelling, just as he initially tries to "cure" himself by visiting Moritz and *telling* him about his illness.

This interpretation, however, does not exhaust the function of narrative repetition in *Ja*. Talking of the beneficial effect of his meeting with the Persian, the narrator admits: "Aber diese Befreiung hatte naturgemäß nur ein paar Tage andauern können, nach zwei drei Wochen war ich schon wieder in einer tiefen Niedergeschlagenheit gewesen, aber das gehört nicht hierher" (Ja 77). By both mentioning his relapse and then suppressing it from the text, the narrator draws attention to the fact that the story he wishes to tell is not the whole story. By mentioning the dejection that set in after the acquaintance with the Persian had run its course, however, the narrator runs the risk of paradoxically foregrounding the parts of the story he wants to conceal, thereby exposing the selective principles at work in the construction of this particular narrative. Repetitive narration, on the other hand, allows the narrator to preserve the shape of his story as moving from crisis to meeting to liberation/salvation. This narrative of liberation recurs with such insistence that the power of the narrator's subsequent relapse to subvert or relativize it is contained by the narrative strategies he employs.

Repetitive narration fulfills a further role. About a quarter of the way into the text, the narrator states: "Aber nicht von mir soll hier die Rede sein, sondern von der Lebensgefährtin des Schweizers, an die ich in den letzten Tagen wieder sehr oft und sehr intensiv gedacht habe" (Ja 42). There is a stark contrast between this assertion and the content of the repeated narratives. "Aber nicht von mir soll hier die Rede sein" implies that the foregoing is merely a digression from the main point, but by that time the digression has taken on momentous proportions. The same rhetorical move can be witnessed later. After a lengthy description of the illness preceding his visit to Moritz's house, the narrator returns to the time he had spent with the Persian, and adds "von dieser Zeit ist hier die Rede" (Ja 77). The structure of the text, however, has by this time already demonstrated that the narrator's agenda is quite different; far from being concerned with talking about the Persian, the structures of repetition betray a fixation with his own life *before* that meeting.

The narrator actually advances an aphorism to justify his own narrative practice: "Aber alles zu Schreibende muß immer wieder von vorne angefangen und immer wieder aufs neue versucht werden, bis es wenigstens einmal annähernd, wenn auch niemals zufriedenstellend glückt" (Ja 43). This could refer to his repeated attempts to write the text we are reading as well as to the strategies employed *within* the text. Nevertheless, by returning again and again to the beginning, the narrator succeeds in writing something that cannot be fully satisfactory according to the explicit demands he places on his own narrative. He contradicts, through the very textual strategies he employs, precisely what he attempts to assert at the level of content, namely that the Persian woman had a beneficial effect on him and that she is the true subject of his story. The circular movement of the narrative, which always returns to the same point in time and space, is a formal analogue of the self-absorbed, even solipsistic existence that the narrator leads, and provides a vivid illustration of his inability to break out of it.

## The Reading of *Ja*

The chapter on *Korrektur* illustrated that the syntagmatic reading of narrative texts through time is structured by means of the hermeneutic code. The creation of an enigma and the promise of a solution account, as Barthes shows exhaustively, for the dynamics of storytelling. Al-

though criticism of Bernhard has largely contented itself with reiterat-
ing and justifying his own statement that he is a "Geschichtenzerstörer," a more differentiated analysis reveals that like any other writer
of narrative, he incites the reader to keep reading by withholding, while
promising to reveal, key information. This can be witnessed throughout
Bernhard's later work, but the hermeneutic code is clearer in *Ja* than in
any of the fiction that precedes or follows it.

There are, in fact, several hermeneutic sequences in *Ja*. The initial
enigma consists of the uncertainty that surrounds the Swiss engineer
and his "Lebensgefährtin." The narrator remarks on their curious relationship: she is totally silent in his presence but evinces an immense
"Redebedürfnis" whenever he is not there (Ja 13). While waiting for
the Persian in the local inn, the narrator muses: "immer wieder habe
ich es versucht, Licht in das Dunkel ihres Verhältnisses hineinzubrin-
gen, aber ergebnislos." But he refuses to ask the landlady for information, partly out of scruple, and partly because he fears that she would
come out with mere sensationalism without revealing the truth (Ja 45).
These are, of course, plausible motives from a psychological point of
view, but they are also justified by the exigencies of narrative design. To
reveal the nature of the relationship between the two newcomers would
conflate the beginning and end of the hermeneutic sequence, and the
storytelling enterprise would collapse.

Another mystery that puzzles the narrator is how the engineer comes to buy the boggy piece of land behind the churchyard — "eine der
ungünstigsten Lagen überhaupt" (Ja 28–9) — at the exorbitant price
demanded by Moritz, and why Moritz had not initiated the narrator
into this unusual business deal before: "Mir war es unverständlich
[. . .], daß sich Leute, die in der ganzen Welt herumgekommen sind
und also viel von der Welt gesehen haben, sich hier in dieser alles eher
als angenehmen Gegend ansiedeln können, aus was für einem Grund
immer" (Ja 54).

A partial response to these questions is provided by Moritz when
the narrator visits him the day after the original meeting with the Swiss
couple. Since the narrator had avoided social contact for three whole
months, he was ignorant of the sale of the "nasse Wiese" simply because of his self-imposed isolation (Ja 93). Moritz fills in the background to the sale and provides "potted biographies" of the couple (Ja
90–120): the engineer is a world-famous builder of power stations and
owes his success to the ambition of his "Lebensgefährtin," who had
abandoned her studies and foregone a career in order to further that of
her partner (Ja 115–7).[5] Now on the eve of retirement, they purchase
the meadow as a "Grundstück für ihren Lebensabend" (Ja 91).

This act of storytelling on Moritz's part fulfills two contradictory functions. It represents both a solution to the narrator's questions concerning the sale of the plot and the couple who purchase it, and establishes a further enigma. Moritz reports the engineer's words when he expresses bafflement at the hasty decision to buy the field: "dem Moritz könne seine, des Schweizers Handlungsweise und also überaus rasche und tatsächlich verblüffend rasche Entscheidung das Grundstück, also die Wiese betreffend, noch so merkwürdig, ja noch so zweifelhaft vorgekommen, er ändere seinen Entschluß nicht" (Ja 97). This does nothing to explain the *reason* for the purchase; the engineer's motives remain obscure.

Light is finally brought into the darkness surrounding the relationship between the Persian and her common-law husband toward the end of the text. During the second of the narrator's walks with the Persian in the larch wood, she explains that her partner bought the plot and built a forbidding concrete house on it "um sich ihrer zu entledigen": it is a form of revenge for the role she has played in his success (Ja 133). She adds: "Es war das abstoßendste Grundstück, das er jemals gesehen hat. Er kaufte es, weil ihm klar war, er finde kein abstoßenderes mehr" (Ja 134). The narrator's reaction to this is not the sympathy or outrage that might be expected. Rather, he exclaims: "Jetzt hatte ich die Erklärung" (Ja 134). The Persian's words are thus important not because they reveal her own hardship, but because they satisfy the narrator's curiosity about the sale of an undesirable piece of land! Just as repetitive narration betrays the narrator's exclusive concern with himself, so, too, do the hermeneutic codes analyzed here. The stories of the Persian and her Swiss protector-cum-persecutor are of significance only insofar as they answer the narrator's questions and allow the construction of an extended narrative. The manipulation of another's suffering as a pretext for storytelling extends to other aspects of the novel.

The hermeneutic codes discussed are interesting because the desire for a solution to the enigma is shared by both narrator and reader. Because the text is focalized exclusively through the first-person narrator, the reader's perceptual horizon is limited by what the narrator knows. We are thus obliged to align ourselves with his point of view and share his curiosity about the seemingly bizarre purchase. There is another enigma, however, that is created by the narrator *in the act of constructing the text*, rather than being experienced by him at the level of the represented world. The question is this: to what does the title of the book refer?

Writing of Balzac's novella *Sarrasine*, Barthes points out that the title itself is responsible for inaugurating a hermeneutic sequence. This is no less true of *Ja*, where the reference of the title is utterly obscure and remains so until the penultimate word of the text. There are several hints scattered throughout *Ja* that the Persian is dead by the time the narrator begins his report (e.g. Ja 95). This is confirmed in the closing pages, where we learn that she has been run over by a cement lorry. Returning to her dilapidated house for the last time, the narrator recalls that he had once asked her whether she would ever commit suicide. "Darauf hatte sie nur gelacht und *Ja* gesagt" (Ja 148) are the last words of the novel. The negative affirmation of this "*Ja*" seems to be an allusion to the last words of Joyce's *Ulysses*, where Molly Bloom responds to her husband's marriage proposal with the words "yes I will Yes." The echo of *Ulysses* in *Ja* is ironic, signaling an acceptance not of eros, but of thanatos, the death-drive. The final irony, though, is that the title and the last sentence constitute the overarching hermeneutic sequence that guides our forward reading of the entire text. *Ja* is thus revealed as a novel that is predicated on the death of the female character it ostensibly sets out to celebrate.

## Death and Narrative Form

The hermeneutic structuring of *Ja* throws an ironic light on Walter Benjamin's famous dictum: "Der Tod ist die Sanktion von allem, was der Erzähler berichten kann. Vom Tode hat er seine Autorität geliehen" (396). This remark occurs in Benjamin's essay "Der Erzähler," which frequently forms the starting point for discussions of narrative, especially within German studies. One of Benjamin's fields of inquiry is the relationship between storytelling and death — be it a real death or the symbolic death represented by the end of a work of narrative. "Ein Mann," writes Benjamin, "[. . .] der mit fünfunddreißig gestorben ist, wird *dem Eingedenken* an jedem Punkte seines Lebens als ein Mann erscheinen, der mit fünfunddreißig Jahren stirbt" (402). Benjamin is alluding to the retrospectivity of narrative knowledge. In order to endow the individual life with narrative meaning, it is necessary to view it with hindsight, from the moment of death or the surrogate of death: narrative closure.

In this light, certain of the narrator's comments concerning his own narrative enterprise begin to signify. Like *Korrektur*, *Ja* abounds in references to the discursive situation. These produce a sense of temporal difference between the time of the story ("erzählte Zeit") and the period during which it is written down ("Erzählzeit"). More importantly, however, they thematize the act of writing itself. The text contains several assurances that what we are reading is authentic, as the narrator claims to possess some kind of eidetic memory (Ja 24, 29). He also attempts to dismiss parts of his tale as mere digressions and to divert the reader's attention from his own solipsistic obsessions (Ja 42, 52, 77). The most interesting comments on the problems of writing, however, concern the narrator's previous inability to complete the project:

> Heute ist es mir möglich, diesen Zustand mit einigem Abstand zu beschreiben, noch vor ein paar Wochen, noch vor ein paar Tagen, wäre mir das noch nicht möglich gewesen. Wie ich auch bis heute nicht imstande gewesen war, diese Begegnung mit den Schweizern und besonders die mit der Perserin, zu beschreiben, aber ich sehe ein, daß eine Beschreibung notwendig geworden ist, will ich tatsächlich eine Analyse dieser Zeit machen, in welcher ich nahe daran gewesen war, umzukippen. (Ja 25)

This demonstrates the retrospectivity necessary for narrative representation, and similar comments recur: we learn that the narrator's previous attempts to write about the Persian have been unsuccessful (Ja 43), and this is attributed to the fact that "der richtige Zeitpunkt dafür noch nicht gekommen war" (Ja 128).

These comments imply that the narrator's earlier attempts to represent his meeting with the Persian had failed because they had been attempted "too soon." Again, this assertion can be read in a psychological light: the narrator's experiences are so traumatic that he needs time to come to terms with them before he can start writing. Such a reading, however, necessarily entails certain assumptions about the nature of narrative, most notably the idea that a sense of closure, or the "sense of an ending" as Frank Kermode puts it, is a prerequisite of the entire narrative enterprise. The ability to look back and locate an endpoint from which retrospective significance can be granted to foregoing events is thus thematized on the level of the discursive situation: the death of the Persian allows the narrator to gain sufficient distance from the events that he can only *subsequently* make into a story.

## Narrative and Gender

Toward the end of *Ja*, the narrator admits that his dual intention in writing the text is "die Begegnung mit den Schweizern und insbesondere mit der Perserin schriftlich festzuhalten und mich dadurch zu erleichtern und mir dadurch möglicherweise wieder einen Zugang zu meinen Studien zu verschaffen" (Ja 128). The narrative is thus intended to have not only a representational but also a therapeutic function. The insistence on the words "mich-mir-mein" in the previous passage suggests that the therapeutic function is in fact the more significant of the two, and this is corroborated by the rest of the discussion so far.

Further evidence for this reading can be found at several points on the level of the discursive situation, where the narrator avows his ignorance about certain key factors in the Persian's life: he does not know how many walks they undertook in the larch wood (Ja 10), is still baffled as to why the Swiss bought the soggy meadow (Ja 54), and has no idea how far the Persian had progressed in her studies before giving them up and devoting her life to her partner's career (Ja 115). He cannot explain why he failed to visit her after she had moved into her new abode (Ja 121), and is ignorant of whether she expressed any wishes concerning the design of the concrete house (Ja 130). Thus while the text is structured by sequences of enigma and resolution, the narrator finds himself, at the moment of writing, in possession of remarkably little knowledge. This throws an ironic light on the hermeneutic sequences, which are foregrounded as devices whose value lies not so much in their gradual revelation of the "truth," as Barthes maintains, but in their performative function of allowing a story to get told. This again suggests that the therapeutic function of the text is privileged over its representational function. Indeed, as a representation of the Persian, the novel is highly deficient and full of lacunae.

The narrative techniques already outlined aid the performative, therapeutic function: the narrative purports to be about the "Perserin" and her relationship with the narrator, but the repetitive narration of the first meeting between them implies that he is actually obsessed with himself. The structures of enigma and suspense are likewise motivated not by concern for the Persian, but by curiosity on the part of a narrator who cynically exploits her death in order to create the suspense necessary for the functioning of the narrative, and to posit a moment of narrative closure from which retrospective significance can be granted to the past events. In other words, the female character is ultimately used — or abused — by the narrator in the service of his own textual and psychological purpose.

Andrea Reiter points out that Endres's feminist assault on Bernhard remains curiously silent on Ja. The reason, she suggests, is that the representation of women in Ja is too diverse to fit in with Endres's rather sweeping thesis. Yet the above analysis would suggest ample scope for feminist critique. Reiter also points out that the narrator of Ja is self-critical to a degree absent in the earlier novels ("Die Bachmann" 156–7, 170). This may be the case, but it could equally be argued that such avowals of blame or guilt actually function as a more sophisticated means of enlisting the reader's acquiescence: they represent an attempt to control the nature and scope of the reader's criticism by inscribing it as a preprogrammed, *intended* response. A more likely reason for Endres's hesitancy in discussing *Ja* is the uneasy irony created by the textual strategies that repeatedly undermine the surface discourse.

The analysis of *Ja* offered here rests on an implicit assumption that the discrepancy between the explicit goals of the narrator's discourse and the implications of its formal properties results in an ironic gap between the narrator and what, in narrative theory, has been called the "implied author," namely an agency — abstracted from the surface of the narrative discourse — whose role consists in the contextual *positioning* of the narrator's account. Manfred Jurgensen points out the ironic moment in *Ja* in his perceptive early discussion of the text, "Konjunktivisches Erzählen" (1980). He exposes the narrator's tendency to coin adages and use the word "naturgemäß" in an attempt to naturalize behavior that is anything but natural, and suggests that this serves to highlight the diremption between Bernhard's views and those of his narrator ("Konjunktivisches Erzählen" 32). What Jurgensen does not address, however, is the fact that this irony affects our reading of gender questions.

The first consequence of the irony in *Ja* is that it allows the text to be read as a diagnosis: the narrator is exposed as a misogynist clothing his tale of exploitation in the language of liberation (see Ja 135). The readings of the text that use this insight to condemn *Bernhard* for his misogyny, however, assume that the critic is cleverer than the text, and has noticed something of which the author was unaware. Although that may be the case, it is unprovable. A more positive interpretation would assume that the divergence between the narrator's "Selbstverständnis" and what the text betrays about him is attributable to an implied author. On this reading, the irony of *Ja* would allow Bernhard to emerge not as a misogynist, but as a critic of misogyny who uses narrative strategies to enable his narrator to condemn himself with his own words.

# Notes

[1] See, for example, Josef König, for whom the narrator of *Ja* is the most autobiographical of Bernhard's characters: *"Totenmaskenball"* 165.

[2] Höller, *Thomas Bernhard* 92–5. See also Huguet 29–30 for an account of *Ja* that foregrounds the psychoanalytic significance of the autobiographical elements.

[3] Bernhard's testament forbade the publication of his correspondence as well as any other material found among his posthumous papers, but the ban on letters holds only insofar as these have "Werkcharakter." Since the correspondence with Hennetmair concerns mainly mundane affairs, its publication does not fall within the terms of the testament.

[4] On lexis, see Pütz; on lexis and character behavior, Görner; on motivic repetition Jahraus, *Die Wiederholung*.

[5] The Persian bears an unmistakable similarity to Joana in *Holzfällen*. Of both texts, Andrea Reiter writes: "Female domination of the male manifests itself in a subtle way. [...] The narrators of both texts are concerned to explain that the sacrifices of the women are voluntary, if rooted in their upbringing and mentality" ("Die Bachmann" 169). The narrative strategies of the texts, however, disallow this kind of positive reading.

# 4: *Wittgensteins Neffe*

## The Problem of Genre

ON THE OUTSKIRTS OF VIENNA there is an immense complex of sanatoria and hospitals situated on the side of a mountain called the Wilhelminenberg. It was here, in the part of the complex known as the "Baumgartnerhöhe," that Bernhard underwent pulmonary surgery in the summer of 1967. This experience forms the starting point of *Wittgensteins Neffe*, for at the same time, Wittgenstein's eponymous nephew was undergoing treatment for his mental illness in a neighboring institution, the mental hospital Am Steinhof. Bernhard sees this "coincidence" as the central and most significant event in his friendship with Paul Wittgenstein, and the time on the Wilhelminenberg serves as a kind of pivot around which Bernhard's other recollections of his relationship with Paul are organized. The text defies any attempts to summarize its "plot"; it is the most fragmentary and anecdotal of Bernhard's late narratives. It is also the most difficult to categorize.

"Aber was ist das Ganze?" asks Marcel Reich-Ranicki of *Wittgensteins Neffe*, "Ein Bericht? Eine Erzählung? Eine psychologische Studie? Ein Porträt? Sind es Erinnerungen? Autobiographische Aufzeichnungen? Das kleine Buch bietet dies alles und noch viel mehr." As this barrage of questions suggests, *Wittgensteins Neffe* occupies a highly ambiguous generic position. It appeared in the same year as the novel *Beton*, and the last volume of Bernhard's "autobiographical" pentalogy, *Ein Kind*.[1] Although it would appear to complement the latter, it has rarely been viewed as a specifically autobiographical work, and none of the major studies of Bernhard's autobiographies discusses it in any detail.[2] This is partly because it was published by Suhrkamp and not by the Residenz Verlag who had published *Die Ursache, Der Keller, Der Atem, Die Kälte,* and *Ein Kind* between 1975 and 1982. By 1982 all Bernhard's fiction was published by Suhrkamp, and so the "institutional frame" guiding the reception of *Wittgensteins Neffe* might have encouraged a "fictional" reading. Furthermore, although the five autobiographies cover a largely continuous time span, there is a gap of some seventeen years between the period covered by *Die Kälte*, whose narrative ends in 1950, and the opening scene of *Wittgensteins Neffe*, which takes place in 1967. This gap, and the fact that *Wittgensteins Neffe* deals not with Bernhard alone but with Paul Wittgenstein, mean that the text does not lend itself to discussion in the same context as the other five autobiographical texts. Franz Eyckeler's comments on *Wittgensteins Neffe* are symptomatic of the problems of generic classification the book raises. It is, he claims, an "explizit autobiographisches Buch," but continues, "in welchem, wie immer, Wahrheit und Lüge, Realität und Fiktion bis zur Unkenntlichkeit miteinander verwoben sind" (151). So how are we to read the text, as autobiography or as fiction?

There are numerous references in *Wittgensteins Neffe* to biographically verifiable people and historically attested events: the narrator is called Bernhard (WN 118)[3] and is the author of *Verstörung* and *Die Jagdgesellschaft* (WN 7, 153), owns a farmstead in Nathal (WN 57, 68, 101, 142–4, 152–3), receives the Grillparzer Prize and the "Kleiner Österreichischer Staatspreis für Literatur" (WN 105–18), suffers from a pulmonary disorder (WN 8 and passim), frequents Viennese cafés (WN 136–42), and so on. It could be objected that Bernhard appears as a protagonist in one of his own playlets, namely "Claus Peymann kauft sich eine Hose und geht mit mir essen," but the character "Bernhard" in that text is devoid of any specific biographical features that would suggest an identity with the "real" Bernhard. Paul Wittgenstein really existed — plates of him are reproduced in Chantal Thomas's monograph and in Sepp Dreissinger's collection of texts and photographs — and the book is full of references to other real people, such as Paul's wife Edith and Uncle Ludwig, conductors Schuricht and Karajan, racing drivers Jackie Stewart, Graham Hill, and Jochen Rindt, actors Paula Wessely and Bruno Ganz, the Austrian Minister of Culture Piffl-Perčevič, and many others. All this, however, is still not sufficient to establish *Wittgensteins Neffe* as an autobiography or memoir, for Bernhard's fictional texts are all, to a greater or lesser extent, autobiographical, and from *Ja* (1978) onward draw more and more heavily on the author's own experience. Furthermore, historically attested people occur in several of his other novels without their ever being read as anything but fiction — *Der Untergeher* being the prime example, which features a pianist called "Glenn Gould" who actually shares little of the real Glenn Gould's biography.

There is an aspect of *Wittgensteins Neffe*, however, that clearly sets it apart from the author's fictional texts, and that is its historical specificity. A passing reference on the opening page to the Six-Day War (WN 7) situates the text in a historical context that is far more precise than in any other Bernhard work. Likewise, the award of the Grillparzer Prize takes place on the hundredth anniversary of Grillparzer's death (WN

106), which historicizes the event to an extent that the setting of Bernhard's play, *Vor dem Ruhestand*, merely "on Himmler's birthday" does not (*Stücke 3* 62–3). This historical specificity justifies reading *Wittgensteins Neffe* as primarily an autobiographical memoir.

Bernhard's autobiographical pentalogy has occasionally been read as transparent autobiography, most recently by Helmut Gross, who did not have the benefit of Louis Huguet's painstaking researches into Bernhard's early life.[4] All five books, however, are highly stylized, self-consciously shaped pieces of work, and can barely be differentiated from Bernhard's fiction in stylistic terms. Consequently, much, if not most critical literature on them has taken formal and thematic concerns as its main focus, rather than questions of information-content and authenticity.[5] The stylization and mingling of fact and fiction is even more apparent in *Wittgensteins Neffe*. At the level of "information," facts are distorted in order to make a narrative point. Hans Höller, for example, confirms: "Weder damals noch heute tragen die Pavillons in der psychiatrischen Klinik 'Am Steinhof' Namen" (*Thomas Bernhard* 104), and yet the narrator of *Wittgensteins Neffe* delights in the irony that his friend Paul has been admitted to the "Pavillon Ludwig" (WN 9). At the level of form, complex manipulations of time structure, the anecdotal fragmentariness of the narrative, and the emphasis placed on the act of remembering and writing direct the reader's attention toward the text's structural principles. So despite the historically attested individuals who people the pages of *Wittgensteins Neffe*, there are aspects of the text that demand the approach to formal issues normally reserved for fiction.

Perhaps because of it generic ambiguity, *Wittgensteins Neffe* is unique in Bernhard's entire body of work in terms of the dearth of critical literature it has inspired. Its importance has never been fully appreciated, yet it raises both thematic and formal concerns that came to dominate the fictional texts that followed it. It is included here for this reason.

## Thomas Bernhard and Wittgenstein's Nephew

If we reconstruct the story of the Wittgenstein family from the fragments scattered throughout the text, Paul Wittgenstein begins to emerge as a typical Bernhard character. He comes, we are told, from "einer der drei, vier reichsten Familien Österreichs, deren Millionen sich in der Monarchie von Jahr zu Jahr wie von selbst vermehrt haben, bis die Ausrufung der Republik zu einer Stagnation des Wittgensteinschen Vermögens geführt hat" (WN 43). Following turn-of-the-century fashion, the "nouveaux riches" Wittgensteins had had themselves painted by Klimt "unter dem Deckmantel des Mäzenatentums," wishing to be seen as patrons of the arts even though they had no real interest in such matters (WN 84). Paul and Ludwig Wittgenstein are presented as the ultimate "spiritual" flowering of the eminently practical Wittgenstein clan: "Ein Jahrhundert haben die Wittgenstein Waffen und Maschinen erzeugt, bis sie schließlich und endlich den Ludwig und den Paul erzeugt haben" (WN 44), but both Paul and Ludwig had to flee the family in order to live the "Geistesexistenz" they craved (WN 102). Now these "facts" are not all strictly true. Karl Wittgenstein, Ludwig's father and Paul's grandfather, had transferred his investments to foreign equities in 1898, thereby avoiding the devastating effects of hyperinflation after the First World War and securing the fortune which, far from stagnating, continues to provide comfortably for his descendants (Monk 7). Furthermore, rather than being philistines with artistic pretensions, the Wittgensteins were highly cultured and artistically gifted. Ludwig's mother Leopoldine and sister Helene were accomplished musicians (Monk 8–9, 13), and his brother Paul had a career as a concert pianist despite losing his right arm in the First World War. It was for the older Paul Wittgenstein that Ravel composed his famous (and difficult) Piano Concerto for the Left Hand.

Bernhard does not disguise the fact that his portrait of Paul Wittgenstein is highly subjective. Toward the end of the text he avows, "diese Notizen bringen das Bild, das *ich* von meinem Freund Paul Wittgenstein habe, auf das Papier und kein anderes" (WN 133), and throughout the narrative of the Wittgensteins he alters facts in order to construct the type of story that occurs in several of his other novels. The version of Wittgenstein family history, according to which they flourished under the Habsburgs but have stagnated since, allows Bernhard to imply criticism of Austria's decline from a major power to a relatively insignificant country in Central Europe. The position of Paul and Ludwig as recalcitrant heirs who give away their share of the family fortune links them to Prince Saurau's son in *Verstörung*, Roithamer in *Korrektur*, the three pianists in *Der Untergeher*, and Franz-Josef Murau in *Auslöschung*, and the fact that Wittgenstein's philosophy still means nothing either to his own family or to Austria as a state is symptomatic of the perfidy and "Geistesfeindlichkeit" that so many of Bernhard's other narrators impute to Austria. Paul Wittgenstein, then, provides an ideal "biographical subject" because he seems to illustrate Bernhard's major thematic concerns: bequest, inheritance, and patrilineage, and the demise of Austrian cultural and intellectual life. The significance of Paul Wittgenstein within the text is considerably wider than this, however, for his relationship with Thomas Bernhard is not only the text's ostensible subject, but also crucial to its rhetoric.

Marjorie Perloff has pointed out that the relationship between the narrator and his biographical subject is constructed around certain pairs of binary oppositions (159–60). She compiles the following list:

> Pavillon Hermann/Pavillon Ludwig
> Lungenkranke/Geisteskranke
> Lungenanstalt/Irrenanstalt
> Lungenkranke/Verrückte
> Philosophie/Verrücktheit
> Der Kranke/Der Gesunde
> Ich/Paul

Perloff goes on to argue that these oppositional pairs are systematically undermined by the text. "The lengthy comparisons and distinctions made between [. . .] paired nouns always backfires," she writes, "all diseases, it appears, are the same disease, the chest patient Bernhard being no 'sicker' or 'healthier' than the mental patient Paul" (158). But an examination of this device at other points in Bernhard's text shows that the case is less clear-cut than Perloff suggests. The Wilhelminenberg narrative, for example, demonstrates that Bernhard and Paul are "gleich und doch völlig anders" (WN 40). Each time it recurs, this episode on the Wilhelminenberg is characterized by an emphasis on the fact that Paul and Bernhard were in the same place but nevertheless separated from each other. This is manifested in the "uns entsprechenden Anstalten" (WN 37), and elsewhere in the opposition of the Pavillon Hermann to the Pavillon Ludwig (e.g. WN 8, 59). It also is stated more explicitly: "Im Pavillon Hermann war ich nur zweihundert Meter von meinem Freund entfernt, aber ich war doch vollkommen von ihm getrennt" (WN 45–6). Conversely, when Paul eventually undertakes the 200-metre trip from the Pavillon Ludwig to the Pavillon Hermann, he gleefully exclaims: "*du da, wo du hingehörst* [. . .] und *ich da, wo ich hingehöre*" (WN 74), but by this time the two of them are in exactly the same place and the distance between them has been reduced to nothing.

This same oscillation between identification and difference can be seen in the following extract:

> Ich wußte, daß mein Freund immer mehrere Wochen oder Monate in Steinhof war schon seit vielen Jahren, und daß er *jedesmal* wieder hinausgekommen ist und so dachte ich, werde auch ich wieder hinauskommen, wenn auch er mit mir überhaupt nicht zu vergleichen war, in keiner Hinsicht, aber ich bildete mir ein, ich bliebe ein paar Wochen oder Monate da und käme wieder hinaus wie er. Und schließlich war dieser Gedanke nicht falsch gewesen. (WN 22)

Here, the similarity between Thomas Bernhard and Paul Wittgenstein is asserted, retracted as merely a necessary fiction to keep hope alive, and then implicitly asserted once more. The same point is exemplified by the one occasion on which the two men manage to meet on a park bench exactly *between* the two pavilions. Paul experiences some kind of physical breakdown: "*Grotesk, grotesk!* sagte er, worauf er zu weinen anfing und nicht mehr aufhörte. Sein ganzer Körper war lange Zeit von seinem Weinen geschüttelt" (WN 74). Here the coming together of Bernhard and Paul in time and space is explicit, but so is a vivid sense of their bodily separateness. Nevertheless, this separateness is again in part negated at a linguistic level by Bernhard's adoption of Paul's phrase "*grotesk, grotesk,*" which is woven into his own discourse when he is describing the final phases of Paul's decline: "An seinen abgemagerten Armen hingen *grotesk, grotesk,* Einkaufsnetze" (WN 148). The point to note is not merely that all attempts at differentiation collapse, but also that all efforts to assert identity come undone.

The similarities between Bernhard and Paul are numerous, and include the preference of travel over arrival, and the "*Zählkrankheit,*" which involves counting the gaps between the windows of buildings when travelling through town on the tram (WN 145).

> Und wir hatten so viele Hunderte und Tausende Vorlieben gemeinsam wie Hunderte und Tausende Abneigungen; uns zogen oft dieselben Menschen an und stießen dieselben ab. Aber das heißt natürlich überhaupt nicht, daß wir in allem und jedem einer Meinung und eines Geschmacks und ein und derselben Konsequenz gewesen sind. Beispielsweise liebte er Madrid, ich haßte es. Ich liebte die Adria, er haßte sie, etcetera. Aber Schopenhauer liebten wir beide und Novalis und Pascal und Velazquez und Goya, während wir von dem zwar wilden, aber doch durch und durch kunstlosen El Greco in gleich großem Maße abgestoßen waren. (WN 147)

Martin Huber writes: "Wenn auch nicht in allem, so stimmen sie doch in vielem in ihrer Meinung überein, und offenbar in den wesentlichen Punkten" (*Philosophisches Lachprogramm* 155). But the differences remain, and to attempt to dismiss them as non-essential is an excessively reductive operation. To return again to Perloff, she cites in conclusion the following passage:

> *er* [war] es oft gewesen, der mich in Verlegenheit gebracht hatte auf jenen Gebieten, die eigentlich die meinigen sind und von welchen ich überzeugt gewesen bin, daß ich in ihnen zuhause bin; er belehrte mich oft eines besseren. Sehr oft habe ich gedacht, *er* ist der Philosoph, nicht *ich*, *er* ist der Mathematiker, nicht *ich*, *er* ist der Kenner, nicht *ich*. (WN 94; Perloff quotes in English translation.)

"The disclaimer, repeated again and again," she comments, "inevitably inverts itself: if 'he' has all 'my' attributes, then of course 'he' *is* 'me'" (161). We have seen, however, that the text is equally emphatic in its simultaneous protestations to the contrary. Ultimately, the conclusion that can be drawn is that "he" *is* and *is not* "me." Bernhard calls into question the binary oppositions that structure his text without, however, totally invalidating them.

The intimation of a possible identity between Bernhard and Paul Wittgenstein is not an unprecedented technique, its *locus classicus* being the mysterious unity of Serenus Zeitblom and Adrian Leverkühn in Thomas Mann's *Doktor Faustus*.[6] But the relationship between Paul Wittenstein and the narrator in Bernhard's text fulfills quite a different function. This becomes clear in those passages that allude to Bernhard's immediate purpose in writing the memoir. He speaks of "Notizen, die ich *mir* über den Paul mache" (WN 31–2), and intends "ihn *mir* aus diesen Notizen [. . .] gegenwärtig zu machen" (WN 161; all italics mine). Bernhard is thus not merely the narrator of the text; he is its explicit narratee. Ultimately he is also its subject: *Wittgensteins Neffe* consists of "Erinnerungsfetzen, die *mir* im Augenblick nicht nur die ausweglose Situation meines Freundes, sondern *meine eigene* damalige Ausweglosigkeit verdeutlichen sollen" (WN 32; italics mine). Paul emerges as a pretext for self-exploration on the part of the narrator; there are numerous episodes in the text where Paul's presence appears largely superfluous to the narration of events, including the prize-giving ceremonies (WN 105–18) and the premiere of *Die Jagdgesellschaft* (WN 153–60). The role he *does* play in these sections is to confirm Bernhard's own condemnation of the Austrian literary and theatrical establishment.

The device of simultaneously asserting that "he" *is* and *is not* "me" represents an attempt to create narrative authority on two levels. First, by implying some kind of identity between Paul Wittgenstein and himself, Bernhard can claim to possess privileged knowledge of his ostensible subject, thereby affirming his right to be the teller of this particular tale. Second, stressing the difference between himself and his friend allows him to add a second voice to the narratorial judgments passed in the text, not only upon Austria, but on a host of other issues ranging from travel to music, disease to the media, philosophy to coffee houses. Ultimately, these two strategies are incompatible, and each undermines the other: if Paul Wittgenstein and Bernhard are in some sense identical, then what Paul says about Bernhard and Austria is what Bernhard says about Bernhard and Austria. On the other hand, if they are different, then Bernhard has no more authority as a biographer than any other of Paul's acquaintances. Once the elaborate manipulation and subversion of binary oppositions is revealed as a self-defeating device, the source of narrative authority has to be sought elsewhere.

## Death and Narrative Authority

For Robert Vellustig, to whom we owe the only extended study of *Wittgensteins Neffe* to date, "Thomas Bernhard and *Wittgensteins Neffe*: Die Bewegung des Hinundher" (1990), Bernhard outlines "eine Form des Personseins, die die individuelle Diskontinuität in Raum und Zeit auf letztlich präkäre Weise als Stabilisierung der Identität erfahrbar macht" (43). The "personale Diskontinuität in der Zeit" is manifested in Paul's Protean and mutable existence and in the constant uncertainty as to whether he controls his illness or vice versa, both of which allow him to elude the restrictions of social norms (43–4). "Existentielle Bewegung im Raum" occurs when Paul's cyclical attacks of madness necessitate movement between Vienna and various psychiatric hospitals, or between Vienna and Traunstein. Also, the movement between places becomes an end in itself, and the emphasis is placed upon the travel rather than the goal: "Lebensraum erschließ sich dem Ich nur zwischen den Räumen." (46). Finally, the "Beobachtungskunst" and "Bezichtigungsmechanismus" developed by Bernhard and Paul Wittgenstein are non-referential ends in themselves, which permit the subject to assert himself against the world and as nonidentical to it (47–8). The "Bewegung des Hinundher" emerges as a means of postponing death, but since its cause is precisely the "Todeskrankheit" of the protagonist, it ultimately proves debilitating; death is inscribed within all attempts to postpone it.

Vellustig pays scant attention to questions of narrative technique. But his discussion of death as the prime mover behind Paul's eccentric behavior provides a neat transition to the concerns of this study, for death is also the motive for Bernhard's narrative. As we have seen, the relationship between death and storytelling forms the subject of numerous reflections scattered throughout Walter Benjamin's seminal essay on the situation of narrative in the modern world, "Der Erzähler." Benjamin first makes the *existential* point that human knowledge and human experience ("gelebtes Leben") assume transmissible form only at the moment of death (395). He then links this to the *aesthetic* point that the reader of novels (or in our case, biographies) must know in advance that he will experience the death of the characters — "Zur Not den übertragenen: das Ende des Romans. Doch besser den eigentlichen" (402). Benjamin is saying that all narratives depend for their meaning on an endpoint from which retrospective significance may be granted to the beginning and middle. "Vom Tode," as Benjamin writes, "hat [der Erzähler] seine Autorität geliehen" (396).

Bernhard claims this authority when he hints that Paul Wittgenstein is dead even before the main text of *Wittgensteins Neffe* has begun; the epigraph possesses the weight of an epitaph: "Zweihundert Freunde werden bei meinem Begräbnis sein und du mußt an meinem Grab eine Rede halten" (WN 6, and in the body of the text, italicized, on 164). And lest any doubt remain, the eventual death of Paul Wittgenstein is announced six pages later (WN 12). The ability of death to endow past experience with authoritative significance is also touched on by Bernhard when he attempts to enumerate those who have played an important role in his life:

> In einem erträglichen Zustand [. . .] kommen wir aber doch ab und zu, weil wir sonst aufgeben müßten, auf drei oder vier, von welchen wir auf die Dauer nicht nur etwas, sondern sehr viel gehabt haben, ja, die uns zu gewissen existenzentscheidenden Augenblicken und Zeiten alles bedeutet haben und tatsächlich auch alles gewesen sind, wenn wir gleichzeitig auch nicht vergessen dürfen, daß es sich bei diesen Wenigen allerdings nur um Tote handelt und also um schon oder längst Gestorbene, weil wir aus unserer bitteren Erfahrung heraus naturgemäß die heute noch Lebenden und mit uns Existierenden und unter Umständen sogar mit uns an unserer Seite Gehenden nicht in unsere Beurteilung einschließen können, wollen wir nicht Gefahr laufen, uns grundlegend und auf die peinlichste und lächerlichste Weise zu irren und also zuallererst vor uns selbst zu blamieren. (WN 131–2)

Death becomes a prerequisite for establishing significance, and the narrative authority that it confers is adduced throughout *Wittgensteins Neffe*.

The announcement of Paul's death in the opening stages of the text means that the story of the friendship moves toward a return, on the final page, to the beginning, while the beginning takes place under the aspect of the end. Even in *Wittgensteins Neffe*, a narrative whose time structure is achronological and involves complex embedding techniques, death is present from the start as some sort of teleological goal toward which the diverse elements of the narrative contribute, and in terms of which they may be integrated in the reading and writing processes. Bernhard seems to realize this when he writes:

> Diese Notizen, die ich in Nathal und in Wien, in Rom und Lissabon, in Zürich und in Venedig gemacht habe, erwiesen sich letzten Endes doch als nichts anderes, wie ich jetzt weiß, als eine Sterbensgeschichte. [. . .] Ich bin im Grunde nichts anderes, als der zwölfjährige Zeuge seines Sterbens gewesen, denke ich. (WN 161)

From the vantagepoint of death, the past can be understood and transmitted.

Since the end of *Wittgensteins Neffe* is known before the narrative proper commences, the narrative act becomes an attempt at recuperation; that which is past and hence absent has to be made present (in both senses of the word) in the process of telling. "Ich beschränke mich darauf," writes Bernhard, "in meinen Notizen jene Stellen zu suchen, die sich auf den Paul beziehen und ihn mir aus diesen Notizen [. . .] gegenwärtig zu machen als den, den ich im Gedächtnis behalten wollte, *den Lebendigen, nicht den Toten*" (WN 161). Bernhard's intention is a resurrection of Paul Wittgenstein in memory and in the text. There are several episodes which dramatize unsuccessful attempts to recover the past in the face of death. After the death of his wife, Paul himself endeavors to restore the past by recreating his former jollity, and as he becomes increasingly aware of his own imminent demise he wears ever more elegant clothes to compensate for his mental and physical decline. Both end in failure, however:

> Er selbst lud mich und meine Freunde nach dem Tod seiner Frau ein paarmal ins Sacher ein, bestellte wie früher Champagner, aber er erreichte damit nur eine noch tiefere Depression. (WN 83)

> Je unbarmherziger sein Verfall, desto eleganter war jetzt seine Kleidung gewesen [. . .]. Seine Kleider, obwohl dieselben eleganten wie vorher, hatten jetzt nicht mehr die weltmännische und in jedem Fall ehrfurchteinflößende Wirkung auf den Betrachter gehabt. (WN 150, 151)

That the past cannot be relived is a lesson learned by Bernhard, t[o] when he realizes that his attempt to rekindle Paul's passion for saili[ng] was also doomed to failure: "Hatte ihn diese erste Segelpartie mit [mir] und meinem Bruder *auf dem See* noch beglücken können, so dep[ri]mierte sie ihn am Ufer bereits und es war ihm klar, daß es sich um sei[ne] letzte gehandelt hat" (WN 86). Repetition is one mode of coming [to] terms with trauma that Freud discusses in his essay on therapeu[tic] technique, "Erinnern, Wiederholen, Durcharbeiten." Freud disti[n]guishes between repeating and remembering. In the compulsion to [re]peat (*Wiederholungszwang*), traumatic material is repressed b[ut] manifests itself in the form of reenactment by the patient as a conte[mpo]rary event rather than as a memory belonging to the past. This [is] what, in a displaced form, Paul Wittgenstein does, desiring to relive t[he] past instead of facing up to the present traumas of his wife's death a[nd] his own increasing infirmity. Remembering, on the other hand, i[s] volves the conscious assimilation of the past trauma into a narrative that recognizes the past as past while preserving its links with the present.

Repetition is thus symptomatic of an incapacity to unify past and present by telling stories, by narrativizing experience. Paul twice endeavors, toward the end of his life, to produce such a narrative by writing his autobiography, the first time renting a room in the environs of Traunstein, the second engaging a secretary to transcribe his dictated memoirs (WN 94–5). But both of these writing enterprises proved abortive:

> Immerhin hat er zehn oder fünfzehn Seiten zustande gebracht. [. . .] [Sein Buch] wäre ohne Zweifel ein sogenanntes *einmaliges* gewesen, aber er war nicht der Mensch, sich wenigstens ein Jahr lang völlig zu isolieren auf ein solches Ziel hin. Aber es ist schade, daß es nicht mehr solcher Fragmente von ihm gibt. (WN 96)

"Fragmente" are all that remain. This is a "macrotextual" analogue to the speech problems that afflict Paul at the level of the individual sentences. Attacks of his so-called insanity are heralded by the inability to finish his sentences (WN 68), and during his last visit to Bernhard's house in Nathal, conversation becomes impossible: "Es war aber auch kein tatsächliches Gespräch mehr zustande gekommen, er redete nurmehr noch in Satzfetzen, die beim besten Willen keinen Zusammenhang mehr ergeben konnten" (WN 152).

This reveals an apparent breakdown in the signifying chain. As we saw in chapter 1, there is a link between this kind of linguistic malfunction and the psyche of the schizophrenic. Personal identity is the effect of a temporal unification of the past and future with one's present, and this unification is a function of language or, more specifically, the sentence: "If we are unable to unify the past, present, and future of the sentence, then we are similarly unable to unify the past, present, and future of our own biographical experience or psychic life" (Jameson, *Postmodernism* 26–7). When the signifying chain breaks down, psychic experience is reduced to a series of unrelated presents in time. Vellustig writes of "personale Diskontinuität in der Zeit." He speaks of Paul's "theatralische Verwandlungskunst" — Paul's tendency to change clothes several times in a single day — as a "rücksichtslose Hingabe an den Augenblick" (Vellustig 43). While this does not necessarily imply that Paul Wittgenstein was a clinical schizophrenic, it is clear that the experience of life as a sequence of present moments also manifests itself as an inability to write an extended life story, and ultimately as a loss of all linguistic coherence.[7] Paul's recreation of the past in language is as unsuccessful as his repetition of the past in life.

*Wittgensteins Neffe*, on the other hand, can be seen as an attempt to make good Paul's failure to write his own life story, to bring to light a tale whose narration has been obstructed by insanity and curtailed by death. The text reasserts the link between past and present and foregrounds the narrator's ability to make and sustain these links by drawing constant attention to the act of writing, and by stressing the importance of *memory*.

The self-conscious construction of this narrative is made apparent by the extensive references to the "discursive situation," the point in time and space at which the narrative is being written. *Wittgensteins Neffe* is peppered with metatextual comments in the present tense that foreground the process of writing and underline the selective principles at work in the text:

> Möglicherweise getraue ich mich später in einer anderen Schrift noch eine Beschreibung jener Zustände in den Geisteskrankenabteilungen zu machen, deren Zeuge ich gewesen bin. (WN 19)

> Aber dieser *Lebensmensch* ist ja nicht der Mittelpunkt dieser Notizen, die ich mir über den Paul mache. (WN 31–2)

> Er [hat] mir die unglaublichsten Berichte gegeben, die es wert wären, weitergegeben zu werden, wofür aber hier nicht der Platz ist. (WN 73)

> Ich könnte jetzt Paulsche Anekdoten zum besten geben, es gibt nicht nur Hunderte, sondern Tausende, die ihn zum Mittelpunkt haben [. . .], aber das ist nicht meine Absicht. (WN 98)

> Ich weigere mich, alle diese Namen aufzuzählen, die dem Minister durch die von ihm zerschlagene Glastür nachgerannt sind, weil ich keine Lust habe, wegen einer solchen Lächerlichkeit vor Gericht zu kommen. (WN 117)

*Wittgensteins Neffe* constantly makes the reader aware that the narrative could have been organized differently, a different story could have been told. The metatextual comments culminate in an assertion of the extremely subjective nature of Bernhard's account of Paul's life: "diese Notizen bringen das Bild, das *ich* von meinem Freund Paul Wittgenstein habe, auf das Papier und kein anderes" (WN 133). As we shall see toward the end of this chapter, this subjectivity, the awareness that a story can always be told otherwise, is precipitated in the narrative form of the text.

The foregrounded discursive situation results in oscillation between past and present. This may be expressed adverbially: "Erinnerungsfetzen, die mir *im Augenblick* [. . .] meine eigene *damalige* Ausweglosigkeit verdeutlichen sollen" (WN 32); or by tense shifts: "Welche Rolle

beispielsweise der Paul bei der sogenannten Verleihung des Grillparzer-
preises an mich *gespielt hat, fällt* mir ein" (WN 105, my italics throughout). The technique of constructing the past in the present becomes
especially evident when Bernhard describes his elation on the morning
of the Grillparzer Prize ceremony: "Möglicherweise zitterten mir sogar
die Hände in der Frühe und es kann auch sein, daß ich einen heißen
Kopf hatte" (WN 106–7). The modalizing terms "möglicherweise" and
"es kann sein" shift the emphasis from the narrated past events to the
act of narration in the present, but Vellustig overstates the case: "Indem Bernhard die erinnerte Vergangenheit immer wieder in die Un-
mittelbarkeit des erinnernden Bewußtseinsvollzugs einholt, rückt er
Momente 'absoluter Gegenwartsfolge' auf gleichsam dramatische Weise
ins Zentrum des poetischen Interesses" (Vellustig 40). The point of
shifting back and forth between the remembered past and the discursive situation is not to produce a sequence of absolute present moments, but rather to assert in the present an ability to make connections
with the past, connections that Paul Wittgenstein could not make.

True to its etymology, then, this *memoir* of Paul is staged as an active process of remembering, and the phrase "ich erinnere mich" occurs
numerous times (e.g. WN 7, 18, 89, 106). This formulation is highly
uncharacteristic of Bernhard; his habitual inquit phrase is "dachte ich,"
and so the foregrounding of "Erinnerung" in this text seems to demand critical attention.[8] Memory plays a privileged role in Benjamin's
meditations on "Der Erzähler": "Das Gedächtnis ist das epische Ver-
mögen vor allen anderen. [. . .] Nur dank eines umfassenden Gedächt-
nisses kann die Epik einerseits den Lauf der Dinge sich zu eigen,
andererseits mit deren Hinschwinden, mit der Gewalt des Todes ihren
Frieden machen" (399). Here, Benjamin's investigation intersects with
Freud's, for whom memory is crucial to the ability to assimilate events
adequately in a conscious narrative, to cope with the pain of loss.
These, I believe, are two of the main functions of *Wittgensteins Neffe*: it
is an attempt to recuperate the past through memory, but it is also a
way of coming to terms with Paul's death in a private act of *Vergan-
genheitsbewältigung*. The way in which coming to terms with death
determines the formal properties of *Wittgensteins Neffe* is the subject of
the final section of this chapter.

## The Confrontation with Death

*Wittgensteins Neffe* begins with an implied announcement of death; the
end is inscribed in the beginning. But a direct progression from the
opening scene in the Pavillon Hermann to Paul's death would collapse

beginning and end, provide a premature curtailment of the story, a failure of the narrative act. Indeed, Paul's life would remain unnarratable. Peter Brooks suggests that a characteristic of narrative is that it should always be on the verge of what he calls "premature discharge" or "short circuit." The reader thus experiences the fear of the improper end and the excitement that such fear entails (Brooks 109). This point applies to novels from a wide variety of traditions: the reader of Jane Austen is always worried that the heroine will marry the wrong man; adventure novels always present the reader with the possibility that the hero might die before winning the hand of the princess or finding the gold; spy thrillers play on the reader's fear that the Western agent might not be able to foil the megalomaniac's plan to take over the world, and so on. In *Wittgensteins Neffe* the fear of death is omnipresent because it has been announced at the outset. One of the tasks of the text's narrative form, then, is to delay the moment of death so that the eventual end is the "right" end. Between the announcement of Paul's death and his burial, the text becomes what Roland Barthes calls "un espace dilatoire" (*S/Z* 82). Within this dilatory space, the reader's desire for an end that will confer meaning on the foregoing is incited and prolonged by the simultaneous promise and retardation of that end, in order to avoid closures that seem premature or short-circuited.

The postponement of death is in fact thematized in *Wittgensteins Neffe*. The pathos of the contrast between Paul's grandiloquent claim, *"Zweihundert Freunde werden bei meinem Begräbnis sein und du mußt an meinem Grab eine Rede halten"* and the final sentence of the text, "Sein Grab habe ich bis heute nicht aufgesucht" (WN 164) signals the narrator's reluctance to face up to Paul Wittgenstein's death, just as he had avoided Paul in the last months of his decline: he flees Paul's flat above the Bräunerhof as soon as he realizes "daß ich ja schon nicht mehr mit einem Lebendigen, sondern mit einem längst Toten zusammensitze" (WN 127). In a rhetorical move that characterizes most of Bernhard's novels, the narrator coins an adage to justify his behavior:

> *Wir meiden die vom Tod Gezeichneten* und auch ich hatte dieser Niedrigkeit nachgegeben. [. . .] Ich zog mich von meinem Freund zurück wie seine anderen Freunde auch, weil ich mich wie diese, vom Tod zurückziehen wollte. Ich fürchtete die Konfrontation mit dem Tod. (WN 148, 149)

At the same time, however, the text effects a progressive approach toward the moment of death; "die Konfrontation mit dem Tod" is achieved within the pages of *Wittgensteins Neffe*. The technique, fundamental to all narrative, of simultaneously promising and deferring the end mirrors at a formal level the narrator's psychological need to both face up to and shy away from his friend's death.

The device that facilitates the deferral of the end in *Wittgensteins Neffe* is the use of repetitive narration, whereby events that happen only once in the story are narrated more than once in the discourse. Repetitive narration functions differently from the compulsive repetition to which Paul Wittgenstein falls prey after his wife's death. It dramatizes the attempt to turn experience into narrative and hence provides a means of working through (Freud's "Durcharbeiten") traumatic experiences, while impeding the linear, forward movement of the text and hence the reading process.

The opening of *Wittgensteins Neffe* is devoted primarily to the Wilhelminenberg period, and the shifts in focus away from this and onto other events and themes ultimately lead back to the crucial months in the Ludwig and Hermann pavilions:

> Aber wie der Paul mit seiner Verrücktheit schließlich immer rücksichtsloser umgegangen ist, bin ich mit meiner Lungenkrankheit und mit meiner Verrücktheit immer rücksichtsloser umgegangen, indem wir sozusagen mit unseren Krankheiten immer rücksichtsloser umgegangen sind, sind wir auch mit der uns umgebenden Welt immer rücksichtsloser umgegangen und dadurch ist unsere Umwelt naturgemäß in umgekehrter Richtung mit uns selbst immer rücksichtsloser umgegangen und wir sind in immer kürzeren Abständen in die uns entsprechenden Anstalten gekommen, in Irrenanstalten der Paul, in die Lungenanstalten ich. Und während wir sonst immer weit voneinander in die uns entsprechenden Anstalten gekommen waren, sind wir neunzehnhundertsiebenundsechzig auf einmal beide gleichzeitig auf den Wilhelminenberg gekommen und haben auf dem Wilhelminenberg unsere Freundschaft *vertieft*. (WN 37)

This passage is almost manic in its hyperbolic accumulations and repetitions, but just as the meeting on the Wilhelminenberg arrests the self-destructive cycles of hospitalization, so the return to it in the text checks a linguistic extravagance that threatens to spin out of control. It acts as an anchor, a centripetal force which prevents the random dispersion of narrative energies, and forces a return to ground that has already been gone over in order to postpone the moment of death. This process intensifies with each return to the Wilhelminenberg (WN 45–6, 50, 59, 71, 73–4, 92), and what is really at stake in these narrative repetitions emerges with the words most frequently associated with it: "Schicksalsberg" (WN 71, 162), and "Freundschaftsvertiefung" (WN 37, 92).

Drawing once more on the structuralist distinction between story and discourse, we may say that the discourse of *Wittgensteins Neffe* begins in 1967, with both Bernhard and Paul Wittgenstein in their respective pavilions on the Wilhelminenberg. The complex temporal ordering of events in *Wittgensteins Neffe*, however, means that as the text progresses this episode soon loses its originary status, for the story actually commences at some unspecified point in Paul's youth. The economy of the narrative structure thus divests the Wilhelminenberg episode of the *temporal* priority that it initially appears to possess, but the periodic returns to it simultaneously suggest another way in which it *is* privileged: paradoxically, it increasingly acquires the significance and function of an ending.

At the time of his hospitalization, Bernhard was told that he could expect to live for "*nur noch Wochen, im besten Fall Monate*" (WN 7), and here we return to the question of death and its capacity for endowing the past with significance:

> Im Pavillon Hermann und letzten Endes *in Todesangst*, ist mir bewußt geworden, was meine Beziehung zu meinem Freund Paul wirklich wert ist, daß sie in Wahrheit die wertvollste von allen meinen Beziehungen zu Männern ist [. . .]. Nun hatte ich plötzlich Angst um diesen Menschen, der mir auf einmal zu meinem allernächsten geworden war, daß ich ihn verlieren könnte, und zwar in zweierlei Hinsicht: *durch meinen*, wie auch *durch seinen Tod*. (WN 59)

Death, here, is symbolic, but as a provisional ending it has much of the force of the literal deaths with which narratives tend to end, for it allows Bernhard to gauge the true significance of Paul's role in his life. The text keeps returning to this episode because it is pregnant with the fear of a premature ending, a short circuit: the friendship between Bernhard and Paul was incomplete, and for either of the friends to have died at this point would not have furnished the "right" or "proper" narrative ending. The Wilhelminenberg is a "Schicksalsberg" because it is here that a decisive turning point takes place: on the one hand is "Todesangst," on the other Paul Wittgenstein, and fate comes down on the side of "Freundschaftsvertiefung" rather than death. By returning to the Wilhelminenberg, Bernhard confronts the traumatic possibility of a premature closure, of life and hence of the text. At the same time, he delays the arrival of the proper closure by forcing a reading that goes backward as well as forward, by returning to a provisional end that precipitates the "Freundschaftsvertiefung" and is hence also a beginning.

It is not *the* beginning of the friendship, however, because that had taken place several years before in the "Blumenstockgassenwohnung" of their mutual friend Irina. The word "begründet" (WN 28) emphasises the foundational moment of the episode, and contrasts with the later "vertieft" (WN 37) and "besiegelt" (WN 92) of the encounter on the Wilhelminenberg. The text takes us back to this moment on three occasions after its initial description on pp. 27–8, and each time the "Blumenstockgasse" is mentioned. Although we do not have to agree with Oliver Jahraus's extreme thesis: "Was sich wiederholt, ist signifikant, und das Signifikante wiederholt sich; Signifikanz entsteht in [Bernhards] Werk erst durch Wiederholung" (*Wiederholung* 21), it is nevertheless the case that repetitions *change* the significance of textual elements. So although the "Blumenstockgasse" initially functions as merely a specification of place, it takes on, through repetition, some kind of talismanic significance and suggests that the organic growth of the "Blumenstock" somehow parallels the taking root and flourishing of the friendship between Bernhard and Paul. Interestingly, Bernhard returns to this first meeting with Paul with increasing frequency as the text progresses (WN 105, 130–2, 133), and it temporarily takes over the function of the Wilhelminenberg episode (to which no reference is made between pp. 92 and 162). The compulsive need to return to origins demonstrates an urgent desire to postpone the inevitable end, to assert the abiding value of friendship in the face of death.

However, the beginning of the friendship with Paul emerges as the end of something else, namely Bernhard's "Depression," "Melancholie," "Selbstmordspekulation," "Selbstmorddenkmechanismus" (WN 129–30). The constant returning to beginnings that turn out also to be ends is a device that takes the *story* further and further from Paul's final death even as the *discourse* approaches it, firstly to the Wilhelminenberg, then beyond that to the origin of the friendship, then yet further back to the depression and suicidal melancholy that preceded that first meeting. This oscillation between ends and beginnings is part of the "Bewegung des Hinundher" of which Vellustig writes, and betrays a desire to recuperate more and more of the past as the moment of loss approaches, to defer the end by situating the beginning at an increasingly distant point and hence expanding the dilatory space in which the narrative can unfold. Just as Bernhard himself had fled from his friend's flat, the text flees into the past and delays the (inevitable) "Konfrontation mit dem Tod."

The way in which each of Bernhard's projected beginnings turns out to be simultaneously an end illustrates Konrad's assertion in *Das Kalkwerk*: "ein Endpunkt ist immer ein Anfangspunkt für einen weiteren Endpunkt und so fort" (Kw 62). It also demonstrates a fundamental point about the nature and functioning of narrative. Fictional narratives, as Frank Kermode has convincingly argued, grew out of the apocalyptic narratives through which man tried to orient himself in relation to imagined beginnings and projected endpoints. In the absence of such macronarratives — which attempt to narrativize the *whole* of human temporality — perceived beginnings and projected ends become arbitrary formal limits placed on the amorphism of time. In the classical novel this arbitrariness was "backgrounded." Henry James wrote in the famous preface to *Roderick Hudson*: "Really, universally, relations stop nowhere, and the exquisite problem of the artist is eternally but to draw, by a geometry of his own, the circle within which they shall happily *appear* to do so" (452). And E. M. Forster expressed the same point with his customary wit in *Aspects of the Novel*: "the more we disentangle [the story] from the finer growths that it supports, the less we shall find to admire. It runs like a backbone — or may I say a tapeworm, for its beginning and end are arbitrary" (41). Bernhard, on the other hand, demonstrates once again the provisional, subjective nature of his narrative account of Wittgenstein's nephew: by showing beginnings and endpoints in *Wittgensteins Neffe* to be effectively interchangeable, he lays bear the arbitrariness involved in narrative form and shows the openings and closures to be necessary fictions that depend ultimately on the selective principles employed by the narrator: "das Bild, das *ich* von meinem Freund habe und kein anderes."

# Notes

[1] Marquardt suggests that *Wittgensteins Neffe* is more akin to *Beton* than to *Ein Kind*, because the main figure is not Bernhard (130). But this is an oversimplification, as we shall see.

[2] See e.g. Parth, Saunders, and Tschapke.

[3] Throughout this chapter I refer to the narrator as "Bernhard," but am aware that the Bernhard of *Wittgensteins Neffe* is an effect of the text rather than its source.

[4] Huguet's valuable and at times fascinating investigations into Bernhard's family and childhood show how he altered his own biographical data in order to construct private myths that draw on archetypal patterns of significance. Especially interesting are Huguet's psychoanalytically oriented discussions of the "Priesterseminar," "Fischkutter," and "Badezimmer" episodes in the autobiographies, and the way in which they are linked to elements of *Ja*, *Korrektur*, and *Frost* (Huguet 11–36). His study as a whole shows how elements of Bernhard's biography, such as the putative rape of his mother and the dissoluteness of his father, are often excluded from the autobiographies but find their way into the fictional texts in displaced form.

[5] In addition to the studies by Parth, Saunders, and Tschapke mentioned above, see the articles by McLintock and Donahue.

[6] A comparison of Bernhard and Mann may be instructive. Alfons Kaiser has seen in the primitive brutality of the postwar, working-class sanatoria in Bernhard's *Der Atem* and *Die Kälte* a transvaluation ("Umwertung") of the pre-1914 decadent luxury of Mann's Davos consumptives in *Der Zauberberg* (77–85). *Wittgensteins Neffe* could provide a kind of satyr play to the portrayal of the relation between genius and madness in the tragedy of *Doktor Faustus*, and the decadent aestheticism of Christian and Hanno Buddenbrook seems to find a parallel in Paul Wittgenstein, the dandified, dissolute, but sickly latecomer to the solid, businesslike line of the Wittgensteins. We will return to Mann's *Buddenbrooks* in Chapter 8.

[7] A further index of Paul's, and indeed Bernhard's, insanity is the section in which the two of them sit in cafés and make connections between their observations and the most diverse and unrelated matters: "So war es nicht selten ganz einfach ein ganz und gar gewöhnlicher Mensch, der seinen Kaffee trank, der uns auf Schopenhauer brachte, oder eine mit ihrem unerzogenen Enkelkind große Strudelstücke verzehrende Dame unter dem erzherzoglichen Gemälde, die uns beispielsweise die Hofnarren von Velasquez im Prado zum Mittelpunkt einer dann unter Umständen stundenlangen Unterhaltung werden ließ" (WN 122–3). The discussion of Foucault (chapter 1) showed that the unlicensed (i.e. not socially sanctioned) perception of similitude comes within the syndrome of madness: the madman is one who sees similarities and signs of similarity everywhere.

[8] This is not to say that "ich erinnere mich" does not occur in, for example, *Der Untergeher* or *Holzfällen*, but its use in those texts is considerably less frequent.

# 5: *Der Untergeher*

## "Ersatzursachenforschung"

THE OPENING SENTENCES of Bernhard's 1983 novel *Der Untergeher* relate an astonishing amount of information, and introduce all the key elements that are to be developed throughout the remainder of the text:

> Auch Glenn Gould, unser Freund und der wichtigste Klaviervirtuose des Jahrhunderts, ist nur einundfünfzig geworden, dachte ich beim Eintreten in das Gasthaus. Nur hat der sich nicht wie Wertheimer umgebracht, sondern ist, wie gesagt wird, *eines natürlichen Todes* gestorben. (U 7)

The narrator stays at the "Gasthaus" or inn on his way to visit the late Wertheimer's hunting lodge, hoping to rescue his former friend's posthumous papers. While he is standing in the inn awaiting the landlady's arrival, he remembers the friendship between himself, Wertheimer, and Glenn Gould, a triple configuration of characters around which the text circles with characteristic insistence. The three friends had made each other's acquaintance twenty-eight years before when they were attending a masterclass given by Horowitz at Salzburg's famous Mozarteum conservatory. Both Wertheimer and the narrator are initially highly promising concert pianists, the former having been an "außerordentliches Talent" (U 152) and the latter "einer der besten Klavierspieler Österreichs, wenn nicht Europas" (U 158). But Gould is the only one to go on to enjoy a successful musical career; the others give up because the distance between Gould's perfection and their own playing renders their efforts pointless and absurd.

The immediate impulse for the writing of *Der Untergeher* is Wertheimer's suicide, and the primary motivation is the narrator's need to explain his friend's death. The problem of causes, beginnings, and origins is a prominent motif in Bernhard's prose. As early as *Das Kalkwerk*, Bernhard's third novel, the form is established in which the death of one of the protagonists sets in motion an investigation of the circumstances surrounding that death and its possible causes. There is a clear link between this kind of narrative strategy and the structure of detective fiction. Tzvetan Todorov proposes two subvariants within the genre of detective fiction, the first of which appears to correspond to the narrative form of *Das Kalkwerk* and *Korrektur* as well as the text that concerns us here, *Der Untergeher*.[1] Todorov terms this subgenre the "roman d'énigme," and writes:

> Ce roman ne contient pas une mais deux histoires: l'histoire du crime et l'histoire de l'enquête. Dans leur forme la plus pure, ces deux histoires n'ont aucun point commun. [. . .] La première histoire, celle du crime, est terminée avant que ne commence la seconde (et le livre). Mais que se passe-t-il dans la seconde? Peu de choses. Les personnages de cette seconde histoire, l'histoire de l'enquête, n'agissent pas, ils *apprennent*. ("Typologie" 11)

Todorov equates these two stories with the Russian formalist categories of *fabula* (the chronological story) and *sujet* (the discourse responsible for its narration), categories that correspond to our "story" and "discourse." He goes on to show that the second story tends to thematize the writing of the book we read: "c'est une histoire qui n'a aucune importance en elle-même, qui sert seulement de médiateur entre le lecteur et l'histoire du crime." Because of its mediatory function, the second story is conventionally highly transparent and should not throw "une ombre inutile sur la première" (13). The structure of the detective novel displays a faith in the ultimate knowability and explicability of the world. It is the hermeneutic form *par excellence*, leading to a revelation of the "truth" in terms of which all the foregoing details may be integrated. The dialectic of the hermeneutic circle, as neatly summed up by Peter Bürger, is in full evidence: "Die Teile sind nur aus dem Werkganzen, dieses wiederum nur aus den Teilen zu verstehen. Das heißt, eine vorwegnehmende Auffassung des Ganzen lenkt die Auffassung der Teile und wird durch diese zugleich korrigiert" (P. Bürger 107).

We have already seen, however, that *Das Kalkwerk* and *Korrektur* problematize the hermeneutic project by failing to provide the certainties that the text encourages the reader to expect. *Der Untergeher* is even more extreme is its subversion of the detective novel structure, and this section will examine the ways in which the subversion is achieved.

### "Hermeneutic" sequences

The tripartite time structure of *Der Untergeher* already suggests that the text might not correspond entirely to the form of detective fiction. Bernhard had already exploited the technique to a limited degree in *Wittgensteins Neffe*. In the earlier text there are several scenes where the narrator recalls a moment in the past, during which he was remembering or thinking about another event lying yet further back. The device manifests itself most clearly when Bernhard flees Paul Wittgenstein's flat, collapses on a park bench and reflects on the friendship: "Ich dachte, da auf der Stadtparkbank sitzend, daß es möglicherweise das letzte Mal gewesen ist, daß ich den Freund gesehen habe" (WN 128). Following this is a description of the beneficial effect that the first meeting with Paul had had on the narrator, before the moment of remembering is once again recalled: "Auf der Stadtparkbank ist mir das alles auf einmal wieder ganz deutlich zu Bewußtsein gekommen" (WN 131). The recollection is then interrupted by an extended reference to the moment of writing, or "discursive situation": "Und ich denke heute, die Menschen, die in unserem Leben wirklich etwas bedeutet haben, können wir an den Fingern einer Hand abzählen" (WN 131); Paul Wittgenstein belongs to "denjenigen, die mir in jedem Fall meine Existenz [. . .] möglich gemacht haben, was mir jetzt, zwei Jahre nach seinem Tod, ganz deutlich bewußt und im Hinblick auf die Jännerkälte und Jännerleere in meinem Haus, keine Frage ist" (WN 133). Finally, we return to the park bench: "Während er, wie ich auf der Stadtpark-bank dachte, [. . .] mit Vorliebe den rechten der beiden Salons des Sa-cherschen Kaffeehauses aufsuchte, bevorzugte ich [. . .] naturgemäß den linken" (WN 134). The oscillation between the primary time level (here: sitting on the bench), the discursive situation, and an excursion into the past ("analepsis") is a constant feature of *Der Untergeher*, *Holzfällen*, *Alte Meister*, and *Auslöschung*.

Ingrid Petrasch discusses these three time levels in *Der Untergeher*. Her "Gegenwartsebene" is the moment of writing. The "Vergangenheitsebene I" — which can be termed the "primary time level" — consists of the narrator's entry into a guest house in Wankham, his conversations with the landlady, his walk to the hunting lodge at Traich, and a conversation there with Wertheimer's servant Franz. The "Vergangenheitsebene II" is constituted of series of flashbacks or "analepses." These narrate an episodic story of the three main characters' lives, leading from the moment when the narrator, Wertheimer, and Glenn Gould meet at Horowitz's masterclass to Wertheimer's burial twenty-eight years later (Petrasch 218–9). Petrasch points out that the primary time level is concerned with the recuperation of the more distant past through the act of memory, and with the "rhythmic" structuration of that past: it dramatizes the "Erkenntnisprozeß des Ich-Erzählers bezüglich der in diesem Rahmen erinnerten Vergangenheit" (221). This emphasis on cognition recalls Todorov: "Les personnages [. . .] de l'histoire de l'enquête n'agissent pas, ils *apprennent*." The situation is, however, more complex, because the primary time level narrates not only a cognitive process, but also a series of events that take on significance in their own right. Although in *Wittgensteins Neffe* the park bench episode is merely a localized structural device, the pri-

mary time level of *Der Untergeher* is constituted of proairetic and hermeneutic sequences that structure the entire forward reading process of
the text.

In Barthes's system of narrative codes, a proairetic sequence is a linear series of actions that derives its logic from the empirical, the "déjà-
fait" or the "déjà-écrit," meaning that we are able to understand and
name action sequences on the basis of lived experience and our acquaintance with a repertoire of literary behavior (*S/Z* 209). Here, they
consist of entering the "Gasthaus," waiting for the landlady, going up
to the bedroom, drinking a cup of tea, talking to the landlady, walking
to Traich, meeting Franz Kohlroser, and so on. This minimal series of
actions establishes a stable, linear primary time level, from which excursions can be taken into the past.[2] These analepses are signaled by
"dachte ich," a phrase whose persistent repetition foregrounds the cae-
sura between the external world and the world of thought; the linear
time of the empirical world here is juxtaposed with the achronological,
subjective time of psychic life.

More significantly, this sequence of actions partakes of the hermeneutic, what Barthes calls the "voix de la vérité," which is operative
within narrative texts and concerns the posing and solving of enigmas.
The narrator's goal is to find Wertheimer's *Nachlaß*:

> Tatsächlich hatte ich die Absicht gehabt und habe sie jetzt noch,
> eventuell von Wertheimer hinterlassene Schriften in Augenschein zu
> nehmen. Wertheimer redete oft von Schriften, die er verfaßt habe im
> Laufe der Zeit. Unsinnigkeiten, so er, aber Wertheimer war auch
> hochmütig, was mich vermuten ließ, daß es sich bei diesen Unsinnig-
> keiten um Wertvolleres handelte, jedenfalls um Wertheimersche Ge-
> danken, die es wert sind, erhalten zu werden, gesammelt, gerettet,
> geordnet, dachte ich und ich sah einen ganzen Haufen von Heften
> (und Zetteln) mehr oder weniger mathematisch-philosophischen In-
> halts. (U 53–4)

These "hinterlassene Schriften" are potentially the bearers of definitive
information about Wertheimer, of a truth that remains concealed:

> Möglicherweise hat Wertheimer auch niemandem außer mir von sei-
> nen Schriften (und Zetteln) etwas gesagt, dachte ich, und hat sie ir-
> gendwo versteckt, so bin ich ihm doch schuldig, diese Hefte und
> Schriften (und Zettel) aufzustöbern und zu erhalten, gleich unter wel-
> chen Umständen. (U 54)

> Vielleicht sind es die Zettel, die dich interessieren und die dich in Att-
> nang Puchheim haben aussteigen lassen, dachte ich.[. . .]. Tausende
> seiner Zettel aneinandergereiht, dachte ich, und unter dem Titel *Der
> Untergeher* herausgegeben. (U 79)

There are actually two hermeneutic sequences operating in parallel here. First, the text throws a certain burden of expectation onto the content of the *Nachlaß*. As Peter Brooks has argued, narratives speak repeatedly of the attempt to bring to light that which remains hidden, and to re-establish it in a circuit of communication (221), hence the rhetoric of concealment and discovery in the above quotations, where "herausgeben" takes on literal force. The forward momentum of the narrative is in part generated by the assumption, shared by both the narrator and his readers, that the discovery of the *Nachlaß* will result in a revelation, that it might shed light on Wertheimer's untimely death. Second, and following on from this, there is also the threat that the desire to locate Wertheimer's writings will be blocked, that the satisfactions of narrative will be thwarted, that the story will be prevented from reaching its intended end. Initially, there is the possibility that the narrator's efforts will be obstructed by Wertheimer's family, who might deny him entry to the *Jagdhaus* (U 54). This is exacerbated by the narrator's additional fear that Wertheimer might have destroyed the "Zettel" himself before taking his life: "Die Einschätzung hatte ich, daß er alle diese Zettel in Traich und Wien vernichtet hat" (U 79). Toward the end of the text a further fear is introduced, namely that Wertheimer's sister could have reached the *Jagdhaus* before the narrator and found the *Nachlaß*: "Im Geiste, wie gesagt wird, sah ich sie jetzt schon in Traich über den Tausenden, wenn nicht Hunderttausenden von Zetteln ihres Bruders sitzen und sie studieren. Dann wieder aber dachte ich, daß Wertheimer nicht einen einzigen Zettel hinterlassen hat" (U 216). Three possibilities are thus kept open: either the narrator will reach the *Nachlaß* first, or Wertheimer's sister will, or there is no *Nachlaß* at all.

The "résolution de l'énigme" takes place only on the final page of the novel, when Wertheimer's former servant Franz Kohlroser reveals that he and Wertheimer had destroyed the entire *Nachlaß*: "Er habe aus allen Laden und Kasten Hunderte und Tausende Zettel herausgenommen und mit ihm, Franz, in das Speisezimmer hinuntergeschleppt, um sie zu verbrennen" (U 242). As an ending, it has a curiously paradoxical effect. It finally resolves the question of whether there is a *Nachlaß*, but at the same time, the narrator's (and by implication also the reader's) desire for and expectation of a final revelation is disappointed. Just as detective fiction relies on the expectation of discovery of the murderer, the projected *telos* of the discovery of the *Nachlaß* is used to structure the primary time level and hence also the entire text. But unlike detective fiction, it reveals itself at the end to be a gap, an absence; there is no final discovery that would provide a solution to the unanswered questions raised in the body of the novel.

Once we have realized this, the story of the trial and conviction of the landlady's uncle takes on immediate relevance. Rather than the somewhat vague connections that Petrasch draws between the so-called "Dichtelmühlprozeß" and the narrator's predicament (223–4), the landlady's uncle's trial functions as a figure for *Der Untergeher* as a whole. It is basically the story of what the narrator terms "einen bis heute nicht zur Gänze aufgeklärten Mordfall" (U 190). The landlady's uncle and his neighbour are accused of murdering a Viennese underwear salesman in order to get hold of the money he had about his person (U 190). During the trial it becomes clear that the defendants are innocent: "ich erinnere mich ja noch ganz genau an die Prozeßberichte und im Grunde hätten die beiden [. . .] unbedingt freigesprochen werden müssen, dafür hatte ja auch schließlich sogar der Staatsanwalt plädiert" (U 194). But the jury convicts them nevertheless. The position of the jury in the trial is analogous to the position of both the narrator and the reader of Bernhard's text. All are presented with a set of data from which they try to draw conclusions. Criminal justice, as Roland Barthes has shown, relies on notions of the literary, of the well-formed plot (*Mythologies* 50–3, 102–5), and in its desire for a neat narrative conclusion, the jury in the "Dichtelmühlprozeß" hastily convicts the uncle and his "accomplice," even though the conviction is clearly unsafe: "tatsächlich nachgewiesen hat man den Mord weder dem Onkel, noch seinem Helfershelfer" (U 192). The story of the "Dichtelmühlprozeß" thus functions as a cautionary tale: the narrator's criticisms of the jury can be read as a warning to the reader that the facts in Wertheimer's "case" may frustrate, or even be incommensurable with, his or her desire for a neat tying up of loose narrative ends.

### Retrospective knowledge and narrative beginnings

The traditional detective novel privileges the explanatory force of the end, to which all details in the text contribute and in the light of which they can be interpreted. In *Der Untergeher*, however, there is profound insecurity about the function of the end; the *telos* structuring the primary time level, namely the discovery of Wertheimer's manuscripts, ultimately turns out to be nothing more than a convenient fiction that allows the tale to get told. On the "Vergangenheitsebene II," however, the death of the protagonist still appears to represent a stable vantage-point from which retrospective significance can be granted to the past in narrative form. The narrator writes, "Jetzt weiß ich, *wie* diese Schrift angehen, ich habe es nie gewußt, ich habe sie immer zu früh angefangen, dilletantisch" (U 109), thereby emphasizing the role of death as a legitimating force in narrative: "Der Tod," as we have noted, "ist die Sanktion von allem, was der Erzähler berichten kann. Vom Tode hat er seine Autorität geliehen" (Benjamin 396). The narrator's previous studies of Glenn Gould have been written "too soon" because death had not intervened to provide that sense of an ending that is so crucial to the functioning of narrative. The narrator uses the benefit of hindsight in order to throw light on certain events from the narrator's past, whose significance becomes apparent only in the light of Wertheimer's suicide. The statement: "Aber Glenn war schon, als er nach Europa gekommen war und den Horowitzkurs besucht hat, das Genie, wir waren zu demselben Zeitpunkt schon die Gescheiterten" (U 82) can be made solely because the subsequent twenty-eight years have shown the narrator and Wertheimer to be — according to their own criteria, at least — failures. Similarly, the word "Untergeher" attains its full significance only in the knowledge of the end: "Aber der Anfang von Wertheimers Katastrophe war schon in dem Augenblick eingetreten, in welchem Glenn Gould zu Wertheimer gesagt hat, er sei *der Untergeher*" (U 218). The same applies to the narrator's own coinage for Wertheimer: "der Sackgassenmensch" (U 208–11). The trouble here is that, as Robert Vellustig points out, these "explanations" for Wertheimer's suicide rely on tautological arguments: "Der Selbstmord Wertheimers erscheint als Beweis für den Begriff, der den Selbstmord begreiflich machen soll; Wertheimer ist ein 'Sackgassenmensch,' weil er in die Sackgasse geraten ist, und umgekehrt" ("Gesprächs-Kunst" 39). Retrospective knowledge, then, is problematic in *Der Untergeher*. Despite the definitive end provided by the deaths of Wertheimer and Glenn Gould, the narrator still cannot determine the significance of the welter of information with which he is presented.

Ingrid Petrasch centers her reading of *Der Untergeher* around the epistemological question of whether Wertheimer's suicide is contingent or determined, arguing that this stands for the wider question "nach der Geordnetheit und damit Sinnhaftigkeit oder Zufälligkeit und damit Sinnlosigkeit der menschlichen Existenz und der Welt schlechthin" (214). It is questionable whether such a large claim is justified by the text, but Petrasch rightly notes: "Einerseits haben sich dem Ich-Erzähler zahlreiche Zusammenhänge in Bezug auf Wertheimers Tod eröffnet, er vermag jedoch nicht zu unterscheiden, welches der zentrale oder ursächliche Zusammenhang ist" (240). Marquardt makes the same point, and adds that the last reason the narrator gives for Wertheimer's suicide would normally be read as definitive due to its position in the narrative, but that this option is thwarted by the disruption of the linearity of the primary time level (53–4). As noted previously, this latter assertion is based on a misreading, but the time structure of the novel is complex enough to prevent the reader from specifying with any reliability the chronological and logical priority of any judgments offered.

Throughout the text the narrator suggests a series of explanations for Wertheimer's death, beginning with the following: "Die Ursache ist sehr oft Scham über die Grenzüberschreitung, die der Fünfzigjährige empfindet, wenn er das fünfzigste Lebensjahr hinter sich hat" (U 52). The suicide is then put down to a desire to copy Glenn Gould and simultaneously teach his sister a lesson (U 75), and this is soon developed further: "Glenns Tod war für ihn, wie sich erwiesen hat, nicht ausschlaggebend gewesen für den Selbstmord, die Schwester mußte ihn verlassen, aber Glenns Tod war schon der Anfang seines Endes gewesen, auslösendes Moment die Verheiratung der Schwester mit dem Schweizer" (U 77; cf. also 88). Rather eccentrically, the narrator tells us that Wertheimer hated the word Chur so much "daß er hinfahren mußte, um sich umzubringen" (U 91), and later decides that Wertheimer killed himself because it was the only way he could achieve any form of self-assertion (U 135), or because he was afraid of losing the unhappiness on which he thrived (U 150). On another occasion it is Wertheimer's recognition of Gould's genius in 1953 that leads to his death twenty-eight years later (U 131, 152). Later still, envy of Glenn's death is re-asserted as the causal factor in Wertheimer's suicide, and the role of his sister's marriage denied (U 211–2). Wertheimer's death is thus overdetermined: it is the result of an excessive number of causal factors. The narrator shows himself to be very aware of the fact:

> Immer wieder fragen wir nach der Ursache und kommen nach und nach von einer Möglichkeit auf die andere, dachte ich, daß Glenns Tod die eigentliche Ursache für Wertheimers Tod ist, dachte ich immer wieder, nicht daß Wertheimers Schwester zu dem Duttweiler nach Zizers ist. Die Ursache sagen wir nicht nur, liegt immer viel tiefer und sie liegt in den Goldbergvariationen, die Glenn in Salzburg während des Horowitzkurses gespielt hat, *das Wohltemperierte Klavier ist die Ursache*, dachte ich, nicht die Tatsache, daß sich Wertheimers Schwester mit sechsundvierzig Jahren von ihrem Bruder getrennt hat. (U 217)

The movement in this passage from the recent past of Glenn's death into the more distant past of the Horowitz masterclass is typical of the text as a whole, and the inability to choose the "zentrale oder ursächliche Zusammenhang" is precipitated in the narrative form of the novel as the problem of how and where to begin. The various connections that the narrator draws are all attempts to fix a narrative beginning from the perspective of the known end (the death of Wertheimer and Gould). As the primary time level moves towards its final discovery that all Wertheimer's "Zettel" have been burned, there is an opposite movement — a typically Bernhardian "Gegenrichtung" — into the more distant past. So, for example, the narrator is invaded by memories of his own previous childhood trips to Chur (U 86–8); the "Wirtin" narrates the history of how she acquired the "Gasthaus" (U 190–7); and, most importantly, Franz Kohlroser reports on the childhood of Wertheimer and his sister before the Nazi era. National Socialism initially crops up in the text in the form of the Nazi sculptures in the house at Leopoldskron (U 112–3), which are sprayed with champagne by Glenn Gould in a highly ambiguous gesture of both desecration and celebration.[3] In Franz's narrative, it is implied that the Nazis ruined the "Lebensform" of Wertheimer's family:

> Er, Franz, erinnerte sich noch genau an die Kinderzeit der beiden Wertheimer, als die beiden noch fröhlich in Traich angekommen seien, lustige Kinder, die zu allem aufgelegt gewesen sind, so Franz. Das Jagdhaus sei der liebste Spielplatz der beiden Wertheimerkinder gewesen. Die Zeit, in welcher die Wertheimerischen in England gewesen sind, in der Nazizeit, so Franz, sei es, während ein Naziverwalter in Traich gehaust habe, auf beängstigende Weise in Traich still gewesen, alles sei in dieser Zeit auch verkommen, nichts ist repariert, alles sich selbst überlassen worden [. . .]. Nachdem die Wertheimer von England zurückgekommen seien, zuerst nach Wien, erst viel später wieder nach Traich, so Franz, hätten sie sich ganz auf sich zurückgezogen gehabt, keinen Kontakt mit der Umgebung mehr aufgenommen. (U 231–2)

As the text moves towards the supposed final revelation in the form of Wertheimer's writings, then, there is simultaneously an excavation of ever deeper layers of the past, which may or may not have a bearing on the present. The problem faced by the narrator at the level of *discourse* is deciding where the *story* actually begins. Although Henry James commented that the novelist's task is to create the illusion that the infinite web of relations appears to have a determinate end, Bernhard's narrative strategy does precisely the opposite: there is a proliferation of possible narrative beginnings whose relevance to the central question of Wertheimer's suicide becomes increasingly uncertain and oblique. Each narrative beginning becomes merely one starting point that can just as easily be replaced by any other of the numerous possible beginnings in a mode of perpetual substitution. Because of this, none of the proposed beginnings can have any binding originary function, and as in *Wittgensteins Neffe*, any starting point has to be regarded as a necessary fiction that provides an arbitrary closure to a process of potentially infinite narration.

## Story and Discourse

The issue of narrative form is complicated by the third time level, that of the moment of writing or "discursive situation." Most commentators on the narrative form of *Der Untergeher* have largely neglected this aspect of the text.

The act of writing is responsible for the recuperation of *both* the other time levels; it has to integrate the narrative of the main characters' past lives as well as the story of the circumstances under which the narrator remembers the past, that is, the trip to Traich. The discursive situation is considerably less prominent than in *Wittgensteins Neffe*, and is indicated merely by three instances of "erinnern" in the present tense: "Ich erinnere mich, daß er gerade während des Horowitzkurses glücklich gewesen ist" (U 146); "ich erinnere mich, daß ich ihn in Traich aufgesucht habe vor zwölf oder dreizehn Jahren" (U 155); "Leute wie wir, haben sich schon frühzeitig vom Tisch des Volkes ausgeschlossen, sagte er, wie ich mich erinnere" (U 207).[4] Nevertheless, the moment of writing is inscribed within the primary time level in the form of *projection*, for there are several passages in which the narrator thinks about how he *will* rewrite the *Versuch über Glenn* upon his return to Madrid and his house on the Calle del Prado:

> Nächste Woche werde ich wieder in Madrid sein und das erste ist, die *Glennschrift* zu vernichten, um eine neue anzufangen, dachte ich, eine noch konzentriertere, eine noch authentischere, dachte ich. (U 108)

> *In Madrid angekommen, gleich die Glennschrift vernichten*, dachte ich, sie muß so rasch wie möglich weg, um mir eine neue zu ermöglichen. Jetzt weiß ich, *wie* diese Schrift angehen, ich habe es nie gewußt, ich habe sie immer zu früh angefangen, dachte ich, dilettantisch. (U 109)

> Ich werde mich in der Calle del Prado einsperren und über Glenn schreiben und ganz von selbst wird mir Wertheimer deutlich werden, dachte ich. Indem ich über Glenn Gould schreibe, werde ich mir Klarheit über Wertheimer verschaffen, dachte ich auf dem Weg nach Traich. [. . .] Indem ich über den einen (Glenn Gould) schreibe, werde ich mir über den andern (Wertheimer) Klarheit verschaffen, dachte ich, indem ich die *Goldbergvariationen* (und *Die Kunst der Fuge*) des einen (Glenn Gould) immer wieder höre, um dann über sie schreiben zu können, werde ich über die Kunst (oder Nichtkunst!) des Andern (Wertheimer) immer mehr wissen und aufschreiben können, dachte ich und ich sehnte mich aufeinmal nach Madrid und meiner Calle del Prado[.] (U 224–5)

These three passages refer to the discursive situation in a mode of "recollected projection," and form a narrative of their own.

Recalling the distinction between *story* and *discourse*, the "Vergangenheitsebene I" is both the *discourse* to the *story* of the "Vergangenheitsebene II," as well as being itself a *story* whose *discourse* is the moment of writing. The function of the discursive situation is thus to recuperate, integrate, and mediate between the story of a friendship, and the story of its recollection. The situation is complicated yet further, however, by the device of recollected projection, for the story of the discursive situation, that is, the process of writing *Der Untergeher*, is told via a series of what Gérard Genette (106–9) terms "external prolepses" (flashforwards that extend beyond the time frame of the novel) in the future tense. This means that the "Vergangenheitsebene I" becomes the *discourse* of the *story* of its own narration. The whole distinction between story and discourse is fundamentally called into question: rather than being fixed categories, story and discourse exist in a relationship that is provisional and reversible. As noted previously, the two stories in the detective novel tend to remain discrete: "Dans leur forme la plus pure, ces deux histoires n'ont aucun point commun." In *Der Untergeher*, on the other hand, there is not only a proliferation of time levels, but they interpenetrate, and the relationships between them are unstable and fluid.

## Perspectivism

The distinction between story and discourse is subverted by other means in the text, too, but these are best approached by way of perspectivism. In *Der Untergeher*, the narrator is acutely aware of the necessarily subjective nature of his report and the judgments contained therein, as well as all conceptions we make of others. After Wertheimer's funeral, the narrator turns down an invitation to lunch with the Duttweilers (Wertheimer's sister and brother-in-law). He then imagines the scene:

> alles hätte ich wieder zum Vorschein gebracht, was besser nicht mehr zum Vorschein gebracht wird, alles Wertheimer Betreffende und mit der mir schon zum Verhängnis gewordenen Ungerechtigkeit und Ungenauigkeit, mit einem Wort Subjektivität, die ich selbst immer gehaßt habe, vor welcher ich aber niemals sicher gewesen bin. Und die Duttweiler hätten auf ihre Weise Wertheimersche Zusammenhänge hergestellt, die eine ebenso falsches und ungerechtes Bild Wertheimers ergeben hätten, sagte ich mir. Wir schildern und beurteilen die Menschen immer nur falsch, wir beurteilen sie ungerecht und schildern sie niederträchtig, sagte ich mir, in jedem Fall, gleich, wie wir sie schildern, gleich wie wir sie beurteilen. (U 213–4)

In similar vein, the narrator adds:

> Ihr Quälgeist ist tot, dachte ich, ihr Zerstörer hat ausgelebt, ist nicht mehr da, wird niemehr, was sie betrifft, etwas zu reden haben. Wie immer übertrieb ich auch jetzt und es war mir vor mir selbst peinlich, Wertheimer aufeinmal als den Quälgeist und den Zerstörer seiner Schwester bezeichnet zu haben, so, dachte ich, gehe ich immer gegen Andere vor, ungerecht, ja verbrecherisch. (U 215)

*Pace* Eva Marquardt, then, the unreliability of the narrator in *Der Untergeher* is not concealed; on the contrary it is explicitly signaled. Her agenda is to demonstrate the narrator's unreliability, and she concludes that his criticisms of Wertheimer are totally arbitrary, and that there is a fundamental tension between his "positive Selbsteinschätzung" and the "Scheitern in seiner Rolle" (56–7). Nevertheless, there is a clear sense in which the narrator is perfectly conscious of his own "failure." Furthermore, it is a failure that is not merely contingent and dependent on the inconsistency of the individual; it is rather a failure that is determined *a priori* by the epistemological limits of perspectivism and the representational relativism that this necessarily entails.

Perspectivism in *Der Untergeher* is underlined by the use of secondary narrators. The final third of the text is devoted to the narrator's conversations with first the "Wirtin" and then Franz Kohlroser, both of whom supply details about the weeks leading up to Wertheimer's suicide. The introduction of these secondary narrators transforms the main narrator into an "intradiegetic" narratee, namely an addressee who exists within the represented world of the text. As narrator, he is responsible for relating the conversations between himself and the other two characters. As a narratee, however, he is placed in the same position as the reader insofar as he cannot know the truth content of the landlady's and Franz's statements. Like the reader, moreover, he is faced with the problem of working out the relationship between the story of Wertheimer's life and the narratives supplied by the "Wirtin" and Kohlroser.

Marquardt points out that the "Wirtin" is labelled as unreliable by the narrator and that her narrative is not only internally inconsistent but also contradicts that of Franz Kohlroser (54). So, for example, she claims: "Die letzten Monate sei er nicht mehr nach Wien gefahren, habe sich nicht einmal für die dort liegende Post interessiert" (U 166), but later adds: "Wochenlang seien sie [Wertheimer's friends] allein in Traich gewesen, ohne Wertheimer, der erst ein paar Tage vor seiner Abreise nach Chur aufgetaucht sei" (U 177). Franz's version of the same events likewise implies that Wertheimer was often present amongst the debauchees: "Wertheimer sei mit ihnen, was allerdings

auch dem Franz aufgefallen war, *ausgelassen* gewesen, ganz und gar
verändert habe er sich in diesen Tagen und Wochen in dieser Gesellschaft gezeigt" (U 237).

These passages of *Der Untergeher* represent an instance of repetitive
narration: the single sequence of the events at Traich in the weeks preceding Wertheimer's death is narrated several times, both by the same
narrator in the form of the landlady and by a different narrator, Kohlroser. This device of multiple — and mutually contradictory — narrators
clearly foregrounds the necessary subjectivism and unreliability of any
perspective. Because there is more than one viewpoint, the notion of
saying anything definitive about Wertheimer's demise becomes ever
more untenable. The multiperspectivalism of *Der Untergeher*, however,
has yet more profound implications for the study of narrative form.

The discrepancies between the various tellings of the same event
foregrounds the device of repetition itself, and steers interpretative attention toward it. It is theoretically possible that the narrator could be
responsible for these inconsistencies (Marquardt 54), but on such a
reading, repetitive narration would serve no purpose beyond exposing
the narrator's unreliability.[5] The narrative schema of *Der Untergeher*
would appear to demand a different approach, namely one that draws
attention not to the *ethical* problem of the narrator's untrustworthi-
ness, but to the *epistemological* problem of narrative representation *per
se*. The narrative of Wertheimer's final bacchanal exists in three forms,
which are in part complementary, but in part mutually contradictory.
The question is thus: what do we know about the weeks before
Wertheimer's death? In other words, *what is the story?* Now we have
seen that narrative theory generally rests on the paradoxical assumption
that a concatenation of events — the story — precedes the act of narration, even though this story is accessible to the reader only by means of
abstraction from the semiotic medium in which the story is couched:
"Story [. . .] exists only at an abstract level; any manifestation already
entails this selection and arrangement performed by the discourse as
actualized by a given medium. There is no privileged manifestation"
(Chatman 37). In abstracting a story from any discourse, the reader is
decoding from surface to deep narrative structures, to put it in structuralist terminology. But what happens in the case of a text like *Der
Untergeher*, where this operation is thwarted by a discourse that sup-
plies contradictory information whose truth value is undecidable? Ultimately, there are parts of the story in this text that remain forever
inaccessible, and any desire for certainty must give way to a kind of
radical doubt. Again, the stability of the story-discourse distinction is
called into question, and the former becomes a matter of conjecture

and potentiality. The narrator's attempts to ascertain the reasons for Wertheimer's death are once again doomed to failure.

"[D]ie ganze Welt," says Konrad in *Das Kalkwerk*, "[...] erkläre man sich aus nichts anderem als aus Ersatzursachen durch Ersatzursachenforschung" (Kw 136). This applies with particular precision to *Der Untergeher*: all the putative causes advanced by the narrator are substituted both for each other and for any notional "true" or "originary" cause, which itself exists solely as a textual absence. The narrative strategies subvert the assumptions of the detective-novel form that the text initially encourages us to expect. Although the narrator (and the reader) starts out expecting to learn more about Wertheimer, he ends up in a state of confusion. The fact that the narrator is currently reading Musil's *Die Verwirrungen des Zöglings Törleß* thus asks to be read as a figure for his own bewilderment (Petrasch 225). The question remains, though: what is the purpose of a text that so systematically undermines the narrative project that subtends it? The final section of this chapter offers an answer to this question in terms of trauma and the need to come to terms with the personal past.

## Writing, Trauma, Therapy

Wertheimer, it is stated, lives his life in the mode of repetition. He is a "Nacheiferer" (U 148) who copies everything from the narrator:

> Alles Wertheimersche ist nicht aus Wertheimer selbst gekommen, sagte ich mir jetzt, alles Wertheimersche war immer nur ein Abgeschautes, ein Nachgemachtes, er schaute sich alles an mir ab, er machte mir alles nach, so hat er auch mein Scheitern von mir abgeschaut und mir nachgemacht, dachte ich. (U 124–5)

Likewise, the philosophy to which he devotes himself is merely an imitative form of aphorising: Wertheimer "versuchte es plötzlich nurmehr noch sozusagen als Zweitschopenhauer, Zweitkant, Zweitnovalis, und übermalte diese pseudophilosophische Verlegenheit mit Brahms und Händel, mit Chopin und Rachmaninow" (U 155). This "Epigonentum" finds a parallel in Wertheimer's inability to appreciate his own uniqueness: "Wertheimer wäre gern Glenn Gould gewesen, wäre gern Horowitz gewesen, wäre wahrscheinlich auch gern Gustav Mahler gewesen oder Alban Berg. Wertheimer war nicht imstande, *sich selbst als ein Einmaliges* zu sehen" (U 133). The desire to be somebody else signals a faulty relationship to questions of time and repetition. It is indicative of a desire to repeat the past in a way that annuls difference: it conflates past and present, then and now; and it threatens to collapse the boundaries between self and other upon which depend, as psycho-analysis has shown us, both a sense of personal identity, and the process of social integration.

It is not merely Wertheimer who is engaged in cycles of repetition, however; the narrator is as well, and their relationship is not as one-sided as it may initially appear. As Petrasch points out, the narrator in his turn repeats certain acts that are carried out by Wertheimer (236–7), and so there is an element of reciprocity in their friendship. This "copying" by the narrator consists primarily of the role played by writing in his life. Wertheimer produces a book entitled *Der Untergeher*, which he never publishes because he constantly changes the manuscript: "die Veränderung seines Manuskripts war nichts anderes, als das völlige Zusammenstreichen des Manuskripts, von dem schließlich nichts als der Titel übriggeblieben ist" (U 79). This not only recalls Roithamer's systematic revision/destruction of his own study "Über Altensam und alles, was damit zusammenhängt unter besonderer Berücksichtigung des Kegels" in *Korrektur*, it also resembles the narrator's essays on Glenn Gould, which he perpetually destroys in order to begin anew.

Much ink has been spilled on the problem of writing in Bernhard, with numerous critics discussing the motif of the "Schrift" or "Studie." The protagonists of *Das Kalkwerk, Korrektur, Beton, Ja, Die Billigesser*, and *Der Untergeher* are all engaged in an intellectual project that never gets written. This is due either to an inability even to begin or, as in *Korrektur*, to an epistemological and linguistic skepticism that casts radical doubt on the possibility of adequately representing or explaining anything. The reason for this failure has been interpreted in various ways,[6] but all commentators agree that the completion of the study would mean death, a view shared by Jürgen H. Petersen whose discussion of the "Schriftmotiv" is of immediate relevance to *Der Untergeher*. Petersen argues that Bernhard's novels up to and including *Korrektur* presuppose a world devoid of meaning, and that the studies in *Das Kalkwerk* and *Korrektur* are arbitrary goals set in order to give life a purpose: "Da der Mensch ein Ziel braucht, um existieren zu können, unternimmt er alle Anstrengungen, diesem Ziel nahezukommen; doch zugleich darf er das Ziel nicht erreichen, sonst besitzt er keines mehr, und dann wäre dem Leben der Halt entzogen" ("Beschreibung" 151). In *Das Kalkwerk*, Konrad's wife perpetually knits mittens, unravels them, and begins knitting again, and Petersen sees this as a cyclical process of setting a goal, reaching it, and then setting it anew (154–5). A similar pattern can be seen in *Der Untergeher*, where the narrator constantly writes, destroys, and rewrites the intended study of Glenn

Gould: "heute schreibe ich diese Unsinnigkeiten, von welchen ich mir zu sagen getraue, sie seien *essayistisch*, [. . .] die ich am Ende doch immer verfluchen und zerreißen und also vernichten muß" (U 158). Writing thus becomes an end in itself, its importance lying in the process rather than in the finished product.

The one crucial difference between *Der Untergeher* and Bernhard's earlier texts is that in the latter case repetition is a means not of coping with a meaningless present so much as coming to terms with a traumatic past. Repetition emerges as the salient method employed by the narrator to cope with the deaths of Gould and Wertheimer. The twin obsessions to which the narrator falls victim are the "Versuch über Glenn" and the Goldberg Variations. Lutz Köpnick has argued that both writing and listening to music have a life-enhancing effect on the narrator, but a consideration of his argument will show that there is something rather different at stake here.

Köpnick argues first of all that the narrator's repeated essays at writing fulfill a therapeutic function:

Ist eine endgültige Loslösung von der traumatischen Erfahrung auf dieser Stufe auch nicht möglich, so bringt die eigentümliche Lust an der Zerstörung von Geschriebenem ein bemerkenswertes Interesse an der Zukunft zum Ausdruck. Durch endlose Variationen ein und desselben Themas schreibt sich das Leben des Erzähler-Autors in die Zukunft. (282)

Köpnick is referring here to the perpetual writing, destruction, and rewriting of the study "Über Glenn" at the level of content, that is, at the level of what the text *says*. But this incessant production of texts is informed by the compulsion to repeat, and rather than signaling an "Interesse an der Zukunft," it betrays an enduring obsession with the past.

Köpnick goes on to suggest that by making the transition from virtuoso to musicologist to recipient, the narrator is able to overcome the destructive power of music and once again enjoy the Goldberg Variations which, as Bernhard's narrator tells us, were originally written "*zur Gemüthsergetzung*" (U 222):

Was einst die Ursache des Traumas war, wird am Ende zum Organon des Eingedenkens. Von seinen beiden wichtigsten Freunden, Glenn und Wertheimer, durch deren Tod geschieden, erkennt der Erzähler gerade in der Musik jetzt eine verborgene Kraft, Vergangenheit und Gegenwart in Konjunktion zu bringen, ohne die Leiden der gewesenen Zeit verstummen zu lassen. Die Rezeption von Musik gilt hier nicht so sehr einem melancholischen Sich-Verlieren an die Vergangenheit, sondern ihrer Rettung und Erlösung durch Aufhebung des Gewesenen in die Gegenwart, durch Aktualisierung. (284)

There are several problems with such a positive approach. First, it conveniently makes music the cause of the trauma, thereby failing to take into account the myriad components of the narrative that thwart any attempt to state what the "Ursache des Traumas" is. Second, a careful reading of the narrator's continual return to the Goldberg Variations suggests that they play a much more problematical role than that of a harmless mnemonic aid. Before the burial, the narrator plays Gould's recording of Bach's piece in his Viennese flat:

> Glenns Goldbergvariationen hatte ich mir übrigens vor meiner Abreise nach Chur in meiner Wiener Wohnung angehört, immer wieder von vorne. War währenddessen immer wieder von meinem Fauteuil aufgestanden und im meinem Arbeitszimmer auf- und abgegangen in der Vorstellung, Glenn spielte die Goldbergvariationen *tatsächlich* in meiner Wohnung, ich versuchte während meines Hinundhergehens herauszufinden, worin der Unterschied besteht zwischen der *Interpretation* auf *diesen* Platten, und der *Interpretation* achtundzwanzig Jahre vorher unter den Ohren von Horowitz und uns, also Wertheimer und mir, im Mozarteum. Ich stellte keinen Unterschied fest. (U 88–9)

In a sense, this does represent an "Aktualisierung": it is *as if* Gould were actually present in the flat. There is also a sense of the "Aufhebung des Gewesenen in die Gegenwart," for he discerns no difference between the two interpretations despite the intervening twenty-eight years. To talk of the past and present being thereby brought into conjunction, however, strikes me as somewhat misleading. Rather than being a means of orienting himself toward the future, the narrator compulsively turns to the Goldberg Variations as a means of reliving (as opposed to understanding) the past, a point underscored by the fact that the final event of the novel sees the narrator once more playing Gould's record of the Goldberg Variations.[7]

This repetition can be understood in the light of Freud's "Wiederholungszwang" or repetition compulsion. In his *Jenseits des Lustprinzips* and the essay on therapeutic practice, "Erinnern, Wiederholung, Durcharbeiten," Freud noted that some of his patients repeatedly lived through a traumatic experience from the past *as if it were present*, despite the fact that it caused them considerable "unpleasure." This, he concluded, was a result of a failure to integrate that experience within a narrative that recognized the past *as* past. One of the therapist's tasks was thus to bring the repressed trauma to consciousness via the act of narrative. In the therapeutic situation, the antidote to compulsive repetition is storytelling. Examining the function of narrative from this perspective allows us to make sense of the narrative project in *Der Untergeher.*

First, it is necessary to posit a distinction between what the text says, and what it *does*, thereby differentiating narration-as-reporting from narration-as-performance.[8] Once we realize that the text we are reading is the final "Versuch über Glenn," it becomes apparent that the "Loslösung von der traumatischen Erfahrung" *is* possible after all: *Der Untergeher* is a narrative that, by dealing with the difficulty of producing an adequate text about Glenn Gould and Wertheimer, has itself become the text whose possibility seems to be denied within its own pages. What the text *does* provides a refutation of what it *says*. While the narrator is still ensnared in unproductive cycles of repetition at the level of story, his discourse is itself that conscious narrative of past trauma that integrates past and present. This is the function of the tripartite time structure: it thematizes the attempt to understand the past by telling stories about it in the present. In order to construct a narrative, an endpoint has to be posited. It is admittedly an endpoint whose immediate "teleological" purpose of revelation is undermined by the text, but it is indispensable in allowing the narrative to be told. It is a necessary fiction. The text of *Der Untergeher* is important less for what it "tells us" about the three central characters than for its therapeutic function as an *act*, a narrative performance. The narrative enterprise on which the narrator embarks is profoundly compromised, but the active process of plotting and the complex interactions between story and discourse foreground the importance of telling stories. Bernhard's fellow Austrian Robert Musil once remarked about his novel *Der Mann ohne Eigenschaften*: "Die Geschichte des Romans kommt darauf an, daß die Geschichte, die erzählt werden sollte, nicht erzählt wird." It is a statement that could be applied to numerous modern novels, including *Der Untergeher*, a text that shows our thirst for information to be ultimately subordinated to our need to tell — and be told — stories.

# Notes

[1] Curiously, Jürgen Petersen fails to link these three, seeing connections between *Der Untergeher* and Bernhard's first two novels, *Frost* and *Verstörung*, which actually have quite different narrative structures and thematic concerns (*Der deutsche Roman* 217).

[2] Marquardt claims that inconsistencies subvert the linearity of the primary time level: "Zu einem Zeitpunkt [...] hält [der Erzähler] eine 'Schale Tee' (U 110) in Händen, die er erst später in seinem Zimmer oben bestellt (U 179) und dann wieder in der Gaststube sitzend erhält (U 189)" (53). This, however, is a misreading. In the passage to which she refers, the comma after

"dachte ich" makes it clear that the "Schale Tee" is being drunk with Wertheimer at some unspecified point in the past (Petrasch's "Vergangenheitsebene II"), and not at the moment of recollection: "nach Traich gehen, bedeutete nur, mich aus meinem fürchterlichen Geisteselend abzulenken und Wertheimer zu stören, Austauschen von Jugenderinnerungen, dachte ich, bei einer Schale Tee, und immer Glenn Gould als Mittelpunkt" (U 110); cf. "dachte ich beim Eintreten in das Gasthaus" (U 7, 28).

[3] On the links between the "Unbedingtheitsanspruch" of Bernhard's overbearing artist figures and the fascist mentality, see Sorg, *Thomas Bernhard* 126–7.

[4] Cf. Petrasch 219. Of the three indicators of the discursive situation she provides, it seems to me that two are in fact flanked by "dachte ich," and hence belong to the "Vergangenheitsebene I," but her point stands nevertheless.

[5] Such a device is not unknown in first-person narratives, but tends to be motivated by other concerns, such as the narrator's desire to hide something or his difficulty in facing up to past events. In Max Frisch's *Homo faber*, for example, the consummation of the incest relation is narrated three times, but this is justified psychologically by Faber's unwillingness to confront the causes of his guilt. The same applies to the putative murder of Mahlke in Günter Grass's *Katz und Maus*, whereas supplying such a psychological "motive" for the repetitive narration in *Der Untergeher* would stretch both the bounds of verisimilitude and the ingenuity of the interpreter, since the narrator has nothing to "hide."

[6] For Huntemann, the studies represent the situation of the modern artist in an uncomprehending world, and their failure resides in a structural and philosophical aporia: how can knowledge of the infinite be communicated in finite form? (*Artistik* 21–45) For Jahraus, the failure is due to a faulty conception of language, signification, and referentiality: the "Studienschreiber" attempt an "originären Benennungsakt [...]. Die Studie will etwas zur Sprache bringen, was nicht bereits zur Sprache gebracht worden ist." So the failure is not empirical or contingent, but "prinzipiell" (*Die Wiederholung* 77). Both these critics would seem to owe a debt to Heinrich Lindenmayr, for whom the failure stems from the contradiction between a mental desire for totality and the necessary specificity of language (77–87). Cf. also Neumeister 99–102.

[7] Despite drawing various parallels between the Goldberg Variations and the narrative form of *Der Untergeher*, neither Köpnick nor Olson ("Art of Fugue") mention the fact that the piece ends not with the thirtieth variation, but with a repetition of the opening aria: a return to the beginning.

[8] Rimmon-Kenan points out this distinction in "Narration as Repetition."

# III.

## The Late Fiction (ii): Reckonings

# 6: *Holzfällen: Eine Erregung*

## Bernhard in Court:
## The background and consequences of *Holzfällen*

IN THE SUMMER OF 1957, Bernhard made the acquaintance of the composer Gerhard Lampersberg and his wife, the singer Maja Weis-Ostborn. Between then and 1960 the couple assisted Bernhard financially and introduced him to many of Austria's most important postwar writers, among them H. C. Artmann, Friedericke Mayröcker, Jeannie Ebner, Ernst Jandl, and the young Peter Turrini. The Lamperbergs' country residence, the Tonhof at Maria Saal in Carinthia (which appears in *Holzfällen* under the thinnest of disguises as "Maria Zaal"), formed the center of a circle of young avant-garde writers and musicians throughout the 1950s. Lampersberg himself was one of the first composers in postwar Austria to adopt the twelve-tone technique of the Second Vienna School, and Bernhard wrote several libretti for him. He also scripted a number of plays for performance at the Tonhof,[1] and produced the short prose pieces *Ereignisse*; publication in book form, however, was delayed until 1969 (see chapter 1). Lampersberg's importance to Bernhard can be gauged from the dedication to *In hora mortis* (1958), Bernhard's second volume of poetry: "Meinem einzigen und wirklichen Freund G. L dem ich im richtigen Augenblick begegnet bin." When the book was reissued in 1987, however, the dedication had been expunged, for Bernhard broke with the Lampersbergs in 1960 in an atmosphere of mutual acrimony (Höller, *Thomas Bernhard* 58). Almost a quarter of a century later, the acrimony apparently erupted, undiminished, in Bernhard's 1984 novel, *Holzfällen: Eine Erregung*.

With the possible exception of Bernhard's 1988 play *Heldenplatz*, *Holzfällen* was the most controversial text of an author who courted controversy. Within four days of its publication in Austria, Bernhard found himself the subject of legal action. It was not the first time. Bernhard's deliberate provocation of the Austrian establishment had begun early in his career. In December 1955, he wrote an article entitled "Salzburg wartet auf ein Theaterstück" for the Catholic newspaper *Die Furche*, dismissing Austria's theatrical life in general and the Salzburger Landestheater in particular as "Dillentantismus," and complaining of the "Schwachsinn and Schweinerei" of the programme. Bernhard was sued by the director of the theater and sentenced to five days' imprisonment or payment of a 300-schilling fine (Ryu 246). Two decades later, Canon Franz Wesenauer successfully sued Bernhard and his publisher Wolfgang Schaffler for libel. Wesenauer had recognized himself in the decidedly unsympathetic boarding-school headmaster "Onkel Franz" in Bernhard's autobiographical text *Die Ursache* (1975). Consequently, the Landesgericht Salzburg ruled that seventy lines of libellous material were to be excised from later editions of the text.[2] In the case of *Holzfällen* the plaintiff was Gerhard Lampersberg, erstwhile dedicatee and patron, who now saw himself as the object of Bernhard's scorn.

Lampersberg instituted legal proceedings because he was upset over the alleged portrayal of himself within the text as the alcoholic, highly obnoxious, superficial socialite Auersberger, a correspondence to which he had been alerted by Hans Haider, cultural editor of the Austrian newspaper *Die Presse*.[3] This resulted in a temporary confiscation by the police of all copies of *Holzfällen* from Austrian bookshops, and gave Bernhard yet more fuel for an extended tirade against his homeland.[4] The hearing ended when Lampersberg dropped the charges in August 1985.

Hans Haider's part in the scandal surrounding *Holzfällen* did not end there, however. He was also the first to suggest that the novel was a *roman à clef,* and spontaneously produced something akin to an affidavit in which he claimed to identify the other "real-life counterparts" of the novel's characters. He saw in Jeannie Billroth a caricature of the novelist Jeannie Ebner, and in Anna Schreker and her husband representations of Friedericke Mayröcker and Ernst Jandl (Löffler 63). The similarities are indeed striking, especially those between Billroth and Ebner. The former is described as "die sogenannte Philosophenichte" (H 216), while the latter is the niece of the philosopher Ferdinand Ebner (who is himself mentioned in *Holzfällen* 167); Billroth is editor of the fictional periodical *Literatur in der Zeit,* while Ebner edited *Literatur und Kritik,* the publication that replaced *Wort in der Zeit* as the official Austrian literary periodical. The main hints concerning the "identity" of Schreker and her husband are that both have received or will receive the Großer Österreichischer Staatspreis (H 256), Mayröcker and Jandl being the only husband and wife pair to have done so. In addition, Schreker is described as a "Gymnasiallehrerin" (H 252), which was Mayröcker's profession for over twenty years before she became a freelance writer (Bjorklund 248).

Merely noting the correspondences between Bernhard's fiction and the reality it depicts, however, is a somewhat sterile occupation. For

this reason, the initial journalistic reception of the text, which interpreted *Holzfällen* as a *roman à clef* and stressed its referentiality, proved
a critical dead end. Subsequent criticism has largely bracketed the
question of reference. For Gerhard Pail, the novel is less a criticism of
society than the "Prozeß einer persönlichen Weiterentwicklung infolge
einer Auseinandersetzung mit einem entfremdeten Umwelt" (63). Ivar
Sagmo reads *Holzfällen* in terms of its relation to Ibsen's *Wild Duck*,
seeing the "Burgschauspieler" as the counterpart of Ekdal, who has
made his peace with life, and Jeannie Billroth as a transformation of the
destructive Edgar, who confronts Ekdal with his "Lebenslüge." Gregor
Hens seeks to demonstrate that the structure of *Holzfällen* is derived
from drama, and argues that the last words of the novel imply an infinite regress that eliminates the narrator, leaving nothing but the "dramatic" core of the action:

> Man versuche nun, diesen Ausgang logisch weiterzuführen: Der Er-
> zähler könnte berichten, wie er nach Hause ankommt, wie er sich an
> seinen Schreibtisch setzt und damit beginnt, über dieses "künstleri-
> sche Abendessen" zu schreiben. Es käme der Punkt, an dem erzählte
> Zeit und Erzählerjetztzeit zusammenfielen. Das *dachte ich* hätte das
> *denke ich* eingeholt, die Erzählerkonstruktion würde notwendigerwei-
> se in sich zusammenfallen. [. . .] [S]obald "*gleich* und *sofort* und *gleich*
> und *gleich*" zu *jetzt* geworden sind, hat sich der Erzähler selbst elimi-
> niert. (122–3)[5]

A feature common to all these approaches is their refusal to address the
question of referentiality, which played such an important role in the
early reception of the book.

Two recent studies have broached the problem of reference, discussing it in terms of the reality-fiction dichotomy. Ryu unfortunately
gets no further than stating that the controversy surrounding *Holzfällen* foregrounds the "Grenzfrage von 'Fiktion' und 'Wirklichkeit'"
characteristic of Bernhard's work (243). More interesting is Barbara
Mariacher's attempt to specify those aspects of Bernhard's late novels
that encourage an identification of author with narrator, textual reality
with external reality. Mariacher argues that the "Verschlüsselung von
Figuren" points not only back toward the concrete person, but also
away from them, "so daß diese 'Vorbilder' gleichzeitig gemeint und
nicht gemeint sind und die Figuren also in der für Bernhards im allge-
meinen charackteristischen Mehrdeutigkeit oszillieren" ( "*Umspringbilder*" 112). Nevertheless, she does not explore how this oscillation
comes about or functions within the text, preferring instead to devote
most of her analysis to the Ibsen connection.

The discussion of *Holzfällen* that follows attempts to deal more adequately with the reality-versus-fiction problem. It treads a middle road between an aestheticizing reading that dismisses the referentiality of the text as irrelevant, and a naively realist reading that assumes a direct correlation between word and world. First, an analysis of the narrator's diagnosis of Austrian cultural malaise will show that the text can be seen as a self-justifying response and solution to the shortcomings it criticizes. An examination follows of those aspects of the text that elude or preclude a realist interpretation and contribute to the referential "oscillation" mentioned in passing by Mariacher. This leads, finally, to a consideration of the critical moment in *Holzfällen*.

## *Holzfällen* as Diagnosis and Response

The narrator of *Holzfällen* sits in a wing-backed chair that is concealed in the partial shadow behind the door of the Auersbergers' living room. From this vantagepoint he observes the other guests, who have been invited to what the Auersbergers call their "künstlerisches Abendessen" and are now awaiting the guest of honor, an actor from Vienna's famous Burgtheater. During the course of the novel, the narrator reports on the happenings at the soirée. At the same time, he reminisces about his intensive artistic friendship with the Auersbergers in the fifties, and about the recent death of their mutual friend Joana, who had been buried earlier that day. Joana's suicide had taken place on the same morning that the Auersbergers encountered the narrator in the Graben and issued their invitation to the "artistic dinner."

The gathering of Viennese writers, artists, and actors allows Bernhard to assemble a microcosm of Austrian cultural life that the narrator can easily dissect. The main thrust of his critique emerges in a highly vitriolic passage toward the end of the text (H 251–61), in which he berates the assembled guests for betraying their talent and abandoning their oppositional attitude toward society in favor of official recognition, state honors, and government handouts. The initially progressive art of the Auersberger circle soon turns into a means of "Anbiederungen an den Staatsapparat" (H 253): they have mutated from avantgarde rebels into the acknowledged representatives of institution art, "vom jungen Talent zur abstoßenden Staatskünstlerin" (H 252), as the narrator says of Jeannie Billroth. Billroth and Anna Schreker have become "raffinierte Staatspfründnerinnen," whose respective obsessions with Gertrude Stein and Marianne Moore have turned into a "literarische Zweck-Pose" with which they can delight the politicians responsible for doling out grants and prizes (H 255). Although feigning progressivism, they have spent the previous twenty years running up and down the back stairs of grant-giving ministries (H 260). This tendency, claims the narrator, is not restricted to those assembled, but infects all Austria's artists:

> Alle österreichischen Künstler lassen sich schließlich vom Staat und seinen niederträchtigen politischen Absichten kaufen und verkaufen sich diesem skrupellosen, gemeinen und niederträchtigen Staat, und die meisten schon von Anfang an. Ihr Künstlertum besteht aus nichts anderem, als aus dem Gemeinmachen mit dem Staat, das ist die Wahrheit. (H 259)

Accounts of the nature of artistic evolution point out that new techniques, initially seen as fresh and potentially subversive, become stale and assimilated with ever-increasing rapidity.[6] This is analogous to the process undergone by the Auersbergers and the other guests at the "künstlerisches Abendessen." Artistic creation, as Fredric Jameson writes, "is not free not to reflect what it reacts against" (*Marxism and Form* 37). The community of artists at Maria Zaal thus initially appears as a means of asserting the self against society, but ends up becoming a microcosm of the superficial society against which it had protested. As a representative of the ultimate artistic compromise with the public, the Burgschauspieler is logically the focal point and *raison d'être* of the "künstlerisches Abendessen."[7] Bernhard's criticism of the Auersberger circle, however, is not merely that their work has been subject to inevitable assimilation by the establishment, but that they have implicated themselves in this process *by their own volition*. Willi Huntemann writes, "Für Bernhards kompromißloses Künstlerethos des radikal auf sich gestellten und für sich schaffenden Künstlers muß ein an Mäzenatentum erinnerndes Verhältnis als Vereinnahmung und Verletzung der Integrität gelten" (*Artistik* 52). The relationship between artists and the state described here is clearly a modern-day form of patronage, and so the critique brings with it the dual accusation of artistic stagnation and a lack of personal integrity — in other words: inauthenticity.

This inauthenticity manifests itself as the repetition of empty forms in order to create appearances: "Den Anschein von allem haben sich diese Leute immer gegeben, wirklich sind sie nichts" (H 164; the word "Anschein" occurs with staggering frequency in *Holzfällen*). Everything about them is derivative:

> Die Auersbergerischen, denen immer ein sogenannter guter Geschmack nachgesagt worden ist, haben im Grunde niemals einen guten Geschmack gehabt, nur einen nachempfundenen guten Geschmack, wie sie ja überhaupt nie etwas eigenes gehabt haben, immer nur ein Nach-

empfundenes, auch kein eigenes Leben, keine eigene Existenz gehabt
haben im Grunde, nur eine nachempfundene. (H 242–3)

This can be seen in the funeral episodes, both embarrassing and comical, where the members of the Auersberger circle stand up, sit down,
sing, and utter responsions either too late or too early (H 107). Furthermore, the Viennese mourners at Joana's funeral are described by
the narrator as "lauter künstlerische Leichen [. . .], lebende Kunstleich-
name" (H 99). The members of the Auersberger circle have thus become   utterly   artificial;   they   have   made   the   transition   from
"künstlerisch" to "künstlich," and this has resulted in artistic death.[8]

Auersberger is the representative *par excellence* of both inauthenticity and artistic stagnation. His desire to be thought of as a member of
the aristocracy leads him to adopt a variety of pretentious habits, but
the text makes it clear that both his social aspirations and his artistic
"achievement" consist in the repetition of what others have done already. The narrator refers to him as a "Webern- und Grafenkopist" (H
96) and as a "*Gesellschaftskopist* als Webern-Nachfolger" (H 153). Indeed, the term "Webern-Nachfolger" occurs nine times (H 14, 38, 62,
96, 97, 153, 179, 213), culminating in his description as a "schon in
den Fünfzigerjahren steckengebliebene[r] Webern-Nachfolger" (H
318); he is an "*unerträglich epigonaler Webern*" whose work consists of
"Kopieren als Komponieren" (H 97).

Anton von Webern was an Austrian serialist composer of the so-called
Second Vienna School. Serialism is a highly sophisticated compositional
technique developed by Arnold Schoenberg in the first decade of the
twentieth century. Schoenberg replaced the structural principle of tonality
— the system of key relationships that had dominated Western music
since the seventeenth century — with mathematically worked-out series
of notes called "tone rows," and every aspect of the composition was derived from this initial series of twelve notes (hence "twelve-tone" or "do-
decaphonic" composition). Despite the text's obsessive reiteration of the
term "Webern-Nachfolger," the thematic relevance of Webern has remained unexplored in the critical literature on Bernhard, but Adorno's
comments on twelve-tone composition in his *Philosophie der neuen
Musik* suggest a way in which we might address this question. At one
level Adorno was a prominent advocate of the twelve-tone technique,
contrasting it favorably with what he saw as the regressive tendencies in
the music of Stravinsky. But his analysis of musical history results ultimately in a critique of serialism, and several aspects of this provide clear
parallels to Thomas Bernhard's tirade against Austrian cultural stagnation in *Holzfällen*.

Adorno analyzes music in terms of the dialectical relationship between subjective expression and objective form. Throughout musical history, he claims, the subjective, expressive impulse steadily emancipates itself from the exigencies of form. Serial music is the culmination of this process, but at the same time it represents the point at which objective form returns to claim control over the subject: "Das Subjekt gebietet über die Musik durchs rationale System, um selber dem rationalen System zu erliegen" (68; see also 110). In serialism, then, Adorno saw an impasse in the dialectic of subject and object in music, since the former is totally eclipsed by the latter: "Mit Webern abdiziert das musikalische Subjekt und gibt sich dem Material anheim" (108). This in turn can be seen as the end of a certain historical phase, for the twelve-tone technique "bringt die Tendenz der gesamten Geschichte der europäischen Musik seit Haydn [. . .] zum Stillstand" (99). It is thus apt that the character Auersberger should be *"der Komponist in der Webern-Nachfolge"* (H 14), for by casting Auersberger as a repetition of the figure who — for Adorno at least — represents the logical conclusion of the Western musical tradition, Bernhard can suggest a sense of stagnation and impasse that connects with other aspects of the Auersbergers' lives. These aspects will emerge in more detail in the following analysis.

For Adorno, twelve-tone music is "geschichtslos in ihrer endlosen Statik" (66). It is a formal method that results in stasis. This represents a further clear parallel to the narrator's critique of the Auersberger circle. Throughout the text, attention is constantly drawn to the fact that nothing in the lives of the Auersbergers or the narrator's other acquaintances has changed: "Tatsächlich haben sich diese auerbergerischen Einladungen nicht geändert, dachte ich, auf dem Ohrensessel sitzend, sie sind wie in den Fünfzigerjahren, wie vor dreißig Jahren" (H 19). Frau Auersberger is wearing the same dress that she used to wear thirty years ago (H 22), the narrator's wing chair is still in the same place that it was thirty years ago (H 31), and the music room is exactly as it was thirty years before (H 240). During the funeral the narrator realizes "daß die letzten zwanzig Jahre, die so Ungeheuerliches über und in die Welt gebracht haben, an den Eheleuten Auersberger tatsächlich spurlos vorbeigegangen sind" (H 148). The whole situation is as though time has stood still (H 75): "die Eheleute Auersberger [hatten] ganz einfach in dem Augenblick auf dem Graben, in welchem sie mich gesehen hatten, die zwanzig Jahre unserer absoluten Kontaktlosigkeit gestrichen" (H 82; cf. 48, 147, 318). In the orbit of the Auersbergers, time becomes static.

*Holzfällen*, then, launches a three-pronged attack at the Auers-bergers and their circle: first there is the question of artistic stagnation; second the accusation of inauthenticity; and finally, the imputation of a failure to acknowledge the passing of time, the difference between the fifties and the present. The functions of *Holzfällen* as a text are to rein-stall the confrontational, oppositional relationship between the work of art and the society in which it is produced, to suggest a solution to the problem of inauthenticity, and to restore temporal difference via a pro-cess of remembering and writing.

Let us now reconsider the purpose of the correspondences between the novel's characters and their "real-life" counterparts. The massive scandal provoked by *Holzfällen* is significant not only as a titillating epi-sode in literary history or as interesting background information to the study of the novel proper, but as an effect that is simultaneously *prepro-grammed* and *justified* by the text itself. As Ferdinand van Ingen points out, *Holzfällen* employs the rhetorical strategies of invective or *vitu-peratio*, and for this genre to function its object must be recognizable as a real person ("Thomas Bernhard's *Holzfällen*" 262–3). But in mounting the *ad hominem* attack at the level of thematic content and rhetorical form *within* the text, *Holzfällen* provides the justification for its existence *as* a text: the conventions of the *roman à clef* are mobilized as a way of avoiding the collusion with the state that the narrator im-putes to Billroth, Schreker, and company. The uproar that greeted the novel is testimony to its success as a response to the criticisms raised within its own pages.

The question of inauthenticity is more problematical, for as well as accusing the Auersberger circle of merely giving the appearance of living, the narrator also admits that his own life is nothing but role-playing:

> Ich habe allen alles immer nur vorgespielt, ich habe mein ganzes Le-ben nur gespielt und *vor*gespielt, sagte ich mir auf dem Ohrensessel, ich lebe kein tatsächliches, kein wirkliches, ich lebe und existiere nur *ein vorgespieltes*, ich habe immer *nur ein vorgespieltes Leben gehabt*, niemals ein tatsächliches, wirkliches, sagte ich mir, und ich trieb diese Vorstellung so weit, daß ich schließlich an diese Vorstellung *glaubte*. (H 105–6)

The interesting point about this passage, though, is that it is full of paradoxes. To admit that one has always "pretended" is to claim for oneself, in the manner of the Cretan liar, some sort of authenticity. Furthermore, if the notion that the narrator has only had a "vorge-spieltes Leben" is itself merely a "Vorstellung," then the passage repre-sents a pretence of pretending — again paradoxically a form of authenticity.[9] Within the text of *Holzfällen*, then, authenticity is reasserted in the recognition of the narrator's own *in*authenticity. In addition, the novel's having touched such a raw nerve in the Austrian establishment attests to its "authenticity" as a diagnosis of cultural malaise. Once again, the social function *of* the text is to act as a corrective to the criticisms elaborated *in* the text.

The third aspect of cultural criticism raised in *Holzfällen* — the collapse of temporal difference — poses a different problem that can only be solved at the level of the novel's narrative form. Let us now turn to the way in which this form re-establishes a more adequate link between past and present.

*Holzfällen* is concerned with the recuperation of past time, as emphasized by Chantal Thomas, who links the structure and import of *Holzfällen* to Proust's *A la recherche du temps perdu*:

> Et c'est alors, tandis qu'il court, à l'aube, dans les rues vides de Vienne, qu'il accomplit le renversement du temps retrouvé, qu'il prend la décision salvatrice de reconquérir par l'écriture la dilapidation du temps pour rien, de la vie non vécue, du temps sacrifié à la mondanité et dont les soirées chez les Auersberger, comme dans *A la recherche* les soirées chez les Verdurin, représentent la quintessence. (Thomas 74)

Bernhard's text, however, attempts more than this, for *Holzfällen* also inscribes the stagnation that must be overcome through the process of writing. The lifestyle of the Auerbergers demonstrates a refusal to acknowledge the passing of time, and this refusal is concretely symbolized by their antique furniture: "In Wirklichkeit sind sie gegenüber ihrer eigenen Zeit so schwach, daß sie sich mit den Möbeln einer längst vergangenen, längst abgestorbenen und längst toten Zeit umgeben müssen, um sich über Wasser halten zu können, wie gesagt werden kann" (H 242). If the Auersbergers attempt to blot out the present by taking refuge in the past, however, the narrator has done the opposite. Indeed, the entire text seems to be predicated on his hitherto inadequate working-through of past experience.[10] The Auersbergers repress the present in favor of the past, whereas the narrator represses the past and concentrates on the present. The task of the text is to overcome these acts of repression.

The psychoanalytic model of the return of the repressed facilitates critical insight into the nature of the beginning of *Holzfällen* and the reminiscences to which it gives rise. Narrative beginnings involve a rupture or crisis within a stable situation, and it is no coincidence that the subtitle of *Holzfällen* is *Eine Erregung*, an "irritation." One of the numerous aphorisms coined by the narrator raises this problem: "[Wir] kommen in eine fürchterliche Erregung hinein, dachte ich jetzt, und können dieser Erregung nicht Herr werden" (H 216). Up to this point, the narrator had adopted the practice of taking his daily constitutional walk in the Graben and other streets in central Vienna, the habitual nature of these excursions emphasised by "iterative" narration: an event that happens numerous times is told only once (H 9–11). The beginning irritation precipitating the narrative in *Holzfällen* is a twofold return of the past, for on the same day the narrator receives a telephone call informing him of the death of his friend Joana *and* meets the Auersbergers while walking in the Graben in search of a tie. Before this meeting, he had had no contact with the Auersbergers for over two decades. They invite him to a "künstlerisches Abendessen," which takes place on the day of Joana's funeral, and this brings about further returns of the repressed as the narrator meets other acquaintances whom he had likewise avoided for decades. The function of the text, from the narrator's point of view, is to come to terms with this sudden resurgence of a buried past.[11]

This is achieved by following a pattern similar to that of *Der Untergeher*. The tripartite time structure is once again in evidence, and consists of the moment of writing, the "künstlerisches Abendessen," and the more distant past stretching from the 1950s to the funeral of Joana in Kilb on the day of the dinner party. By incorporating references to the moment of writing, the narrator thematizes the attempt to integrate the past within the present through the process of storytelling. The device has, however, an additional significance in *Holzfällen*, for the most prominent phrase signaling the discursive situation in *Holzfällen* is "wie ich jetzt/heute denke," transformations of which occur a dozen times in the course of the novel (see especially H 87, 253, 261, 263). The emphasis on "jetzt" and "heute" implicitly restores a sense of temporal distance, as the reader is reminded that the opinions the narrator holds about the Auersbergers today are incompatible with those of his juvenile enthusiasm: "Der Auersberger, den ich allen Ernstes einmal als einen *Novalis der Töne* bezeichnet habe, wie ich mit Abscheu vor mir selbst denke, war längst *unzurechnungsfähig* gewesen" (H 261). Thus there is a constant confrontation between the narrator's current perspective and his perspective as a young man.

The shifting time levels, and the consequent juxtaposition of the "Abendessen" with reminiscences of the narrator's past life, likewise illustrate this contrast. Upon seeing Frau Auersberger in her yellow dress, for example, the narrator remarks, "ich hatte ihr vor dreißig Jahren Komplimente gemacht wegen dieses Kleides, das mir damals so außerordentlich gefallen hatte an ihr, während es mir jetzt überhaupt nicht mehr gefiel, im Gegenteil" (H 22). The process of disillusionment is amply demonstrated in the diremption between "Damals" and "Jetzt": "Damals war ich zweiundzwanzig Jahre alt und in alles, das Maria Zaal und die Gentzgasse gewesen ist, verliebt und schrieb Gedichte. Jetzt ekelte mich aber vor den widerlichen Bildern, die ich selbst vor dreißig Jahren ungeniert mitgemacht habe" (H 23–4). This device restores temporal difference: the reader is constantly made aware of the divergence of the narrator's past and present opinions, which acts as a foil to the Auersberger's stagnant repetition of the past as if the intervening thirty years had not happened.

We have seen that the artificiality and malaise of the Auersberger set is in part a function of repetition. As in *Der Untergeher*, the narrator of *Holzfällen* is not exempt from the charm of repetition. Several episodes, notably Joana's funeral and the initial meeting with the Auersbergers on the Graben, are narrated several times with almost obsessive regularity. Once again, however, we can draw a distinction between what the text says and what it does. The repetitious lifestyles of the Auersberger circle at the level of content are counterbalanced by the narrator's attempts to come to terms with the past, not by merely repeating it in his actions, but by working through it in narrative form. The narrative repetitions are a means of integrating the traumatic experiences of Joana's death and the meeting with the Auersbergers within a coherent narrative, unifying past and present. Far from being compulsive, ritualistic copyings, the returns to key episodes of the recent past maintain the dialectic of difference within similarity that is the prerequisite of productive repetition. Each time the meeting with the Auersbergers is narrated, for example, more information is conveyed in a way that gradually builds up a more complete image of the event itself. This in turn foregrounds the narrator's efforts to come to terms, through the act of storytelling, with his own emotional reactions to such an unexpected eruption of the past. The same applies to the early morning telephone call from Kilb, and the funeral of Joana: repetitive narration is dynamic rather than static because each return to familiar ground carries a germ of novelty. The significance of the Graben and funeral episodes is contained in their repetition as well as in what the narrator actually says about them, for they imply a notion of time that is diametrically opposed to that of the Auersberger circle.

Repetitive narration, then, serves the same function as the juxtaposition of narrative time levels and the shifts between the narrator's youthful enthusiasms and middle-aged disillusionment. All three devices indicate the continuation of the past into the present, but unlike the Auersbergers' notion of time-as-stasis, they also contain within themselves a sense of rupture, of nonidentity between then and now. This introduces a vital element of temporal difference, and prevents the conflation of past and present which, in the case of the Auersbergers, had led to the artistic and social stagnation that forms the target of the narrator's abusive criticism.

The narrative form of the text can be seen as a solution to the problem of temporal stasis to which the content of *Holzfällen* alerts us. Robert Menasse alluded to the "Geschichtslosigkeit" of Bernhard's early work in "Die sozialpartnerschaftliche Ästhetik": "Es wird eine enthistorisierte Meta-Zeit konstruiert, in der sich etwa in der Abfolge nicht näher datier-ter Tage [. . .] eine Reihe historisch nicht konkretisierbarer, oft archaisch anmutender Begebenheiten ereignen" (*Überbau* 97). In the explicit for-mal confrontation of the 1950s with the 1980s, however, *Holzfällen* at-tempts to re-establish a degree of historical specificity and as such also represents the restoration of a more genuinely historical consciousness.

## The Text as Construct

Both the function and the form of *Holzfällen* have been seen here as a response to the problems the text itself diagnoses. In the course of the discussion, we moved from a consideration of the text's reception to an analysis of its key formal features, thereby drawing attention away from its referentiality and toward the text as artifact or construct. Although the elements of narrative form thus far discussed are not incompatible with the realist reading, which stresses the correspondence between *Holzfällen* and the external world, there are other features of the novel that such a reading cannot adequately address. An examination of these aspects follows.

### Narrative Dynamics

Storytelling, as this study has shown, is dependent on granting events retrospective significance from the vantagepoint of the end. *Holzfällen* is no exception, but the benefit of hindsight here serves the function of stressing the rift between experience and consciousness. The narrator speaks of "diese Fürchterlichkeiten vor allem *nach* dem Begräbnis [. . .], die so unglaublich gewesen sind, daß ich erst nach und nach imstande sein werde, sie zu begreifen; noch hatte ich nicht die Klarheit in meinem Kopf, die für ein solches Begreifen notwendig ist" (H 85). The narra-tor's own behavior at Joana's funeral is likewise a matter for retrospective analysis. He claims not to have been aware of his guilt at the time of the funeral and becomes conscious of it only while sitting in the wing-backed chair (H 102). Similarly, he is shocked to realize that his behav-ior had been governed not by grief but by curiosity, and that he had "aus der Gemischtwarenhändlerin mehr herausgepreßt [. . .] am Telefon, als ihr lieb war" (H 103). The narrator is thus engaged in a perpetual attempt to come to terms with that which has already taken place: events can be adequately judged, and their significance gauged, only once they have ended, even if the sense of an ending is merely provisional.

The drama of divergence between experience and consciousness is enacted on a formal level by the hermeneutic and proairetic codes. In *Holzfällen*, the title itself inaugurates the hermeneutic code.[12] It poses an enigma before we have even opened the book, and invites the question: to what does it refer? The answer is that until page 302, we have not the slightest idea. The "künstlerisches Abendessen" appears to have nothing to do with felling trees. Furthermore, Bernhard's narrator avoids all "hermeneutic morphemes" that might guide the reader toward the "résolution de l'énigme." It is only in the closing stages of the novel that the words of the Burgschauspieler provide a solution: "*In den Wald gehen, tief in den Wald hinein*, sagte der Burgschauspieler, *sich gänzlich dem Wald überlassen*, das ist es immer gewesen, der Gedanke, nichts anderes, als selbst Natur zu sein. *Wald, Hochwald, Holzfällen, das ist es immer gewesen*" (H 302).

At this point, however, the narrator admits that he has been vaguely aware of the actor repeating these words all evening:

> Während ich selbst aufgestanden bin, hatte ich gedacht, daß der Burgschauspieler schon im Verlauf des Fogoschessens und dann auch noch immer wieder einmal im Musikzimmer, diese drei Wörter *Wald, Hochwald, Holzfällen* gesagt hatte, ohne daß ich schon gewußt hätte, was er damit meinte. Meine Aufmerksamkeit während des Essens und auch danach im Musikzimmer, hatte sich ja lange Zeit naturgemäß nicht auf den Burgschauspieler, sondern auf die Jeannie Billroth konzentriert gehabt. (H 303)

At the level of story, the withholding of this information is motivated (somewhat ironically) by the narrator's absent-mindedness, the necessity of retrospection in the attempt to decide what is significant. But the hermeneutic sequence is also motivated by the formal exigencies of the narrative. These demand that the forward momentum of the text is established by keeping the enigma open, simultaneously frustrating and maintaining the reader's desire for a solution. Since *Holzfällen* is a retrospective narrative, the narrator is in possession of all the information before starting his tale and could in principle divulge the meaning of the title at a much earlier stage, for example during the dinner itself. All retrospective narratives must, of course, withhold information from the reader if they are to function at all. But by *admitting* that the Burgschauspieler has been muttering "Wald, Hochwald, Holzfällen" all evening, the narrator draws attention to the divergence between the chronological position of the solution in the *story*, and the position of its narration in the *discourse*. We are made aware of the narrator's structuring role in his deliberately withholding information from the reader. The device of the hermeneutic code emerges as a fiction that creates the tension necessary to maintain a degree of forward momentum and establishes the textual "dilatory space" in which the drama of the narrator's consciousness and social mores can be expanded.

The proairetic code fulfills a similar function. A term frequently used in connection with Bernhard's fiction is "handlungsarm," and indeed the amount of action in *Holzfällen* is negligible. For the first 172 pages, the narrator sits in his "Ohrensessel" and observes the guests invited to the dinner party as they await the arrival of the Burgschauspieler. This sets up the macrosequence "waiting," which is primarily proairetic, but also hermeneutic by dint of establishing suspense as to whether the actor will ever arrive. The sequence finally ends when the actor turns up, but the narrator is asleep at that moment and misses the event itself. The "waiting" sequence is thus robbed of its potentially climactic effect, dramatizing in comic fashion the failure of consciousness to keep up with experience. The narrator "oversleeps" the expected endpoint of the sequence, suggesting that it is not the end itself which is important, but that raising the expectation of an end permits the narrative to stretch itself over 172 pages. The "hermeneutic sequences," then, are foregrounded as a device. They call attention to themselves, thereby emphasizing the constructed nature of the text.

## Possibility and Narrative Choices

A curious feature of *Holzfällen*, one that is hardly present in Bernhard's other prose works and has attracted scant critical attention, is the preponderance of sentences in the conditional perfect tense ("Konjunktiv II"). The narrator would have been destroyed by the Auersbergers if he had not left their circle at the right moment (H 20); it would have been better if he had stayed at home, read and played the piano (H 21, 80); the Auersbergers would not have spoken to the narrator if they had not had the pretext of informing him of Joana's death (H 58); the Auersbergers could have ignored the narrator in the Graben (H 81); without Joana he would have embarked upon a different career (H 89); Joana would have killed herself earlier if she had not met John, her "*Zufluchtsmensch*" (H 127); Fritz would never have become the world-famous artist that he was without Joana's influence (H 135, 136); the Burgschauspieler would not have regarded Ekdal as his favorite role if he had not had such a great success with it (H 177); the production of Ibsen's *The Wild Duck* would have been more successful with a better cast (H 178); the Burgschauspieler would not have remained in Austria if he had not bought a villa in Grinzing (H 186), would willingly have played Gregers if he had had the opportunity in his youth (H 203), but would have lost his post at the Burg if he had gone to Düsseldorf to play the role (H 204); the narrator would have been destroyed by Jeannie if he had not left her at the decisive moment (H 218); he would not have gone to the artistic dinner if he had known that Jeannie would be there (H 238), and neither would the Burgschauspieler (H 296); and finally, the actor would willingly have been somebody else, but would have had to have had different parents (H 301).

This somewhat tedious list of examples is necessary because it not only conveys an impression of the quantitative predominance of such constructions, but also makes explicit a feeling which attends upon the reading of *Holzfällen*, namely the sense that the events of the text are the result of a progressive narrowing down of possibilities. This opens up the opportunity for two (ultimately complementary) readings, depending on whether the device is attributed to the narrator or to an external agency — the "implied author" or even the real author.[13]

Within the narrative world of *Holzfällen*, the conditional sentences show that events could have happened otherwise if different circumstances had prevailed, or if certain pivotal encounters had not taken place, implying that the "künstlerisches Abendessen" in all its facets is the result of a set of determinate causal factors. The narrator is sitting in the wing chair in the Auersberger's flat in the Gentzgasse due to his having met them in the Graben, which was in turn due to Joana having committed suicide that very morning, which was itself due to the failure of her marriage and career, which was a result of the destructive effect of Vienna . . .etc. As in *Der Untergeher*, however, the narrator faces the problem of controlling the proliferation of causal connections: when the Burgschauspieler mentions that he would have required different parents in order to have been someone else, causality not only extends back beyond the individual's birth, but also threatens to degenerate into the self-evident and platitudinous. The decision as to which unrealized possibilities are significant and which are not begins to look decidedly arbitrary.

If we attribute the conditional sentences to an implied author, however, they can be seen as a metafictional hint to the reader that the narrative choices could have been different, and that a different story could have been told. On this reading, the narrative world of *Holzfällen* is not a deterministic one governed by proliferating causal chains *within* the text, but is utterly arbitrary, dependent on the whim or rhetorical purpose of a manipulative implied (or real) author *outside* the text. This implies that the narrative is not an immediate representation, but rather a conscious construction produced in order to attain goals that are rhetorical in nature. The strategy of narrowing down possibilities, then, can be subjected to a dual reading: it is a device that simultaneously supports and refutes the realist assumptions underlying the scandal that greeted *Holzfällen* on its publication.

### Aphorisms and Narrative Motivation

The motivation of narrative is a formal problem as well as one of verisimilitude. In other words, what characters do in fiction is dictated by the ends of a particular narrative design at least as much as it is determined by conceptions of human psychology and motive. Again, it is to Roland Barthes that we turn in order to investigate the problem of motivation in the eccentric texts of Thomas Bernhard. One of the key concepts in Barthes's *S/Z* is the "referential code." This is basically a set of cultural assumptions that are held by the narrator (and by implication his readers), and which create the illusion, within the text, of a reference to reality:

> Quoique d'origine entièrement livresque, ces codes, par un tournement propre à l'idéologie bourgeoise, qui inverse la culture en nature, semblent fonder le réel, la "Vie." La "Vie" devient encore, dans le texte classique, un mélange écoeurant d'opinions courantes, une nappe étouffante d'idées reçues. (211)

Indicators of the referential code include aphorisms and generalizations, clichés, statements of opinion, explicit addresses to the reader, and references to other forms of writing with which it is assumed we are familiar. The first of these is particularly pertinent to a discussion of Bernhard's texts. Indeed, the use of gnomic sayings in Bernhard amounts to a parody of the referential code.

One of Barthes's insights into the functioning of the Balzacian text concerns the way in which maxims — supposedly carrying received wisdom — are coined in order to lend plausibility to the psychology and behavior of the characters. Several critics have pointed out a similar tendency in Bernhard. Referring specifically to Oehler in Bernhard's early narrative *Gehen*, Willi Huntemann remarks, "Sprachliches Charakteristikum in Oehlers Vortrag und bei Bernhard überhaupt ist das didaktische 'wir,' das zugleich den Anspruch des Gesagten auf kategorische Allgemeingültigkeit signalisiert" (*Artistik* 186). This is perhaps an oversimplification. Manfred Jurgensen is nearer the mark when he suggests that the generalizations are ironic ("Konjunktivisches Erzählen" 30), but the nature and function of this irony has remained largely unexplored.

In a way reminiscent of Balzac's texts, the narrator of *Holzfällen* attempts to "naturalize" his own behavior by generalizing aspects of his own psyche and conduct, as if to suggest that his idiosyncrasies are in fact an integral part of the human condition. The result, however, demands to be read ironically because of the exaggerated discrepancy between the narrator's maxims and the reader's empirical experience of accepted modes of behavior. This unmasks the gnomic sayings themselves as a narrative device, creating a set of textual norms against which the actions of the narrator and/or main characters would appear perfectly self-explanatory. This unmasking is achieved not only through the deviant notions of motive which Bernhard's generalizations presuppose, but also through ridiculous excess: the length of generalization that proceeds from a minor incident at the level of story heavily foregrounds the act of generalization itself:

> Wir hängen uns jahrelang an einen Menschen, dachte ich, der Jeannie jetzt ins Gesicht schauend, sind von diesem uns faszinierenden Menschen vollkommen abhängig schließlich und ihm nicht nur mit Haut und Haaren, wie gesagt wird, verfallen, sondern ihm tatsächlich vollkommen ausgeliefert, wenn wir ihn verlassen, wie wir glauben und wie ich damals geglaubt habe, erledigt und gehen doch eines Tages nicht mehr hin, geben gar keinen Grund an, warum, suchen ihn nicht mehr auf, diesen Menschen und *meiden ihn* von da an, fangen an, ihn zu verachten, ja zu hassen, treffen ihn nicht mehr. Und dann treffen wir ihn und kommen in eine fürchterliche Erregung hinein, dachte ich jetzt, und können dieser Erregung nicht Herr werden. (H 219)[14]

In Balzac, such generalizations serve to conceal the ontological gap between word and world, and it is only their preponderance that calls attention to them, "underlining (and sometimes undermining) precisely what they were designed to conceal, the arbitrariness of any narrative decision" (Chatman 244–5). If, as Chatman argues, Balzac needed generalization to lend plausibility to his characters in a historical epoch in which motivation was no longer clarified by known and accepted codes (245), then this problem is all the more acute for a writer of the late twentieth century. In Bernhard, gnomic sayings are revealed as necessary fictions that draw attention to their own arbitrariness and hence to the arbitrariness of all behavior in the text. Far from concealing the ontological gap between word and world, they actually serve to highlight it. In this light, the confiscation of *Holzfällen* by the Austrian authorities — a move that can be justified only if one takes a naively realist approach to the literary text — begins to appear vaguely absurd. In a bizarre reversal of the hierarchy of the real and the fictional, Gerhard Lampersberg's action merely confirmed the Burgschauspieler's assertion: "Wir leben ja ununterbrochen in Absurdität" (H 285).

## Double Reading and Critique

*Holzfällen* is arguably Bernhard's most contradictory fiction. It is, first of all, referential to an unusually high degree. With the possible exception of *Ja*, it is the most autobiographical of his novels: the narrator shares much of Bernhard's own biography, and the text contains a large number of characters whose "real" counterparts are easily traced. At the same time, it foregrounds narrative devices to a greater extent than Bernhard's other fictional works: the hermeneutic code, the use of the "Konjunktiv II," and the generalizing maxims emphasize that the text creates a world rather than merely reflecting one that already exists. This leaves the reader and critic of *Holzfällen* in a curious position, for on the one hand we are presented with a text that lends itself to interpretation as a *roman à clef*, but on the other we are perpetually made aware of the text's status as a verbal construct. It is this phenomenon that accounts for the "oscillation" mentioned by Mariacher, but whereas she talks in vague terms about "Mehrdeutigkeit," the oscillation in question is clearly of an ontological nature. The members of the Auersberger circle belong to the distinct ontological realms of textual and extratextual reality *at the same time*.

A similar ontological problem infects other aspects of the text. The second section of this chapter explored the nature of the cultural malaise diagnosed within *Holzfällen* and suggested that the formal attributes of the text can be regarded as a response to the ills it identifies. This device can itself be read in two ways. Because the novel refers to a recognizable external reality, it would be possible to offer a realist reading that emphasized the pertinence of the critique, in which case *Holzfällen* would emerge obviously as a critical text. It would be equally possible, however, to claim that the text's polemical moment is undermined by the fact that the solution to the problems addressed at the level of story is proffered solely within the text, at the level of discourse. In other words, the diagnosis and the response belong to distinct ontological spheres, and although we can employ reading strategies that conflate these spheres in order to make critique and solution commensurable, this can be achieved only at the expense of ignoring the numerous facets of the text that work against such a realist reading.

In chapter 1, Wendelin Schmidt-Dengler talked of the simultaneous existence of a "stets zurückgenommene[r] Realismus" and a "stets zurückgenommene Symbolik" in Bernhard's work. *Holzfällen*, however, displays a "stets zurückgenommene[r] Realismus" combined with a "stets zurückgenommene Metafiktionalität." Thus, any attempt to read *Holzfällen* as a critical or polemical text is constantly foiled by the foregrounding of the text as verbal construct, while any attempt to produce a formalist reading falls short because it cannot account for the referential moment that is a preprogrammed effect of the text. The "double reading" offered here negotiates a path between the text's two contradictory impulses — the referential and the metafictional — and ultimately suggests a way in which they may be synthesized: *Holzfällen* teaches us that referentiality in fiction is a textual effect created by choices made by the narrator and, in the final analysis, the author.

## Notes

[1] One of the libretti was later published as *die rosen der einöde* (Frankfurt am Main: Fischer, 1959); another, entitled *Köpfe*, was performed at the "Tonhof" on 22 July 1960 along with three one-act plays: see Dittmar, *Werkgeschichte* 39–40. For interesting accounts of the "Tonhof" circle, see the interviews, especially those with Lampersberg and Jeannie Ebner, in Fialik. See also Höller, *Thomas Bernhard* 55–8.

[2] Dittmar, *Werkgeschichte* 166; Löffler 60. The "missing" passages of *Die Ursache* are signaled by asterisks in the dtv paperback edition so that the interested reader can check the deleted lines in a copy of the first edition.

[3] Löffler, pp. 62–3. Ferdinand van Ingen points out that like Bernhard's Auersberger, Gerhard Lampersberg removed the "-er" suffix from his name ("Thomas Bernhards *Holzfällen*" 260–1).

[4] For a select documentation of the affair, see Dittmar, *Werkgeschichte* 270–8, and Schindlecker, "Dokumentation."

[5] The word "logisch" in Hens's argument is somewhat misleading, since the self-elimination of the narrator in a process of infinite regress is by no means a logical entailment; it is merely a possibility that is in fact present in a great many first-person ulterior narratives.

[6] See Jameson, *Prison-House* 52–4.

[7] Bernhard, conversely, was notoriously blasé about his audience. In connection with his dramas he claimed, rebarbatively, to write solely for actors and to have nothing but contempt for his audience and readers ("Bernhard Minetti" 38–9). In an interview, he also once remarked, "Von mir aus müßte von jedem Buch nur ein einziges Exemplar gedruckt werden: für mich" (Müller 24).

[8] On the issue of artificiality, see Sagmo, the title of whose article is a misquotation from *Holzfällen*. It should read "in dem heillosen Wahnsinn der Künstlichkeit" (H 301).

[9] The accusation of the pot calling the kettle black is also pre-empted by the narrator's claim that he can criticize others because he is always more ruthless

in his *self*-criticism (H 83). This notion can be traced back to Montaigne who, in his "De l'experience," advances the argument that he who mercilessly observes himself gains the right to judge others (1053). Bernhard stresses the significance of Montaigne for his own work in *Die Ursache* and the short story "Montaigne."

[10] See, for example, his claim to have forgotten how he came to know the Auersbergers (H 159). It is only through the process of narration that he is able to recall meeting them through Jeannie Billroth (H 216).

[11] Cf. Pail, for whom the narrator's inability to resist the invitation suggests that the engagement with the past that it provokes is a "quasi therapeutische Notwendigkeit" (60).

[12] Investigation might well reveal that this is the case with the majority of novels: the function of the title is not only to give an indication of contents, but also to activate the reader's desire to find out what the referent and significance of the title *are*. For a discussion of novel titles as authorial game-playing, see O'Neill, *Fictions of Discourse* 124.

[13] The implied author, in narrative theory, is an agency abstracted from the text whose role is to position the narrator's account contextually and to determine how the narrator's discourse is read: do we take it at face value, or are we dealing with an unreliable or ironic narrator?

[14] See also the similar constructions on pages 27, 73–4, 76, 85, 98, 138, 139, 140, 157–8, 160, 161, 219, 220, 224, 232, 236, 245, 267, 274, 298, 299, 308–9, 311, 313, 315.

# 7: *Alte Meister: Komödie*

## Fragmentation and History

IN STRUCTURAL TERMS, *Alte Meister*, published in 1985, returns to the technique of quotation that characterizes *Frost*, *Verstörung*, and *Korrektur*. The narrator, Atzbacher, relays the words of the main character Reger, a widowed scholar of private means who writes articles on music for the London *Times*. Reger is unique among Bernhard's protagonists, for despite being a self-confessed misogynist (AM 196), he is the only one whose relationships with women have not been mutually antagonistic and destructive. On the contrary, the happy marriage that he had enjoyed leads him to question the ability of art and the intellect to compensate for human relationships. The fact that Reger's wife is eighty-seven when she dies (AM 247) alludes to the death, at the same age, of Hedwig Stavianicek. Bernhard had met Staviancek — whom he often apostrophized as his "Lebensmensch" — in 1949, and despite being thirty-five years his senior she remained his constant companion until her death in 1984. Reger's relationship with his wife, then, can in part be seen as a belated tribute to the woman who had taken over from Bernhard's grandfather, Johannes Freumbichler, as the most important person in his life.

The main subject of *Alte Meister: Eine Komödie*, however, is indicated by its title: it is an at times uproariously comic reckoning with the cultural past in general and the Habsburg legacy in particular.

It is no coincidence that *Alte Meister* is set in a museum. As noted in chapter 1, Austria's "Selbstverständnis," its national identity, is intimately tied up with the Habsburg past, of whose cultural achievements modern Austria considers itself the proud guardian. As Robert Menasse puts it, "Wir definieren uns über unsere Kultur und unsere Geschichte, und unsere Kultur besteht aus einem selektiven Umgang mit Geschichte, und Geschichte ist für uns die herzeigbare geerbte Kultur" (*Land ohne Eigenschaften* 25). Thus Reger's exclamation, "dieses ganze Österreich ist ja nichts anderes, als ein Kunsthistorisches Museum" (AM 307), is an enunciation of the ideology that implicitly pervaded — and continues to pervade — the cultural politics of the Second Republic.

The secondary literature on *Alte Meister* that concentrates on Reger's approach to art interprets his "Zerlegungs- und Zersetzungsmechanismus" (AM 226) in purely personal terms. Reger's technique consists in subjecting paintings and other great works of art to such intense scrutiny that they all reveal themselves to be imperfect: "Noch in jedem dieser Bilder, sogenannten Meisterwerke, habe ich einen gravierenden Fehler, habe ich das Scheitern seines Schöpfers gefunden und aufgedeckt" (AM 42). For Huntemann, *Alte Meister* offers a solution to the destructivity of art as manifested in *Der Untergeher* and *Holzfällen*: the art-life dichotomy — which had destroyed Wertheimer and Joana — is here faced in a spirit of skeptical compromise: "Einerseits sind Kunst und Philosophie *sub specie naturae* lächerlich und vergeblich, andererseits aber, *sub specie individui*, als 'Überlebensmedikament' notwendige Fiktion" (*Artistik* 59–60). Sorg's commentary on the text emphasizes the more negative aspects of the art-life divide. For him, Reger aims for a

> Hierarchisierung von Leben und Kunst, die zunächst den Geist als Erlöser von den Qualen der Körperlichkeit und der Empirie feiert, aber in letzter Instanz die Ohnmacht der Kunst vor der Existentialität der Individualgeschichte erkennt und ihre Unterlegenheit konzediert. (*Thomas Bernhard* 117)

Mittermayer, on the other hand, stresses that the technique of "Zerlegung" and "Zersetzung" is a survival strategy, undertaken to protect the self from an awareness of its *own* imperfections and inadequacy (*Thomas Bernhard* 129–30). In light of the setting of *Alte Meister* and the extended reckoning with the Habsburg legacy that takes place within its pages, however, the significance of Reger's theory of artistic reception transcends the existential concerns of the individual, having wide-ranging implications for the understanding and representation of history.

The question of history is addressed by Ingeborg Hoesterey, who argues, in a discussion of the narrative form of the text, that the metaphor *Alte Meister* signifies the "burden of the tradition that every artist has to face whether he paints or writes." Thus, underlying Reger's tirades is Harold Bloom's concept of the "anxiety of influence," according to which "it is an emotional necessity for every creative consciousness to refute, and often dramatically so, the master discourses while striving to develop an individual creative idiom" (117). The phenomenon of the "anxiety of influence" is narrated via the "painting effect," which causes the *Weißbärtiger Mann* to follow the observer for sixteen meters in the Bordone-Saal (120). Although this argument is perhaps problematic in its excessive reliance on the reader's empirical experience of the Tintoretto painting, it highlights a key aspect of *Alte Meister* that other critics have tended to treat only in passing (if at all), namely the relationship between narrative structure and the burden of the past, especially in the form of cultural and intellectual history. There is a clear correlation between the mode of reading — be it of books or of paintings — advocated by Reger, and the mode of representation adopted by Atzbacher in *Alte Meister* as a whole.

Reger's concept of art criticism involves reducing even the greatest works of art to the status of an imperfect fragment. This privileging of the fragment also pervades Reger's method of reading books, which can be summed up in the statement, "Wer alles liest, hat nichts begriffen" (AM 40). The role of the recipient is not to read *in extenso*, but to flick through the pages and pick out details in order to scrutinize them "tausendmal gründlicher als der normale Leser" (AM 39). Chantal Thomas reads this anarchic mode of reading as a refusal of author/ity (80), and such "resistant" reading can be seen as another way of overcoming the anxiety of influence. In formal terms, the technique of atomizing or fragmenting the text involves a rejection of linearity, a refusal to allow one's reading of a text to be dictated by the syntax of narrative or argument. It is a mode of reading that is radically antinarrative. As this study illustrates, narrative events typically acquire significance only in the light of the end — even if their significance turns out to be their meaninglessness, like the red herrings in detective fiction. To privilege the fragment at the expense of wider narrative or argumentative coherence is to reject the aspect of texts that is generally regarded as "sinnstiftend," namely the aspect of temporal progression, and this is mirrored in the spatial metaphors for reading that Reger employs:

> Ich betrete ein Buch und lasse mich darauf nieder, mit Haut und Haaren, müssen Sie denken, auf ein oder zwei Seiten einer philosophischen Arbeit, als wäre ich dabei, eine Landschaft zu betreten, eine Natur, ein Staatsgebilde, ein Erddetail, wenn Sie wollen, um ganz und nicht nur mit halber Kraft und mit halbem Herzen, in dieses Erddetail einzudringen, es zu erforschen, und um dann, ist es erforscht mit aller mir zur Verfügung stehenden Gründlichkeit, auf das Ganze zu schließen. (AM 40; cf. 260)[1]

Such imagery, in conjunction with Reger's exhortation to "umblättern" rather than read (AM 39), foregrounds a conception of the text as a spatial entity. Once the reader is freed from the tyranny of narrative syntax, the text, like a painting, can be "read" in any order one chooses.

Similarly, Reger's discourse seamlessly juxtaposes artists from various epochs and representing a variety of genres. This technique, as Uwe Betz points out, represents the very antithesis of the layout of museums in general and the Kunsthistorisches Museum in particular, where paintings are strictly grouped in individual galleries according to the era in which they were produced. Reger's monologue possesses an "entzeitlichende Kraft" that transforms the museum into what Betz calls a "polychronen Raum der 'Posthistoire'" (75). The concept of "posthistoire" is neither explained nor elaborated upon by Betz. His discussion implies that Reger's monologue destroys the narrative ordering that museums, with their notions of progression and periodization, construct as the tacit framework within which art is made available for interpretation by the general public. "Posthistoire" thus refers to a cultural condition or predicament in which linear narrative is no longer an adequate means of representing the prevalent "Zeiterfahrung" and has lost its ability to organize the tradition. It is replaced by a pervasive sense of stasis, which facilitates a mode of reception that, like Reger's, is characterized by breaks, jumps, and the celebration of discontinuity.

This approach to art carries over into Reger's entire attitude toward heredity and history; his "Zersetzungsmechanismus" (AM 70) ultimately becomes a means of dealing with life itself. Atzbacher quotes Reger as saying "Die höchste Lust haben wir ja an den Fragmenten, wie wir am Leben ja auch dann die höchste Lust empfinden, wenn wir es als Fragment betrachten, und wie grauenhaft ist uns das Ganze und das fertige Vollkommene" (AM 41). The concept of the fragment, then, is broader in its significance. We learn, for example, that Reger is a descendant of Anton Bruckner, Adalbert Stifter, and Martin Heidegger, and his parents were keen to broadcast this kinship: "Mit Stifter sind wir verwandt, mit Heidegger sind wir verwandt, und mit Bruckner auch, haben meine Eltern bei jeder Gelegenheit gesagt, so daß es mir oft peinlich gewesen war" (AM 97–8). Heidegger appears somewhat anomalous in this triumvirate. Bruckner and Stifter, on the other hand, are clear representatives of the Habsburg tradition. Bruckner was court organist in Vienna from 1867, and his devout Catholicism had a profound influence on his musical output, which included a large body of sacred choral works as well as the nine symphonies (Jelavich 122). He thus embodies the intimate association of church and state that so often forms the target of Bernhard's criticisms of Austria, both past and present. Stifter's novel *Der Nachsommer* has been read by Ulrich Greiner as depiction of the stasis and security represented by the Habsburg regime in the nineteenth century: that is, as an icon of what has become known as the "Habsburg Myth."[2]

Reger's exaggerated and often hilarious denunciation of Stifter and Bruckner, then, is of a piece with his method of reading paintings, which is likewise directed at manifestations of the Habsburg past: "Nun ja, die Habsburger haben genau den dubiosen katholischen Geschmack, der in diesem Museum zu Hause ist. Das Kunsthistorische Museum ist genau der dubioser habsburgische Kunstgeschmack, der schöngeistige, widerliche" (AM 32; cf. also 305). Both represent a rejection of the continuities of the Habsburg tradition. Furthermore, the fact that Reger is related to Bruckner and Stifter shows that even in connection with his own family history the continuities of the tradition are rejected. While his parents boast of their august lineage, Reger lays the emphasis on the less honorable aspects of the family past, which includes a double murderer:

> Ich selbst habe mich nie gescheut, zu sagen, ein Verwandter von mir habe in Stein und in Garsten eingesessen, was wohl das Schlimmste ist, das ein Österreicher über seine Verwandtschaft sagen kann, im Gegenteil, ich habe es öfter gesagt, als notwendig [. . .]. Wir haben mit unserer Verwandschaft zu leben, ist sie wie immer, sagte er. Wir *sind* ja diese Verwandtschaft, sagte er, *ich in mir bin ja alle zusammen.* (AM 100)

This desire to draw attention to the shady aspects of family history is a corrective to Reger's parents' selective attitude toward their ancestry: not only does Reger debunk the representatives of a glorious collective and personal past; he substitutes for it an alternative history of crime and incarceration, which is the very obverse of the "herzeigbare geerbte Kultur" and the "selektiven Umgang mit der Geschichte" of which Menasse writes.

Toward the end of *Alte Meister*, Atzbacher quotes Reger's reflections on the incapacity of art to compensate for human loss: "Ohne Menschen haben wir nicht die geringste Überlebenschance, sagte Reger, wir können uns noch so viele große Geister und noch so viele Alte Meister als Gefährten genommen haben, *sie ersetzen keinen Menschen*" (AM 291). After his wife's death, the only writer who offered Reger any comfort was Schopenhauer.

> Aber natürlich habe ich auch bei Schopenhauer nur deshalb eine Überlebenschance gehabt, weil ich ihn für meine Zwecke mißbraucht und *tatsächlich auf die gemeinste Weise verfälscht* habe, so Reger, indem ich ihn zu einem Überlebensmedikament gemacht habe, das er in Wirklichkeit gar nicht ist[.] (AM 287)

This returns us, in a sense, to the anxiety of influence. "Mißbrauchen" and "verfälschen" are clearly a type of deliberate misreading: the only way to assimilate the discourses of the past is to misread them, just as the only way to tolerate personal and collective history is to "misread" it, to refuse the satisfactions of traditional modes of narrative ordering and transmission by fragmenting the discourse of temporality. The notion of the "notwendige Fiktion" alluded to by Huntemann is thus not merely a practice carried out by Reger *in* the text; as we shall see, it also informs the very production and structure *of* the text. *Alte Meister* represents an illustration, at the level of form, of the thesis expounded by Reger within its pages.

## Fragmentation and Form

*Alte Meister* takes the minimising of the hermeneutic and proairetic codes to its probable extreme. Action on the primary time level is greatly reduced; indeed, in comparison with *Alte Meister*, novels such as *Der Untergeher* and *Holzfällen* appear positively swashbuckling. The first 173 pages narrate Atzbacher's hour-long wait between his arrival in the Kunsthistorisches Museum and his appointment with Reger, during which he observes the latter from an unseen corner of a gallery adjacent to the Bordone-Saal. The remainder of the text narrates Atzbacher's and Reger's conversations while the two of them sit on a bench in front of Tintoretto's "Weißbärtiger Mann" in the Bordone-Saal.

The chronological framework is maintained by occasional references to the time: the narrator arrives in the museum at 10.30 (AM 7), he observes Reger leave the Bordone-Saal at 11.20 (AM 127), is still waiting for the latter's return at 11.28 (AM 171), and keeps his appointment at 11.30 on the dot (AM 173). At midday the two are still seated in the Bordone-Saal (AM 204). This short list gives some impression of the manipulation of time on the "primary time level." The most striking thing is that a relatively large expanse of text narrates a highly compressed amount of story time. Just as a line can be divided into an infinite number of points, so a moment in narrative can be expanded indefinitely, and Atzbacher makes full use of this possibility. Such "retardation" devalues the present moment and shifts the emphasis of the text onto the past, and it is no coincidence that Reger claims to feel out of place in the present: "Ich gehöre nicht zu den Leuten, die die Gegenwart genießen, das ist es, ich gehöre zu diesen Unglücklichen, die die Vergangenheit genießen, das ist die Wahrheit, die die Gegenwart immer nur als Beleidigung empfinden" (AM 270–1). Despite this manipulation of the primary time level, however, it is still a stable aspect of the text's time structure. Indeed, as we shall see, it is the only stable aspect.

The even greater degree of retardation between 11.20 and 11.28 contributes to the "hermeneutic" sequence by deferring the moment of the meeting in order to heighten the reader's desire for the culmination of the first half of the novel. Within the skeletal time structure discussed above, the text gains its forward momentum by posing a single enigma at the beginning, which is solved only at the very end. Atzbacher, the primary narrator,[3] has been asked by his friend, the music critic Reger, to come to the Kunsthistorisches Museum in Vienna for the second day running, whereas it has been Reger's habit for the last thirty-six years to attend the museum only on alternate days. The mystery on which the narrative depends is thus: what reason does Reger have for summoning Atzbacher to the museum on consecutive days?

It is an enigma that is reformulated on several occasions. "Aus was für einem Grund Reger heute da ist, weiß ich nicht," writes Atzbacher (AM 23), and later: "Sicher war es ihm eine wenn auch sozusagen selbstverschuldete Strafe Gottes, daß er sich ausgerechnet an diesem Samstag mit mir im Kunsthistorischen Museum verabredet hat, dachte ich, und fragte mich, zu welchem Zweck? und konnte mir keine Antwort geben" (AM 136). Reger himself brings up the question of why he has summoned Atzbacher:

> [I]ch sitze schon stundenlang hier auf der Sitzbank und denke darüber nach, *wie* ich es Ihnen sagen soll, *warum* ich Sie *auch für heute* ins Kunsthistorische Museum gebeten habe. *Später, später,* sagte Reger, *lassen Sie mir Zeit.* Wir begehen ein Verbrechen und sind nicht imstande, es ganz einfach umständelos mitzuteilen, sagte Reger. (AM 184–5)

At this point, the enigma appears to be one of considerable gravity: Reger speaks of a crime and Atzbacher talks of the consequent divine retribution (which is admittedly given a comic edge by the fact that it consists in visiting a museum). Willi Huntemann points out that the ultimate solution of the riddle is comic because it is clothed in the garb of an existential decision (*Artistik* 85). But he fails to note that the mock seriousness of these comments is already undermined when a "résolution paritelle" is offered: "Ja, habe ich in aller Frühe gedacht, du triffst dich mit Atzbacher im Kunsthistorischen Museum, um ihm einen Vorschlag zu machen, und weißt ganz genau, daß du ihm einen völlig unsinnigen Vorschlag machst und wirst diesen Vorschlag machen" (AM 245–6). Here, the notion of crime gives way to that of an impending suggestion, and when the suggestion is finally made on the third from the last page of the novel, it is revealed to be one of quotidian banality:

> Ich glaubte, meinen Ohren nicht zu trauen, als er sagte, er habe *zwei Eintrittskarten, ausgezeichnete Parkettplätze für den Zerbrochenen Krug im Burgtheater* gekauft und der *eigentliche* Grund, warum er mich heute schon wieder ins Kunsthistorische Museum gebeten habe,

sei der, mir den Vorschlag zu machen, mit ihm zusammen den *Zerbro-chenen Krug* in Burgtheater anzuschauen. (AM 309)

The triviality of the hermeneutic sequence is debunked even further by the final lines of the novel, "Die Vorstellung war entsetzlich" (AM 311). This is tantamount to a parody of the hermeneutic code: even the most insignificant "mystery" can be foregrounded in such a way that it serves as the dynamic force which gives the narrative its momentum. The meeting in the Bordone-Saal is revealed as literally a pretext that structures both excursions into the personal and collective past, and reflections on the present.

The significance of meeting in the Bordone-Saal on two consecutive days is perpetually reasserted at a lexical level by Atzbacher's use of the deictic adverbial "gestern." Since this implies a subsequent "heute," it initially seems to lay exaggerated stress on the fact that Reger and the narrator are meeting two days running.[4] Nevertheless, close reading reveals that the use of deixis is much more complex and ultimately much more problematic.

Deictics are those parts of speech whose reference is dependent on the spatio-temporal location of the speaker: this, that, here, there, now, then, you, I, tomorrow, yesterday.[5] In the case of "ordinary" speech, deictics can be interpreted only if the addressee knows where and when the speaker is speaking. In written narrative, deictics are severed from an immediate act of enunciation, and correspondingly undergo a functional shift: rather than *presupposing* knowledge of the temporal and spatial situation of the utterance, they serve to *construct* it. Typically, deictics help the reader to orientate him- or herself, and to establish temporal and spatial relationships, within the fictional world. It is also possible, however, to employ deixis in order to disorientate the reader, and this possibility is exploited by the narrator of *Alte Meister*.

As in Bernhard's other novels of the 1980s, the discursive situation is signaled by verbs of cognition in the present tense, primarily in this case "denke ich" (AM 24, 61, 62). But proximal temporal deictics, which in all of Bernhard's other fiction signal the discursive situation, function in a rather odd way. "Heute," for example, is combined with the preterite and refers to the day of the meeting in the Bordone-Saal (AM 137). The same applies to "jetzt, einen Tag später also" (AM 117), whereas in conventional usage both would refer to the discursive situation. Likewise, Atzbacher's use of "gestern" *should* refer to the day preceding the act of enunciation, *not* the meeting with Reger in the museum. Its reference is ambiguous in the first instance:

Da er im sogenannten Bordone-Saal gegenüber Tintorettos *Weißbärti-gem Mann* seinen Vormittagsplatz hat, auf der samtbezogenen Sitzbank, auf welcher er mir gestern nach dem Erläutern der sogenannten *Sturm-sonate* seinen Vortrag über die *Kunst der Fuge* fortgesetzt hat, [...] mußte ich im sogenannten Sebastiano-Saal Aufstellung nehmen. (AM 7)

Here, it is possible that "gestern" could refer to the day preceding the act of writing, and that the disquisition on Beethoven and Bach could have taken place *since* the Saturday rendezvous in the Bordone-Saal. Nevertheless, as the first half of the text progresses, it becomes clear that "gestern" refers, in fact, to the day preceding that meeting.

This opens up two interpretative possibilities. The first is that it is a highly deviant use of "gestern." Käte Hamburger has shown that such deviance is one of the characteristics of third-person narrative:

[D]ie Vergangenheitsadverbien in der realen Rede [...] können mit dem Imperfekt nur in bezug auf das Jetzt des Sprechenden verbunden werden: Gestern geschah dies und das. Diese Verbindung ist aber in der Wirklichkeitsaussage nicht mehr möglich für eine in bezug auf das Jetzt des Aussagenden schon vergangene Zeit. Versetzt sich der jetzt und hier Sprechende an einen zurückliegenden Zeitpunkt, etwa: am 15 Juli geschah dies und das, so kann er durch ein "gestern" ebenso-wenig ein vor diesem Tag Geschehenes bezeichnen wie durch ein "morgen" etwas, was sich nach ihm zugetragen hat. Hier sind Adver-biale wie "am Tage vorher" (bzw. "darauf") erforderlich. Aber wir brauchen nur einen beliebigen Roman [...] aufzuschlagen, um zu bemerken, daß diese der Wirklichkeitsaussage sozusagen eingeborenen logisch-grammatischen Gesetze ihre Gültigkeit verloren haben. (70)

Any novel, that is, so long as it is narrated in the third person. For Hamburger's system regards first-person novels as "fingierte Wirklich-keitsaussagen," whose grammar is bound by the same rules as genuine "Wirklichkeitsaussagen." Since *Alte Meister* is a first-person narrative, the use of "gestern" to refer to the point in time preceding the day of the meeting is highly deviant with respect to normal grammatical us-age, involving a breakdown in the narrator's (and consequently the reader's) ability to orient themselves temporally.

The second possibility, however, is that the moment of utterance, that is, the discursive situation, is situated on the same day as the meet-ing in the Bordone-Saal and the subsequent visit to the theater. Verisi-militude would speak against such a reading: how could Atzbacher have written a 310-page text upon returning from the performance of *Der zerbrochene Krug*? But there are also grammatical reasons to discourage this interpretation, most prominently the sentence, "Tatsächlich bin ich am Abend mit Reger ins Burgtheater und in den *Zerbrochenen Krug* ge-gangen, schreibt Atzbacher" (AM 311). "Am Abend" would seem to be at odds with the repetition of "gestern," and the use of "jetzt" and "heute"; one would expect the adverbial "heute Abend."

The temptation to discuss *Alte Meister* within the framework of temporal relations used for the foregoing chapters, then, is thwarted by deictic particles that ultimately create a certain temporal disorientation, destabilizing the relationship between the three categories of discursive situation — primary time level — analepses far more radically than was the case even in *Der Untergeher*. The same effect is produced by the use of tense, Atzbacher mixing perfect, imperfect, pluperfect, and a hybrid form along the lines of "hatte gemacht gehabt" with a total lack of consistency.[6]

This destabilization of time levels is also apparent in the quotation technique of *Alte Meister*. Bernhard's early texts often involve a narrator who largely effaces himself behind the quoted monologues of another central character. *Frost* (1963) consists largely of a trainee doctor's reporting the words of the painter Strauch; and in the final and longest section of *Verstörung* (1967), Fürst Saurau's words are relayed with the minimum of narratorial intervention. *Gehen* (1971), *Korrektur* (1975), and *Die Billigesser* (1980) are informed by similar structures of quotation, and temporal relations remain relatively stable and unproblematic in all of them, despite the associative, nonlinear nature of the quoted monologues. The situation in *Alte Meister*, however, is complicated because Reger's monologues, already achronological in themselves, are also *narrated* achronologically. That is, each of them appears to be contextualized within a concrete communicative situation, but the order in which these situations are narrated diverges from the deducible order of their occurrence, and the boundaries between them are fluid.

We have seen that in the first part of the text, the phrase "sagte er gestern" renders the context of the utterance indeterminate, subverting the conventional role of deixis and possessing no stable temporal referent. Although in much of the central part of the "Komödie" Reger's monologue is clearly located on the day of the meeting, toward the end of the text Atzbacher recalls other, earlier situations in which Reger had digressed on a variety of topics, and the text shuttles between these in an ostensibly arbitrary fashion. Atzbacher reports words spoken by Reger in the Hotel Ambassador during their first meeting after the death of Reger's wife (AM 246–52), during Atzbacher's first visit to Reger's "Singerstraßenwohnung" (AM 252–62), the second visit to the Singerstraße (AM 262–3), in the Bordone-Saal (AM 263–85), again in the Ambassador (AM 285–98), once more in the Bordone-Saal (AM 298–9), and again in the Ambassador (AM 299–300) before the text closes in the Bordone-Saal. To give page numbers for these passages, however, is in a sense misleading. Phrases such as "so/sagte Reger damals im Ambassador" establish, through extensive repetition (fifteen times in five pages, AM 248–52) a stable communicative context. Nevertheless, "so Reger damals im Ambassador" or "so Reger damals in der Singerstraßenwohnung" are at times replaced with the simple "so Reger," which results in a certain textual drift or slippage: it is not always clear where and when a given statement was actually made, and the structure of the text implies temporal instability.

The fragmentation of works of art, the privileging of the detail over the whole in the reading process, and the rejection of the familial and cultural tradition find their formal analogue in the disruption of temporal relations at the level of narrative form: any sense of continuity within the novel is undermined not only by the associative structure of Reger's ramblings — for this is shared with several of Bernhard's other fictions —, but also by the ambiguities of the time structure at all levels of the text. This accounts for the highly ironic deployment of the hermeneutic code to structure the primary time level: as a means of representing personal and collective history, linear narration is profoundly compromised, and can be used only if it simultaneously inscribes its own inadequacy or redundancy.

In its engagement with both personal and collective history, *Alte Meister* forms a comic prelude to the final reckoning with Austria and its past which Bernhard undertook with considerably more seriousness in his final novel, *Auslöschung*. It is this novel that forms the subject of the next chapter.

## Notes

[1] Cf. the extended metaphor in *Ritter, Dene, Voss*, in which the study of philosophy is compared to entering a "Gasthaus" (*Stücke 4* 196–7).

[2] See the long introductory essay in Greiner. The phrase "Habsburg Myth" was coined by Claudio Magris. His book *Der habsburgische Mythos in der österreichischen Literatur* investigates the appeal of an idealized, stable Habsburg past for Austrians writing during the crisis and dissolution of the Habsburg empire.

[3] Like *Beton* (1982) and *Auslöschung* (1986), *Alte Meister* also contains a higher narrative instance than the primary narrator (in this case Atzbacher), for the first and last sentences of the text include the phrase "schreibt Atzbacher." Apart from introducing another narrative level and hence increasing the distance between narrator and reader, however, the device seems largely

redundant. It is backgrounded to such an extent that it plays no significant role in the reading of the text, and seems to serve merely as a demarcation line between the fictional world of the text and the real world of the reader. This anonymous narrator acquires a much more significant role in *Auslöschung*, as we shall see.

[4] See AM 7, 8, 44, 63–7, 71–2, 76, 80, 90, 99, 103, 106, 108, 116, 123.

[5] This list is borrowed from Toolan 263. See also Culler, *Structuralist Poetics* 164–70.

[6] On Bernhard's highly idiosyncratic use of the past tenses, see McLintock.

# 8: *Auslöschung: Ein Zerfall*

## On the Dating of *Auslöschung*

THE NARRATOR OF *Auslöschung: Ein Zerfall* is Franz-Josef Murau, yet another scholar of private means who has left his native Austria and now leads his "Geistesexistenz" as a teacher of German literature in Rome. At the start of the novel he has recently returned from Austria, where he had attended the wedding of his sister Caecilia to a south-German "Weinflaschenstöpselfabrikant."

On the opening page of the first vast chapter "Das Telegram," the eponymous telegram arrives at Murau's home, informing him that both his parents and his elder brother, Johannes, have been killed in a car accident. Throughout the rest of the chapter Murau rearranges the family photographs on his desk, reminiscing about Wolfsegg, his past life, and his family. The death of his father and brother leaves him in the unexpected position of being the sole heir of Wolfsegg, a large stately home and agricultural estate in Upper Austria, which Bernhard had also used as the location of the short story "Der Italiener" (1962) and its filmic version (1970). Having decided that he would settle in Rome for good, Murau is now obliged to return to Wolfsegg to participate in the funeral ceremonies and take over the administration of the properties that have fallen into his ownership.

The second chapter of the novel, "Das Testament," narrates Murau's activities in and around Wolfsegg during the twenty or so hours between his arrival and the funeral. Just as the photographs had done in the first chapter, the things he sees in the grounds of the ancestral home function as stimuli to the storytelling impulse and cause him to make extensive narrative excursions into the past. Like the numerous other country estates with which Bernhard's protagonists are encumbered, notably in *Ungenach* and *Korrektur*, Wolfsegg represents in spatial form the burden of individual and collective history. It is the site of traumatic childhood experiences within an oppressive — even hostile — family setup. It is also a relic or museum piece, still governed by a basically feudal form of social organization. As such, it stands for inherited traditions and, ultimately, for Austrian history itself.

*Auslöschung*, Bernhard's longest novel, forms a large-scale attempt to come to terms with this past. It can be seen as a final re-working of the thematic and formal issues that had obsessed Bernhard throughout his literary career, and has with some justification been described as a "Bilanz und Zusammenfassung" (Mittermayer, *Thomas Bernhard* 110).

*Auslöschung* was also the last of Bernhard's novels to be published. Nevertheless, within the space of a few years conjecture arose as to the actual composition date of the text, and it has since become *de rigueur* for Bernhard's critics to devote at least some space to the problem. The first commentator to suggest that the novel was in fact completed in the early 1980s was Ulrich Weinzierl. He advances two main points of evidence. The first is stylistic and concerns the frequency of the expression "nurmehr noch," which, claims Weinzierl, is comparable to the usage of the same words in *Beton* (1982). The second is a conversation with Bernhard's half-brother (and not "step-brother," as Weinzierl would have it), Peter Fabjan, who allegedly told him, Weinzierl, that *Auslöschung* had been written in 1981–2 and kept in a safe for several years. Fabjan knew of no later revisions made to the text (193–4).

Several of Bernhard's critics have since subscribed to Weinzierl's view, but the whole issue is by no means clear-cut. The first of Weinzierl's proofs — the frequency of "nurmehr noch" — is, to say the least, far-fetched. It might be more persuasive if the phrase occurred nowhere else in Bernhard's output, but it also crops up extensively in *Der Untergeher* and *Alte Meister*. (Indeed, one wonders whether Weinzierl trawled those texts for evidence, too; presumably not). The second piece of evidence, namely the conversation with Fabjan, is not totally reliable; even less conclusive is Wendelin Schmidt-Dengler's similar statement:

> Ich verdanke es einem glaubwürdigen Gewährsmann, dem Thomas Bernhard am 5. November 1986 mitgeteilt hat, er, Bernhard, habe die *Auslöschung* vor fünf Jahren fertiggestellt, das Manuskript für den Fall, daß ihm etwas zustoße, seinem Bruder zur Aufbewahrung übergeben und dann doch schließlich veröffentlicht. (Qtd. in Mariacher, "Beziehung" 241)

The number of speakers in this communicative chain is reminiscent of the embedded speakers in Bernhard's own texts, and the effect in terms of reliability is the same. One suspects in this case that Bernhard was once again retrospectively stylizing and revising his biography as he had done so many times before, the most conspicuous example being the alleged job as a librarian in London, of which no records exist (Höller, *Thomas Bernhard* 147). In addition, Fabjan's claim that Bernhard made no changes to the typescript between placing it in the safe and publication can be refuted by the facts that a) the manuscript itself bears the dates "1981–1986," and b) even in this ostensibly completed version the narrator and main character is called Pöttinger, not Murau.[1]

Even if the above objections could not be raised, there is a sense in which the date of composition is less important than the date of publication. As one recent voice of sanity has noted, Bernhard clearly *chose* to bring out *Auslöschung* when he did (Nickel 9).[2] The date of publication is at present the most reliable one we have, and although the debate concerning the composition date of *Auslöschung* is interesting conjecture, it can have no binding effect on our interpretation of the novel until the results of current work being undertaken in the Bernhard archive are made public.

## "Herkunftskomplex"/"Zukunftskomplex"

Toward the beginning of *Auslöschung* there is a curious and ostensibly unmotivated passage that describes the narrator's horror at the manic pickling activities of his mother and sisters:

> Die Aussicht, die in diesen Gläsern gehortete, von meiner Mutter und meinen Schwestern beschriftete Marmelade in den nächsten Jahrzehnten aufessen zu müssen, hatte sich in mir schon sehr früh als permanenter Haß gegen alles Eingekochte und insbesondere gegen Marmelade überhaupt festgesetzt. In den Speisekammern hatten wir auch immer Hunderte von Gläsern mit Hühner-, Fasanen- und Taubenschenkeln, vor deren trübem Gelb es mir jedesmal, wenn ich ihrer ansichtig wurde, ekelte. Obwohl es mit der Zeit immer weniger Marmelade gebraucht, immer weniger sogenanntes Eingewecktes gegessen worden ist in Wolfsegg, haben meine Mutter und meine Schwestern immer mehr eingekocht und eingeweckt; sie waren tatsächlich von einem Einkoch- und Einweckwahn besessen, solange ich denken kann und von diesem Einkoch- und Einweckwahn nicht mehr zu heilen gewesen. Aus altgewordenem Brot hatten sie jede Woche Brösel gemacht und ganze Galerien von Gläsern mit Bröseln aufgehoben, die niemals gebraucht wurden, weil in Wolfsegg kaum mehr paniert worden ist, weil wir keine Schnitzel mehr gegessen haben ganz einfach, die Wiener Art nicht mehr gefragt und nicht mehr gegessen wurde. (Aus 101–2)

The image of preserving plays a major role in another great "Zeitroman" of the 1980s, Salman Rushdie's *Midnight's Children* (1981), whose narrator, Saleem Sinai, is the owner of a pickle factory. It is worth quoting one of the relevant passages from that text in order to establish what is at stake in Bernhard's transformation of the motif:

> In the spice bases I reconcile myself to the inevitable distortions of the pickling process. To pickle is to give immortality, after all: fish, vegetables, fruit hang embalmed in spice-and-vinegar; a certain alteration, a slight intensification of taste, is a small matter, surely? The art is to change the flavour in degree, but not in kind; and above all (in my thirty jars and a jar) to give it form — that is to say, meaning. (I have mentioned my fear of absurdity.)
>
> One day, perhaps, the world will taste the pickles of history. They may be too strong for some palates, their smell may be overpowering, tears may rise to eyes; I hope nevertheless that it will be possible to say of them that they possess the authentic taste of truth. (461)

In Rushdie, the image of pickling serves as a potent metaphor for the self-conscious artistic engagement with history, for the need to preserve the past in a way that takes account of the falsifications inherent in any form-giving enterprise. Most important, however, is the faith that the pickle jars of history will be opened once again. The "Einkoch- und Einweckwahn" of Murau's mother and sisters, on the other hand, is merely a process of bottling up, in both the literal and figurative sense of the term: there is an ever-decreasing possibility that their preserving jars will ever be reopened, but they continue to hoard foodstuffs away in an unreflective, indeed compulsive, manner.

The passage thus begins to signify once we realize that it forms part of an extensive complex of images of repression characterizing Wolfsegg under the ownership of Murau's parents. These images are offset by opposite images of the lifting of repression. During the frequent hunting parties at Wolfsegg, for example, the house is full of guests: "Auch viele Italiener sind bei solchen Gelegenheiten Gäste in Wolfsegg, dann werden die Speisekammern geleert, hatte ich zu Gambetti gesagt, und die *Marmeladegläser zu Dutzenden aufgemacht* und es gibt sogar die vielfältigsten Salate, *Kompotte*" (Aus 186, my italics). Here, the preserving jars are opened under the influence of outsiders, and this can be read as a metaphorical analogue of the lifting of repression as it is undertaken by Onkel Georg, the younger brother of Murau's father, whenever he "invades" Wolfsegg from his adopted home of Cannes. Onkel Georg encourages a rediscovery and liberation of culture from the stuffy confines of library and statuary. He opens up bookcases, the "jahrhundertelang versiegelten Behälter des Geistes" (Aus 148), and this act is repeated by Murau as soon as he inherits the Wolfsegg estate: "Die Bibliotheken müssen aufgesperrt werden, sagte ich. Alle diese Bücher müssen an die frische Luft kommen. Wir wissen gar nicht, was das für Schätze sind, ungelüftet, verstaubt, sagte ich" (Aus 401; cf. also 150).[3]

One reason for Murau's avowed admiration of his uncle is that he works against the "museum culture" and revivifies the otherwise torpid

Wolfsegg: "Mit ihm konnte in keinem Falle eine wie immer geartete Langeweile aufkommen" (Aus 40). Onkel Georg conceives of culture as something living and dynamic:

> Mein Onkel Georg hat mir die Musik und die Literatur aufgeschlüs-selt und mir die Komponisten und Dichter als lebendige Menschen nahegebracht, nicht nur als jährlich drei- oder viermal abzustaubende Gipsfiguren. [. . .] Ich habe durch meinen Onkel Georg keine toten, sondern sehr lebendige Städte kennengelernt, keine toten Völker auf-gesucht, sondern lebendige, keine toten Schriftsteller und Dichter ge-lesen, sondern lebendige, keine tote Musik gehört, sondern eine lebendige, keine toten Bilder gesehen, sondern lebendige. (Aus 45)

The dominant imagery in these passages, valuable treasures being allowed to gather dust, suggests that Wolfsegg represents the "museum culture" that crops up as a recurrent motif in Bernhard's writings. It occurs as early as 1966 in the essay "Politische Morgenandacht" — where Austria is described as "eine Mischung aus Freilichtsmuseum für ordinäre Weltenbummler und Irrenanstalten" (12), — and finds its way into *Alte Meister* where Reger states, "dieses ganze Österreich ist ja nichts anderes, als ein Kunsthistorisches Museum" (AM 307). This is by no means an idle metaphor, for as we have seen in previous chapters, the dominant conception of Austria's postwar cultural identity has been that of guardian of the glorious cultural heritage rather than as a vi-brant cultural force in the present. Thus when, toward the beginning of *Auslöschung*, Onkel Georg exclaims, "Ihr lebt ja in einem Museum! Alles schaut aus, als wäre es jahrelang unbenützt" (Aus 40), he is im-plicitly drawing parallels between Wolfsegg and Austria as a whole in a way that echoes the explicit metaphorical link between the two drawn by Murau himself: "Dieser Staat ist wie meine Familie" (Aus 460).[4]

The metaphorical identification of Wolfsegg with Austria is not confined to questions of culture, for the Murau family's involvement in recent Austrian history is considerably more sinister. When Murau ex-presses his interest in family history, the image of a hidden past which has to be brought to light once more predominates: "Und ich hatte angefangen, in unseren jahrhundertealten Schriften zu blättern, die in großen Kisten auf den Dachböden gelagert waren, von welchen sie immer Kenntnis gehabt, die sie aber niemals näher in Augenschein ge-nommen haben. Sie fürchteten unliebsame Entdeckungen" (Aus 56–7). The implication here is that the Murau's family history is governed by suppression and repression, which contrasts with Murau's thirst for history in its totality:

> Die Geschichte interessierte mich, aber nicht so, wie *sie* sich für unsere Geschichte interessierten, sozusagen nur für die als zu Hunderten und

Tausenden aufeinandergelegten Ruhmesblätter, sondern als Ganzes. Was sie niemals gewagt hatten, in ihre fürchterlichen Geschichtsab- gründe hinein und hinunter zu schauen, hatte ich gewagt (Aus 57).

At this point family history intersects once more with collective history, and in particular Austria's role in National Socialism.

Again it is Onkel Georg who attempts to lift the repression of the Nazi past by Murau's parents. We are told that Georg had left Wolfs- egg and participated in the resistance movement during the Second World War, though in precisely what capacity remains unspecified (Aus 193). On his last visit to Wolfsegg he reminds Murau's father that the latter had been a long-serving member of the Nazi party. "Darauf war mein Vater aufgesprungen," writes Murau, "und hatte seinen Suppen- teller auf der Tischplatte zertrümmert und ist aus dem Speisezimmer hinausgestürzt. Meine Mutter hatte meinem Onkel Georg noch die Wörter *gemeiner Kerl* an den Kopf geworfen und war ihrem Mann ge- folgt" (Aus 195). Silke Schlichtmann, drawing on Alexander and Mar- garete Mitscherlich's renowned psychoanalytic study of "Vergangen- heitsbewältigung," *Die Unfähigkeit zu trauern*, points out that the concept of "Wiederholungszwang" facilitates an understanding not only of individual, but also collective behavior (84–5). She argues that silence about the Nazi catastrophe contains within it the danger that the crime will be repeated: the repressed can return only in the form of renewed violence, hence Murau's father's spontaneous aggression when reminded of his Nazi affiliations by Onkel Georg (85).

The attitude of Murau's family toward their implication in Nazism is a question not only of psychology, but of discourse. Murau believes that his uncle had documented Wolfsegg's Nazi past in his own auto- biographical text "Antiautobiografie." This work, however, was never found among Georg's posthumous papers — indeed, Murau suggests that his mother might be to blame for its disappearance (Aus 188) — and this represents one more example of the blockage and curtailment of a narrative that deserves to be told. "Da diese Antiautobiografie meines Onkels nicht mehr da ist," writes Murau, "habe ich selbst ja so- gar die Verpflichtung, eine rücksichtslose Anschauung von Wolfsegg vorzunehmen und diese rücksichtslose Anschauung zu berichten" (Aus 197). The intention of Murau's narrative, like that of Bernhard's other "late" texts, is thus to bring into a circuit of communication that which has been hitherto buried, repressed, and lost from view in the three spheres of cultural, individual, and collective history.

Murau's "rücksichtslose Anschauung" of Wolfsegg, however, is threatened by the possibility that he, too, will fall prey to the tempta- tions of repression. At one point he says to Gambetti: "Ich könnte

[. . .] Ihnen beispielsweise von Morden sprechen, die mit dem Jägerhaus in Zusammenhang stehen und mit dem Nationalsozialismus, aber
dazu habe ich jetzt, in dieser noch alles in allem glücklichen Atmosphä-
re, keine Lust" (Aus 196). There are also episodes in which Murau
threatens to succumb to a kind of "Wiederholungszwang" such as we
have seen in *Wittgensteins Neffe*, *Der Untergeher*, and *Holzfällen*. One
of his intended projects now that he has become the sole heir and
master of Wolfsegg, is to restore the "Kindervilla" in a symbolic attempt to recapture and relive his childhood (Aus 184, 399–400). He
also attempts to combat insomnia in the night before the funeral by re-
reading Jean Paul's *Siebenkäs* (Aus 540), just as *Siebenkäs* had provided
an escape and refuge from the family when Murau had been a child
(Aus 264–8).

Nevertheless, he realizes the futility of these enterprises. Of the
Kindervilla Murau writes:

> In der Kindervilla suchte ich nach der Kindheit, aber ich fand sie na-
> türlich nicht. In alle Räume trat ich, auf der Suche nach der Kindheit,
> ein, fand sie natürlich nicht. Zu welchem Zweck eigentlich, dachte
> ich, richte ich die Kindervilla her? [. . .] [D]as ist aber absurd, nur dar-
> an zu denken, denn die Kindheit läßt sich nicht mehr herrichten, in-
> dem ich die Kindervilla herrichte, dachte ich [. . .]. [W]ir glauben,
> wenn wir in ein Haus hineingehen, in welchem wir so glückliche
> Kindheitsstunden oder sogar -tage verbracht haben, wir schauen in
> diese Kindheit hinein, aber wir schauen nur in diese berühmt-
> berüchtigte *gähnende Leere* hinein. (Aus 597–8)

The desire to read *Siebenkäs*, on the other hand, is thwarted by Murau's
preoccupation with his current problems. The compulsion to repeat,
then, is avoided, and the text of *Auslöschung* is an attempt to work out
and work through an attitude to temporal process that is more productive, more satisfactory, than mere repetition.

In other words, Murau's purpose in writing *Auslöschung* is to come
to terms with what he himself calls his "Herkunftskomplex" (Aus 201).
Numerous critics have pointed this out,[5] but it has gone unremarked
up to now that Murau also writes of the "*Zukunfts*komplex Wolfsegg"
(Aus 386, my italics). Wolfsegg, then, represents not only the burden
of the past, but also the burden of the future: Murau suddenly finds
himself in the unexpected position of having to deal with the vast property that has been left to him. This interplay between a need to recuperate personal and collective history and a need to orient oneself
toward an uncertain future accounts for the formal dynamics of
*Auslöschung*, which have largely been ignored in the vast body of secondary material on the text, but which can be seen as a solution, at the

level of form, to the problems of history and inheritance raised on the
level of the represented world.

## Narrative Dynamics

Toward the midpoint of the novel, Murau confesses: "Das Zögern ist
meine Art" (Aus 333). At that juncture, it is a justification for his reluctance to enter the grounds of Wolfsegg and his voyeuristic desire to
observe the gardeners at work without being seen himself. But it can
also be read as a metatextual comment on the way in which the narrative strategies of *Auslöschung* rely on complex forms of delay and deferral.

There are several embedded narratives within the text that dramatize
this process. Upon his return to Rome after his sister's nuptials, Murau
reports on his trip to Gambetti, but his "Bericht" is "zu ausführlich, ja
tatsächlich zu geschwätzig" (Aus 10), which attests to a certain unwillingness to reach the end of his narrative. This pattern is repeated in
modified form at those points where an intended disquisition upon a
particular topic is interrupted by lengthy digressions on ostensibly unrelated subjects. Murau announces to Gambetti: "ich werde versuchen,
Ihnen eine präzise Beschreibung von Wolfsegg zu geben" (Aus 153),
and then launches into a speech on the difficulty of understanding philosophy. "Ich war auch an diesem Abend," he realizes, "anstatt gleich
die angekündigte Beschreibung von Wolfsegg zu geben, die Gambetti
noch auf der Flaminia versprochene, auf einen meiner von mir selbst
immer am meisten gefürchteten Exkurse gekommen" (Aus 156; cf. also
162). The same happens when Murau begins narrating the *Siebenkäs*
episode, in which he became so engrossed in Jean Paul's novel that he
missed a family mealtime and was incarcerated in his bedroom as a punishment. Having barely embarked on his narrative, however, Murau
soon turns to the time spent helping his mother to sort her letters on
Saturday afternoons (Aus 264–6). Once again, he is aware of his digression: "Aber ich wollte ja etwas anderes sagen, Gambetti, hatte ich zu
diesem auf dem Pincio gesagt" (Aus 266). The digressions in these two
passages are indicative of the general tendency in *Auslöschung* to resist
closure and avoid coming to the point.

Murau's difficulty in telling the story he sets out to tell is symptomatic of the overall functioning of form and the manipulation of strategies of enigma and suspense in *Auslöschung*. If we return to the
embedded narratives quoted above, it becomes clear that the digressions are a mode of postponing a narrative confrontation that would
cause Murau some form of "unpleasure." In the first instance, this is an

engagement with Wolfsegg, and instead of facing the concrete problem of his "Herkunftskomplex," Murau retreats into the comparative comfort of abstract philosophical discourse. In the second, it is the showdown with his family and his subsequent solitary confinement as he is banished to his bedroom for three days. The narration of this punishment is deferred as Murau recalls the relatively pleasant Saturday ritual of "Briefeordnen," the sole occasions on which he was aware of any maternal affection.

Embedded narratives can be related to the primary story either syntagmatically or paradigmatically: syntagmatically by providing explanatory information that contributes to the linear reconstruction of events, and paradigmatically by functioning as a metaphor for the telling process itself. Almost all the embedded tales in *Auslöschung* fall into the first category, and tend to be linked to the minimal narrative on the primary time level in terms of chronology and causality, however remote. As we shall see, however, the two narratives above are also related to the text of *Auslöschung* in a mode of similarity: they replicate in microcosm the dynamics of the text as a whole.

The opening of *Auslöschung*, for example, is striking for its curious and indirect approach to the event which triggers off the entire narrative, namely the arrival of the telegram informing Murau of his parents' and brother's deaths. The subordinate clause with which the text begins defers the main clause narrating the arrival of the telegram until the fifteenth line of the page, a device that is the first of many delaying tactics Murau uses to postpone having to consider the implications of the telegram.

At certain points during the first chapter, he draws the reader's attention to such strategies. In connection with the dream narrative involving a meeting in the Grödnertal to discuss Schopenhauer's philosophy and Maria's poetry, he writes: "ich habe mich, das Telegramm in Händen, vom Telegramm ablenken wollen auf alle Fälle und so war mir der Traum als das günstigste Mittel für eine solche Ablenkung von diesem zweifellos furchtbaren Telegramm erschienen" (Aus 212).[6] A little later, Murau asks himself how his sisters will greet him now that he has become the heir of Wolfsegg and executor of his parents' will, and wonders whether they will welcome him "in dieser, wie es mir scheint, *unverschämten Weise*" (Aus 250). Significantly, though, he adds, "Ich getraute mich nicht, diesen Gedanken fortzuführen, ich hütete mich davor." This again draws attention to the fact that the narrative relies on strategies of postponement. And lest there be any doubt, Murau — who is nothing if not a self-conscious narrator — spells it out:

ich [bin] jetzt durch das Telegramm dazu gezwungen [. . .], in der
kürzestmöglichen Zeit nach Wolfsegg zurückzukehren. Diese Selbst-
verständlichkeit aber glaubte ich jetzt, durch absolute Untätigkeit,
*hinausschieben* zu können, indem ich einfach am Schreibtisch sitzen
blieb und die Fotografien betrachtete. (Aus 254, my italics)

The second chapter is structured in like fashion. While waiting in
front of the gates to Wolfsegg, Murau thinks, "ich ziehe meinen tatsächlichen Auftritt in Wolfsegg auf die ungeheuerlichste Weise hinaus"
(Aus 329). He feels unable to face up to the deaths of his parents and
Johannes by viewing their laid-out corpses in the orangery, and it is
only some sixty-five pages later that this sequence of deferral comes to
an end: "ich wollte das furchtbare Unumgängliche nicht mehr hinausschieben" (Aus 394). Before that happens, however, he self-consciously
puts off the meeting with his sisters, declaring that he has no desire to
go up to see them straightaway, preferring to wait for a few minutes in
the lobby (Aus 359). As we have seen in the discussion of *Holzfällen*,
motivation in fiction is not merely psychological, but is dictated by narrative design. Here, then, the desire to defer confrontation with the
implications of the telegram — meeting his sisters, viewing his parents'
corpses — can be read psychologically as a desire to avoid "unpleasure," and narratively as a structuring procedure that allows the expansion of the "dilatory space" within which Murau's excavations of the
past can unfold.[7]

What all these examples have in common is that they simultaneously
posit and defer an endpoint, whether the latter be conceived as a physical action or as an act of storytelling. They thus illustrate *in nuce* the
conflict between the two contradictory narrative impulses: on the one
hand the desire for closure, and on the other a resistance to the end.
This clearly corresponds, at a formal level, to Murau's declared aim in
writing *Auslöschung*: the orientation toward the past (the "Herkunftskomplex"), which the various structures of deferral facilitate, is structured by, and included within, an orientation toward the future (the
"Zukunftskomplex").

These analyses of embedded narratives apply *mutatis mutandis* to
the text of *Auslöschung* as a whole. As in most of Bernhard's novels, the
retarding elements, such as embedded narratives and extended passages
of what might loosely be termed interior monologue, are dominant in
*Auslöschung*, but they are embedded within sequences of enigma and
suspense that provide the text with its forward momentum towards the
*telos*. As in *Holzfällen*, the first of these "hermeneutic sequences" is in-
augurated by the title of the text: what, precisely, is to be extinguished,
obliterated, erased? The word "Auslöschung" turns out to be polyse-

mous, and the "enigma" of *Auslöschung* is solved in a variety of ways. As Silke Schlichtmann has shown, it has a threefold field of usage: it is an act of social violence carried out by governments and the Catholic church in order to destroy nature, culture and the individual subject; it refers to Murau's individual act of writing: "mein Bericht ist nur dazu da, das in ihm Beschriebene auszulöschen, alles auszulöschen, das ich unter Wolfsegg verstehe, und alles, das Wolfsegg ist" (Aus 199); and finally, it possesses a metatextual function and refers to the final text of "Auslöschung," that is, Murau's report itself. This report is the text we read, with the exception of the interjections of an extradiegetic narrator that introduce and conclude the monologue: "schreibt Murau, Franz-Joseph" (Aus 7) and "schreibt Murau (geboren 1934 in Wolfsegg, gestorben 1983 in Rom)" (Aus 651; cf. Schlichtmann 23–7).

Schlichtmann also undertakes an interesting analysis of the distribution of the various words within the semantic field of destruction, but does not link this to the narrative dynamics of the text. What seems to me significant is that the third sense of "Auslöschung" predominates in the final third of the text, occurring four times (Aus 457–8, 542–3, 612, 651), while the other usages are absent. In the reading process, the hermeneutic sequence surrounding the title is kept open because of a constant oscillation between the possible solutions, but the "metatextual" solution to the enigma is the one that finally has priority and subsumes the other two meanings. Thus the functioning of the title itself guides the text through openness to closure by keeping the sequence open until the final stages, when a univocal solution asserts itself. Other hermeneutic sequences operate in a similar fashion.

The final sentence of the first chapter of *Auslöschung* reads: "Was das Telegramm bedeutete, wußte ich" (Aus 310). This represents at once Murau's finally facing up to the implications of his parents' accident and a further sequence of deferral, for there is a discrepancy between what the narrator knows and what the reader knows; we are still in ignorance as to what the telegram "means." This creates an enigma and incites the reader's desire for the knowledge that Murau is deliberately withholding. Throughout "Das Testament" this enigma is reformulated on numerous occasions, keeping the sequence open and delaying the end, which is conceived in terms of how Murau is going to distribute his inheritance. Indeed, the entire second chapter is abundant in Murau's claims to nescience as far as the future is concerned. When his sisters demand that he protect them, he states,

> Aber so wenig, wie sie es selbst wissen konnten, was nun geschehen werde, so wenig wußte ich es selbst, denn die Tatsache, daß mir und zwar ausschließlich mir der ganze Komplex mit allen seinen Aus- und

> Einwirkungen zugefallen war, hatte ich noch nicht einmal im gering-
> sten überlegt gehabt, weder am Vortag in Rom, in Anbetracht des
> zweifellos schockierenden Telegramms, noch bis zu diesem Zeitpunkt
> [. . .] (Aus 386)

Similarly, when the cook refers to him as "den *Herrn*," he says that the
implications of that title had not yet sunk in (Aus 408); and when his
sisters question him about the immediate future, he does not answer
them because, so he claims, he is as ignorant as they about the immediate future of Wolfsegg (Aus 527). The function of Caecilia and Amalia
is, in a sense, to guide the reading of the text: they ask the questions
that are also those of the implied reader, and Murau keeps us — as well
as his sisters — in ignorance.

Murau's protestation that he has no idea what he intends to do with
the estate, however, is disingenuous, for his frequent reformulations of
the enigma of Wolfsegg's future are punctuated by hints that form, if
not the definitive "résolution de l'énigme," then certainly a set of
"leurres" and "réponses partielles." The expressed desire to have the
Wolfsegg paintings valued (Aus 374), the intention to restore the
paintings as well as the "Kindervilla" and the dairy (Aus 399–400), and
the decision to open up all the libraries attest to a certain restorative
impulse, a kind of rehabilitation of Wolfsegg.

However, such renovative intentions are undermined by a parallel
sense that the estate will be dissolved. When wondering what will happen to Caecilia and Amalia, Murau claims to have no precise idea of
what they will have to endure, "aber doch eine Ahnung davon, daß diese Ahnung eine böse war, war mir klar" (Aus 423). We soon learn that
they would certainly not be staying in Wolfsegg with Murau (Aus 432),
and that the latter's plans for the "Weinflaschenstöpselfabrikant" involve his unceremonious expulsion from the property (Aus 476). Already, the thought that he could pay his sisters off has occurred to him
(Aus 388), and it appears again later: "ich dachte von Anfang an mehr
an eine Auszahlung der Schwestern, denn an eine Wolfsegger Teilung
mit ihnen" (Aus 527). The general assumption that he will take over
the administration of Wolfsegg is described by Murau as "ein ganz und
gar absurder Gedanke": he is utterly unwilling to give up the life he has
made for himself in Rome (Aus 482). The hermeneutic sequence is
thus kept open by constant oscillation between three possibilities. Either Murau does not know what he plans to do with Wolfsegg, or he
intends to renovate and restore it, or he intends to banish his sisters
and brother-in-law and return to Rome.

The final page offers a definitive solution, but even here Murau's
manipulatory strategies are in evidence:

Ich hatte schon einen Plan für Wolfsegg und alles, das auch in Nie-
derösterreich und im Burgenland und in Wien dazugehört, im Kopf,
als ich mich mit den Schwestern [. . .] über die Zukunft von Wolfsegg
unterhalten habe bis zwei Uhr früh. Am Ende der Unterhaltung
konnte ich den Schwestern nicht sagen, was mit Wolfsegg geschehen
wird, obwohl ich es zu diesem Zeitpunkt schon gewußt habe, ich
sagte ihnen, [. . .] ich wisse nicht, was mit Wolfsegg geschieht, hätte
nicht die geringste Vorstellung in dieser Frage, während ich doch
gleichzeitig fest entschlossen war, mich bei Eisenberg in Wien zu mel-
den auf ein Gespräch, in welchem ich ihm ganz Wolfsegg [. . .] der Is-
raelitischen Kultusgemeinde in Wien anbieten wollte. (Aus 650)

His treatment of Caecilia and Amalia here mirrors, at the level of story,
his treatment of the reader at the level of narration, for because the
mode of narration in *Auslöschung* is ulterior, Murau would have been
in full knowledge of the "résolution de l'énigme" before starting his
tale. Murau's professed ignorance about his plans for Wolfsegg is a device that prevents the collapse of the end into the beginning. It is a
necessary fiction that facilitates the construction of a primary time level
from which he can explore his "Herkunftskomplex."

Like several other novels discussed in this study, *Auslöschung* involves an excavation of the past even as it moves forward into the future. This future, the "Zukunftskomplex," is embodied in the
hermeneutic code: the primary time level is propelled forward by manipulation of the reader's desire for knowledge, and the final narrative
closure is provided by the satisfaction of that curiosity, namely the
revelation of Murau's decision to donate the entire Wolfsegg estate to
the "Israelitische Kultusgemeinde in Wien." This is an issue to which
we shall return in the final section of this chapter.

## Narrative, Perspectivism, and Laughter

We have seen that Murau's narrative seeks to restore a sense of history,
not as merely "zu Hunderten und Tausenden aufeinandergelegten Ruhmesblätter, sondern als Ganzes" (Aus 57). In terms of narrative form, this
project relies on the techniques of deferral discussed previously. Yet the
desire for history-as-totality is undermined by Murau's simultaneous recognition of the perspectivism inherent in narrative representation.

Unlike their twentieth-century counterparts, nineteenth-century
historical novelists were not concerned with the question of perspectivism. Realism, the dominant mode of nineteenth-century fiction, rested
on the assumption that there was an external object-world that was
knowable to human subjects and capable of representation through the

transparent medium of language. Like most fiction writers of the period
— and, indeed, most historians — historical novelists tended to locate
the narrator at the pole of maximum covertness, thereby obscuring his
ideological and organizational functions.[8]

While the historical novel largely went into eclipse during the Modernist period, the reemergence of historical fiction in the past four decades has been accompanied by an awareness of the structuring role of the
narrator, and the ideological context in which he or she is writing has
been heavily foregrounded.[9] This can be seen in the work of numerous
post-1945 German novelists, including (to quote merely some famous
examples) Thomas Mann's *Doktor Faustus*, Günter Grass's *Danziger
Trilogie* and *Der Butt*, Siegfried Lenz's *Deutschstunde*, Christa Wolf's
*Kindheitsmuster*, and Heinrich Böll's *Gruppenbild mit Dame*. In all these
novels, the first-person form is the main device that contributes to this
end, making the reader aware that the narrative design is the product of
a single organizing consciousness. The time structure, too, throws the
structuring role of the narrator into even greater relief: references to the
moment of writing make it clear that what can be known and transmitted about the past is that which can be (re-) constructed in the present.
In *Auslöschung*, references to the discursive situation are signaled as usual
by present tense verbs and proximal deixis.[10]

*Auslöschung*, however, extends and complicates the tripartite temporal
structure that was developed by Bernhard in *Wittgensteins Neffe* and re-
fined in the texts that followed it. A device new to *Auslöschung*, which
again stresses the moment of construction, is the introduction of a further, unspecified time-level on which Murau's conversations with his
"pupil" Gambetti take place. These conversations are signaled by phrases
such as "hatte/habe ich zu Gambetti gesagt," or merely by the periodic
insertion of a vocative "Gambetti." They are located at an intermediate
stage between the primary time level and the more distant past of Murau's childhood and early adulthood, and they function within the narrative economy to show that the completed narrative, *Auslöschung*, is the
result of numerous fragmentary and provisional narrative acts that cannot
be — or at least *are* not — integrated into an overarching macronarrative
(Korte 92; Gößling, *"Eisenbergrichtung"* 8; Finnern 21). In addition,
they situate Murau's utterances in a concrete communicative context, for
they all take place in Rome, and certain of them even at specific periods in
specific geographical locations (Aus 153–4).

Contextualization in itself is a relativizing device: the narrative is
shown to be determined by the circumstances of its production. The
relativization is likewise achieved through the inclusion of an intradiegetic narratee (that is, a narratee who is part of the represented

world). Bernhard's texts are, admittedly, abundant in intradiegetic narratees, but they are generally themselves the primary narrators of the text and exist as narratees only insofar as they report the words of another central character: the "Famulant" in *Frost*, the narrators of *Verstörung*, *Das Kalkwerk*, *Gehen*, *Korrektur*, and *Die Billigesser*. In *Auslöschung* this structure is reversed: Murau relates not what another character has said to him, but rather what he has said to another character.[11] By also reporting his interlocutor's reactions, however, he opens up a self-critical perspective, which again calls into question the reliability of his judgments.

Like all narratives, the stories Murau tells to Gambetti can be conceived as performances whose aim is to produce a certain effect in the narratee, be it to persuade, convince, amuse, win sympathy, or gain power. One of the difficulties in *Auslöschung*, however, is to establish the extent to which the eventual effect is intended or not. Does Gambetti refuse the role of passive listener, refuse to succumb to the power of the teller, and inscribe dissent within his response? Or are his reactions precisely what Murau intends? For his usual reaction to Murau's diatribes against Austria and Wolfsegg is to laugh.

After denouncing Wolfsegg as a "Puppenhaus" and "Puppenwelt," Murau writes: "Gambetti hatte laut aufgelacht und mich einen maßlosen Übertreiber genannt, mich als typisch österreichischen Schwarzmaler bezeichnet, als grotesken Negativisten" (Aus 123–4). This structure, whereby Murau's denunciations are followed by Gambetti's laughter, recurs throughout the text (Aus 163, 183, 576, 610), and the net result is that Murau is himself drawn into the "Gambettilachen": "Die Fotografie ist ihre Rettung, Gambetti, hatte ich gesagt, worauf Gambetti gelacht und mich einen *Vormittagsphantasten* genannt hat, einen Ausdruck also verwendet hatte, den ich noch niemals gehört hatte, was meinerseits ein Gelächter zur Folge hatte" (Aus 128), and later: "Gambetti hat meine Theorie schließlich nur lachend aufgenommen, ich hatte mich an seinem Lachen beteiligt" (Aus 480; see also 611).

One thing that can be said for this device is that it appears to be endorsed by the text: by joining in with the laughter, Murau is aligning himself with Gambetti's — and by implication the reader's — laughing reception of his narratives. Korte suggests that *Auslöschung* can be read as the parodic inverse of the *Bildungsroman*: "Unermüdlich zwar redet der Erzähler auf Gambetti ein, aber er breitet monoton und monoman das eigene Leid aus," and the relationship between the two highlights isolation, not integration (Korte 95–6). Gambetti's laughter, too, turns the traditional relationship between pupil and mentor on its head: "einmal bin ich der Lehrer Gambettis und er ist mein Schüler, dann wieder ist Gambetti mein Lehrer und ich bin sein Schüler, und sehr oft ist es der Fall, daß wir beide nicht wissen, ist jetzt Gambetti der Schüler und bin ich der Lehrer oder umgekehrt" (Aus 10). As Andreas Herzog writes: "Daß genaue Zuhörerschaft nicht Hörigkeit bedeutet, signalisiert das Lachen von Muraus Vorzugsschüler Gambetti, wenn Murau und Bernhard wieder einmal übertrieben haben" ("Vom Studenten" 120).

Helga Schultheiß's review, enticingly entitled "Wie überleben? Alles weglachen!" is disappointingly silent on the role of laughter in *Auslöschung*, but laughter fulfills an important dual function. First, it amounts to a recognition of perspectivism that, as in *Wittgensteins Neffe* and *Der Untergeher*, is also explicitly signaled by the narrator at numerous points in the text. Murau emphasizes that he can only represent Wolfsegg as *he* sees it, because every representation is inescapably determined by the perspective of the observer (Aus 197). Similarly, he is aware that the reports of his parents' accident given by the newspapers and his sisters are necessarily discrepant, even though they are talking about the same accident (Aus 414); and that personal identity, too, is a function of perspectivism: "Jeder sieht immer einen anderen, wenn er auch denselben beschreibt, dachte ich. So viele Beschreiber, so viele Seher, jeder aus einer andern Richtung, aus einem andern Blickwinkel heraus auf dieselbe Person" (Aus 550).

Laughter, by both Murau and Gambetti, thus serves as implicit self-criticism, a relativization of Murau's own conceptual categories and structuring procedures. Certain passages of the text make explicit Murau's realization that his habit of passing negative judgments on Wolfsegg and his family is possibly unjust, and determined by his need to assuage what psychoanalytically oriented studies have identified as his guilt (Klug, "Interaktion"; Treichel 62–3; Gößling, *"Eisenbergrichtung"* 23–7): "Diese Gewohnheit ist eine Waffe, die im Grunde eine Infamie ist, mit welcher wahrscheinlich nur ein schlechtes Gewissen befriedigt werden muß" (Aus 105). Furthermore, Murau is aware that the denigration of others is a means of asserting the self:

> wir geben so lange nicht Ruhe, bis wir aus dem guten, liebenswürdigen, einen schlechten, nichtswürdigen gemacht haben, weil es uns paßt, weil wir zu einem solchen Mißbrauch bereit sind, wie wir ja zu allem Mißbrauch bereit sind, um uns beispielsweise aus fürchterlich quälenden Stimmungen herauszuretten, in die wir hineingekommen sind, ohne zu wissen, wodurch. (Aus 596)

Bernhard's characters, as Christian Klug has pointed out, are not always blind to the "blind spots" in their own thinking: "nachträglich kann ihnen klar werden, was sie gesagt haben, und zuweilen auch, wie peinlich ihre Selbstinszenierung gewesen ist" ("Interaktion" 19). This clarity is partly a function of the narrative technique of the intradiegetic narratee and his infectious laughter. Nevertheless, it need not lead to an acknowledgement of "Peinlichkeit," but can rather give way to an almost joyous awareness of perspectivism, which undermines the potentially monological, monolithic nature of Murau's narrative.[12]

This leads us to the second function of laughter in the text — the debunking of all that occupies an elevated position in the hierarchies of power. This can be seen in the previous quotation, where the hierarchies of "gut-schlecht" and "liebenswürdig-unliebenswürdig" are turned on their heads. It also manifests itself in Onkel Georg's comic debunking of the work ethic and regimented lifestyle of his elder brother, Gambetti's debunking of his "teacher" Murau, and Murau's own mirth at his mother's belief that Jean Paul's *Siebenkäs* was in fact a ruse, invented by Murau himself to irritate her (Aus 207).

This aspect of the laughter in *Auslöschung* becomes especially evident at the point where Murau views a painting of the Madonna and Child:

> Der Hals der Muttergottes auf diesem Bild ist so lang, wie ich noch niemals einen gemalten Hals gesehen habe, allen Erfahrungen der Anatomie vollkommen widersprechend. Das Jesuskind auf dem Bild hat einen Wasserkopf. Der Anblick dieses Bildes hat mich schon immer belustigt und er belustigte mich auch jetzt. Ich mußte laut aus mir herauslachen, mir war es gleichgültig, ob man mich gehört hat oder nicht. (Aus 523)

This is a denigration of religious iconography that as Mikhail Bakhtin has shown, was a prominent aspect of the carnivalesque. Renaissance parody and grotesque realism "degrade, bring down to earth, turn their subject into flesh" (20), which is precisely what Murau does here: by concentrating on the comical physical attributes of the Madonna and Child, he robs them of their exalted spiritual status and reduces them to the level of common humanity.

For Bakhtin, the philosophical meaning of Renaissance laughter was to see the world "in its droll aspect, its gay relativity" (66–7), a meaning that was lost in the seventeenth century as laughter was displaced into what Bakhtin calls the "low genres" and became narrowly satirical in its aims (11). Although it would be overstating the case to cast Murau in the role of Renaissance fool, there are nevertheless certain moments in *Auslöschung* where the carnivalesque spirit does manifest itself, and this has no precedent in Bernhard's writing. Those critics who accused Bernhard of producing the merely old under the guise of novelty were blind to the subtler variations of narrative technique, for the role of laughter and its all-embracing critical and defamiliarizing import is a function of the totally new device of the intradiegetic narratee: Gambetti.

This technique is not without its problems, though. By means of laughter, Murau criticizes and debunks power, and undermines authority. At the same time, however, the laughter is turned against him, which threatens to divest his critique of any legitimacy it might have possessed. In other words, Murau's own critical standpoint is destabilized by the very techniques he uses to establish that standpoint in the first place. The issue of legitimation is fundamental to his whole narrative enterprise, and is the subject of the next segment.

## History and Legitimation

Although the achronological, associative time structure and the use of embedded perspectives situates *Auslöschung* firmly within the formal tradition of Modernism, it draws on the thematics of the family saga, a fictional subgenre that was dominant in the nineteenth century but tends to occur in the twentieth either as nostalgia (Evelyn Waugh's *Brideshead Revisited*) or in the mode of satire (Doderer's *Die Merowinger*). In Germany, the most conspicuous example is Thomas Mann's *Buddenbrooks: Verfall einer Familie*, a text that is at once the apotheosis and negation of the nineteenth-century tradition.

Schlichtmann has drawn attention to the similar subtitles of *Buddenbrooks: Verfall einer Familie* and *Auslöschung: Ein Zerfall* (39). Although a comparison of the two novels falls outside the scope of both her analysis and the present study, there are certainly conspicuous similarities between Murau and Hanno Buddenbrook. They are both, for example, the sickly, artistic latecomers of a robust dynasty that now appears doomed due to historical circumstance. They are also both aware that they are the last of the line. Hanno's moment of insight comes when he draws a thick horizontal line across the family chronicle kept by his father, stammering the excuse, "Ich glaubte . . . ich glaubte . . . es käme nichts mehr . . ." (523). Murau gains a similar awareness during his nocturnal visit to the "Kindervilla":

> Zu welchem Zweck eigentlich, dachte ich, richte ich die Kindervilla her? Wo gar niemand mehr da ist, der die Kindervilla genießen, sie ausnützen kann, dachte ich und darauf, daß es doch sinnlos wäre, die Kindervilla, so wie ich es bis zu diesem Augenblick vorgehabt habe, herzurichten, aus ihr wieder die Kindervilla zu machen, die sie einmal gewesen ist *uns Kindern*, dachte ich, das ist eher absurd[.] (Aus 597)

One issue we need to address, then, is Bernhard's treatment of the literary topos of upper-class decline at a time when such a theme appears almost a century "out of date."

Family sagas deal with the problem of authority and its transmission from generation to generation. In the section on *Verstörung* in chapter 2, we noted Dorothy Dinnerstein's assertion that the production of an heir and the passing of the father's name from one generation to the next were a patriarchal compensation for men's lack of bodily connection with the child. Commenting on this passage, Jonathan Culler goes on to suggest that men tend to value metaphorical relations — "relations of resemblance between separate items which can be substituted for one another, such as obtain between the father and the miniature replica with the same name, the child" — over metonymic maternal relationships based on contiguity (*On Deconstruction* 60).

Murau's depictions of Wolfsegg emphasize precisely those aspects of male succession enumerated here: his father's marrying for no other purpose than to produce an heir (Aus 294), and the fact that his son Johannes turns into a younger version of himself: "wie sein Vater, dachte ich, führt er das Leben eines von Millionen von Duplikaten dieser alten Gesellschaft" (Aus 352). Johannes adopts not only the external trappings of his father's lifestyle, but threatens to appropriate his very being:

> Mein Bruder wird immer mehr zu meinem Vater, habe ich oft gedacht. Er hat sich ihm in letzter Zeit schon ganz angenähert, es dauert nicht mehr lange, habe ich bei der Hochzeit gedacht, und *er ist unser Vater*. [. . .] Der erstgeborene Sohn ist sozusagen von Anfang an bestimmt gewesen, der Vater zu sein und wird es bald sein, habe ich gedacht. Es ist das nur noch eine Frage der kürzesten Zeit. Und manchmal habe ich ja auch, wenn der Bruder spricht, das Gefühl, es spricht der Vater, höre ich den Bruder gehen, es geht der Vater, denkt der Bruder, es denkt der Vater. (Aus 353)

Onkel Georg goes so far as to comment that before long, Johannes will have not only taken *on* the bitter and disappointed facial features of his father, but taken them *over* in the same way that people take over property (Aus 92).

Metaphorical identification, then, is linked to the transmission of property from father to son, a process that places the son in the same *metonymic* relation to the property as the father.[13] These metonymic links — subsumed, of course, within the larger metaphor — are established through exchange, the passing of material goods from one generation to the next. This implies an unproblematic sense of historical continuity whose authority and legitimacy are conferred by the symbolic act of bequest and inheritance.

Its discursive correlative is the "zu Hunderten und Tausenden aufeinandergelegten Ruhmesblätter" (Aus 57) mentioned earlier. These constitute an example of history as annal or chronicle, which Walter Benjamin contrasts with "historiography" or narrative history:

> Der Historiker ist gehalten, die Vorfälle, mit denen er es zu tun hat, auf die eine oder andere Art zu erklären; er kann sich unter keinen Umständen damit begnügen, sie als Musterstücke des Weltverlaufs herzuzeigen. Genau das aber tut der Chronist, und besonders nachdrücklich tut er das in seinen klassischen Repräsentanten, den Chronisten des Mittelalters, die die Vorläufer der neueren Geschichtsschreiber waren. Indem jene ihrer Geschichtserzählung den göttlichen Heilsplan zugrunde legen, der ein unerforschlicher ist, haben sie die Last beweisbarer Erklärung von vornherein von sich abgewältzt. (397)

Events are not rendered meaningful through integration within a narrative uniting beginnings and middles under the aspect of the end. Rather, they are "aufeinander gelegt," that is, piled up unreflectively — in a manner akin to the pickle jars with which we began — and their very inclusion in the list functions as guarantee of their legitimacy. The presupposed framework of meaning that grants automatic significance to the individual acts of the Murau family is no longer Christian eschatology, but rather a secular assumption of the correctness of the social order and the tradition of bequest and inheritance. Benjamin's point, however, facilitates a crucial insight into the nature of Murau's narrative task.

In order to escape the authority of the tradition, Murau refuses to conform to the metaphorical pattern: he is not *like* his father, cannot be *substituted* for him:

> Der Bruder hatte sich zum Idealbild erziehen lassen, ich hatte mich immer dieser Zumutung entzogen, ich war an der Darstellung eines solchen elterlichen Idealbildes niemals interessiert gewesen, ich verabscheute ein solches, weil ich, kurz gesagt, niemals einem Vorbild entsprechen habe wollen und dadurch auch niemals ein Idealbild hätte sein können. (Aus 354)

This rejection of the paternal tradition has been linked by Chantal Thomas to the diatribes against photography in *Auslöschung*:

> Produire des doubles, c'est l'objet de la photographie, c'est le désir des géniteurs. La méditation sur les *êtres photographiés* à quoi se réduit la famille se confond avec une réflexion sur des êtres qui n'existent que dans et par la famille, et dont l'existence était déjà programmé en tant que continuité de celle des parents. Je ne serai pas un double, se défend Murau. (229)

He also severs any remaining metonymic links with his family by escaping to Rome.

Murau's rejection of these links, however, also entails a relinquishment of the authority bestowed by the family tradition. This means that rather than being immediately comprehensible in terms of a pre-existent structure of meaning, Murau's narratives have to deal with the burden of explanation: he is, as Benjamin puts it, "gehalten, die Vorfälle [. . .] auf die eine oder andere Art zu erklären," and his narratives have to create their own strategies of legitimation. One means by which this is done is through the establishment of an ersatz tradition. Murau attempts both to *follow* and to *be* a "Vorbild" in a metaphorical mode that is even more radical than that of habitual patrilinear succession. He achieves this by substituting for the biological family a genealogy of the intellect that relies exclusively on metaphorical connections.

This tendency is manifested in the short story "Montaigne." It can be read as a forerunner of *Auslöschung*, and involves the narrator's escaping from his family into the library. Here he settles to read, and explicitly sets up a family of philosophers in opposition to his biological family, speaking of

> meiner unendlich großen philosophischen Familie, die ich doch nur als eine unendlich große französische Familie bezeichnen kann, in welcher es immer nur ein paar deutsche und italienische Neffen und Nichten gegeben hat, die aber alle, muß ich sagen, sehr früh gestorben sind. (14)

Later he writes that he has never had a father or mother, but always "his" Montaigne (15).

Murau likewise replaces the family — and more specifically the father — with the art and philosophy of the past (Sorg, *Thomas Bernhard* 129; Vogel 186). In addition, he sets up a "spiritual paternity" consisting of Onkel Georg, a relationship which is structurally identical to that between Johannes and his father: "Wenn ich dich sehe, sagte mein Onkel Georg, sehe ich im Grunde immer mich" (Aus 57). Murau's life then repeats that of Onkel Georg in numerous ways. He escapes to the Mediterranean South, devotes himself to a life of the intellect, and conceives of his "Auslöschung" as a repetition of Onkel Georg's "Antiautobiografie" (Aus 197). He also reproduces Georg's liberating act of opening the bookcases (Aus 147, 150). Of the greatest significance, however, is the fact that the Onkel Georg-Murau constellation is repeated in Murau's relationship with Gambetti:

> in Wirklichkeit bringe ich ihn aber ganz konsequent von seinen Eltern und deren Ideen ab, dachte ich, [. . .] ich spiele die Rolle des Onkels Georg, dachte ich, der mich aus Wolfsegg vertrieben hat mit seinen Gedanken und Eröffnungen über Wolfsegg und was das bedeutete, bis mir Wolfsegg einfach unmöglich gewesen ist, daß ich Gambetti,

wie mich mein Onkel Georg aus Wolfsegg, aus der Welt seiner Eltern vertreibe. (Aus 208)

Schlichtmann points out that the positive figures in *Auslöschung* represent a compensatory counter-history of humane values and "geistige Kultur" (67). For her, this is the antithesis of the negative teleology of historical degeneration that she discerns in Murau's report (39–65). In fact, this structure of repetition from Onkel Georg through Murau to Gambetti sets up a parallel genealogy to rival the Wolfsegg line and provides a replacement tradition of authority whose function is to *legitimize Murau's very telling* of an alternative history to that represented by the continuity of Wolfsegg.

Following on from this, the second strategy of legitimation adopted by Murau is a function of the text's complex embedding procedures. The transmission from generation to generation here is no longer a question of property, but of narrative. Onkel Georg's extended monologues to Murau (e.g. Aus 48–59) and Murau's lengthy narratives addressed to Gambetti are both the *result* of the authority provided by the rival genealogy and, paradoxically, also the means by which that authority has to be perpetually re-created. Because the "alternative" history of Wolfsegg is not sanctioned by the self-legitimating tradition, each narrative act has to legitimize itself through its narrative design, whose purpose is to create an authority that allows events to be granted meaning in that particular way.

As we have seen, the construction of meaningful narratives entails positing an end. It is noteworthy that Onkel Georg and Murau are the only characters in the novel who actually tell stories, and they are able to narrativize their experience because their time at Wolfsegg has been brought to a close, furnishing them with a provisional ending. This allows them to interpret diverse and disparate events from their childhood as leading up to the final departure from Wolfsegg. Furthermore, this departure functions as a provisional point of closure for the reader, who can apprehend the numerous fragmentary micronarratives that constitute the text as belonging to the same order of meaning and leading to the same end. The functioning of *ultimate* narrative closure in this text, however, is by no means a simple matter.

## " . . . schreibt Murau . . ."

Although Murau's gift of Wolfsegg to the Israelitische Kultusgemeinde forms the end of the discourse of *Auslöschung*, it is not, strictly speaking, the end of the story. In the final sentence of the text we are informed that Murau returned to Rome, where he wrote the text we have just read. We also learn, via an odd kind of prolepsis supplied by the anonymous third-person narrator, that Murau is now dead. *Auslöschung* is more secure in providing the satisfactions of narrative endings than some of the other Bernhard texts discussed here, for Murau's projected end is an assumption of his own imminent demise.

This is partly a function of the epigraph from Montaigne: "Ich fühle, wie der Tod mich beständig in seinen Klauen hat. Wie ich mich auch verhalte, ist er überall da," but there is a problem of attribution attendant on this motto. It could have been placed there by Murau, by the anonymous extradiegetic narrator, or may be attributed to the real author. Nevertheless, there are echoes of this epigraph in Murau's own discourse: "Meine Zeit, die mir noch bleibt, ist auch nur noch die kürzeste, wenn ich meinen Bericht nicht bald anfange, ist es zu spät. Ich weiß es nicht, aber ich fühle es, hatte ich zu Gambetti gesagt, ich habe nicht mehr viel Zeit" (Aus 199). Furthermore, Murau has a lower-than-average life expectancy (Aus 432), and has been told by doctors that he can expect a short, indeed the shortest life (Aus 620). It is the assumption of his own end that allows Murau to begin and complete his "Auslöschung":

> Die Schwierigkeit ist ja immer nur, wie einen solchen Bericht anfangen, wo einen tatsächlich brauchbaren ersten Satz einer solchen Aufschreibung hernehmen, einen solchen allerersten Satz. In Wahrheit, Gambetti, habe ich ja schon oft angefangen mit diesem Bericht, aber ich bin schon in dem allerersten aufgeschriebenen Satz gescheitert. (Aus 198)

As we have seen, "Der Tod ist die Sanktion von allem, was der Erzähler berichten kann." Murau's eventual death thus validates the narrative, which becomes, as it were, his own obituary.

There are also symbolic deaths at the end of *Auslöschung*. The desire for knowledge about the future of Wolfsegg provides Murau's narrative with its forward impulse, and this desire is expertly maintained by the interplay of the hermeneutic morphemes discussed previously. Nevertheless, the narrowing-down of narrative possibilities results in the ultimate satisfaction of the reader's curiosity, which coincides with the closure of the narrative. The past time of the "Herkunftskomplex" is redeemed, while the "Zukunftskomplex" is transformed from a set of possibilities into a *fait accompli* in the course of the primary time level. The resolution of the enigma and the "end" of the future, which the close of the story represents, are the narrative equivalents of death.

The final sentence of the novel, then, embodies two endings and two acts of transmission: on the one hand, the dissolution of the Wolfsegg estate and its transmission to Eisenberg; and on the other, Murau's individual end and the transmission of his life-story. There is, of course, a structural similarity in these two sets of closure and transmission, for they can be carried out only in the secure knowledge of an endpoint. If death acts as the guarantee of transmissibility of a person's life story, then the death of a family, the lack of future generations allows the bequest of their property to an external beneficiary.[14] Wolfsegg is the "Nachlaß" of the Murau dynasty, and in the knowledge that the dynasty has come to an end, Murau can bequeath the estate to Eisenberg. Like *Watten* of 1969, *Auslöschung* is also "Ein Nachlaß," Murau's "Nachlaß," and in the light of his own death can be transmitted to the readers of the narrative.

The fact that *Auslöschung* ends with the death of the main narrator sets it apart from Bernhard's other texts of the 1980s, and raises once again questions concerning narrative transmission. The problem of transmission beyond the grave had already been thematized in *Auslöschung* through the disappearance of Onkel Georg's "Antiautobiografie"; more significantly, it is dramatized in the narrator's quest for Wertheimer's absent "Zettel" in *Der Untergeher*. In this text, the absence of Wertheimer's "Nachlaß" robs the end of the structural function that the narrator (and reader) assumes it will possess, and modifies its capacity to endow the foregoing with meaning. The projected *telos* turns out to be different from that which arrives, and the reader is, as it were, cheated of that final moment of revelation that would guarantee the significance and transmissibility of all that went before. The end of *Der Untergeher* forces the reader to revise her understanding of the rest of the text, for the various possible reasons for Wertheimer's suicide are not superseded by a definitive revelation in the form of his own writings. Because of this, no single cause can be granted priority over the others, and the end of the text curiously seems to reopen the possibilities which would typically be closed down as the narrative progressed.

The success of narrative transmission in *Auslöschung*, however, is evident in that the text is in front of us and can be read at all. The extradiegetic narrator, despite his being only minimally signaled, is highly significant in this connection, and criticism of *Auslöschung* to this point has failed to adequately address his role.

Those critics who suggest that he represents an editor of Murau's "Nachlaß" have no textual evidence on which to base the claim (Gößling, *"Eisenbergrichtung"* 39; Korte, 99; Marquardt 58), but they have obliquely grasped the fact that he is vital to the transmissibility of the narrative that might otherwise have been lost, like Wertheimer's "Zettel" and Onkel Georg's "Antiautobiografie." Just as Murau functions as a kind of posthumous "Nachlaßverwalter" of the Wolfsegg estate, so the anonymous extradiegetic narrator fulfills the same role in relation to Murau's narrative. We may also draw a parallel between the function of the anonymous narrator and Murau's relationship with Gambetti: the former describes his pedagogical role as a "literarischer Realitätenvermittler [. . .] ich vermittle literarische Liegenschaften sozusagen" (Aus 615): an analogous act of transmission to the one taking place here.

What is curious about the extradiegetic narrator, however, is that in a novel so concerned with questions of contextualization, he remains utterly uncontextualized: we know absolutely nothing about him. Indeed, my very use of the word "him" is a product both of convention and prior knowledge of Bernhard's texts, none of which has a female narrator; but there is no textual evidence for the extradiegetic narrator's sex. The function of this device seems once again to be the assertion of narrative authority, but here it is not context-dependent: while, as I have argued, the individual micronarratives of which the text is composed rely for their legitimacy on the situation of enunciation, the final authority of the extradiegetic narrator seems to claim an absolute, self-sustaining legitimacy.

There are two possible readings of this, the first linked to Bernhard's own career and literary legacy, and the second to do with the wider problematic of the novel, namely its self-imposed task of uncovering the buried Nazi past.

Hans Höller's biographical monograph on Bernhard opens with a discussion of Bernhard's sensational will, a paragraph of which reads:

> Weder aus dem von mir zu Lebzeiten veröffentlichten, noch aus dem nach meinem Tod gleich wo immer noch vorhandenen Nachlaß darf auf die Dauer des gesetzlichen Urheberrechtes innerhalb der Grenzen des österreichischen Staates, wie immer dieser Staat sich kennzeichnet, etwas in welcher Form immer von mir verfaßtes Geschriebenes aufgeführt, gedruckt oder auch nur vorgetragen werden.
>
> [. . .] Nach meinem Tod darf aus meinem eventuell gleich wo vorhandenen literarischen Nachlaß, worunter auch Briefe und Zettel zu verstehen sind, *kein Wort* mehr veröffentlicht werden. (Qtd. in Höller, *Thomas Bernhard* 7)

Among other things, Bernhard is here preventing posthumous anonymous editors from disseminating his unpublished works. In this light, Bernhard can be seen, in *Auslöschung*, to be pre-empting such editorial interventions by having his fictional extradiegetic narrator exercising control over the posthumous life story and "literarischen Nachlaß" of his protagonist and surrogate, Franz-Josef Murau.

More problematically, the function of the extradiegetic narrator is intimately connected with questions of history and narrative closure. At numerous points in the text, Murau articulates the need to remember and represent the Nazi past. The avowed task of the whole "Auslöschung" project is to lift what Murau perceives as the tendency of Austrian society to repress and remain silent about the less noble aspects of its past (Aus 193–7), and indeed, we have seen how this is manifested in both the imagery and the structure of the narrative.

Nevertheless, there seems to be some kind of conflict between the need for openness on the one hand, and on the other the definitive closures and acts of transmission with which this narrative concludes, and which all narrative appears to demand. Murau's gift of Wolfsegg to the "Israelitische Kultusgemeinde" has generally been viewed by critics as a positive gesture of atonement for the atrocities perpetrated against the Jews by the Nazis, but Irene Heidelberger-Leonard proposes a more negative reading. She argues that Eisenberg represents not the Jew as victim, but as one who, in Murau's dream at least, successfully resists his persecutors. "Eisenberg, der *über* den Geschichtsabgründen schwebende Erlöser mit Bart und langem schwarzen Mantel, inszeniert durch die Annahme des Tributs, das ihm Murau entrichtet, die unverhoffte politische Lösung, die Versöhnung der 'Menschheitsgeschichte'" (190).[15] She sees in Murau's refusal to take over Wolfsegg — which is a spatial symbol of the Nazi past — an "Akt der Verdrängung schlimmster Art," tantamount to a refusal to bear the burden of Austrian history: "Aber indem Thomas Bernhard Murau die Schenkung vornehmen und uns durch den Herausgeber mitteilen läßt, daß die 'Selbstauslöschung' geglückt ist, entzieht er sich dem lebenslänglichen Kampf um die Korrektur der Geschichte, den er noch zu führen gedachte" (191).

There is something of an aporetic moment in the structure of *Auslöschung*. On the one hand, as we have seen, the sense of an ending is a prerequisite of narrative, and it is only by positing some kind of end that the history of Wolfsegg and its Nazi past can be narrativized at all. On the other hand, the imposition of an endpoint, be it in discourse through the limit of the narrative, or within the represented world in the form of Murau's "Erbverweigerung" and death, implies accomplishment and closure.

In this light, the extradiegetic narrator (whom Heidelberger-Leonard terms the "Herausgeber") fulfills a dual function. Because he possesses the noncontextualized authority discussed earlier, there is a sense in which his closing interjection "(geboren 1934 in Wolfsegg, gestorben 1983 in Rom)" is quite literally the last word: despite the delays and deferrals, the end has been reached, the narrative is over, the subject is closed. However, by his very act of framing the narrative, he brings it into the public domain. His act of transmission, with which the text ends, is the act that facilitates the reader's engagement with the beginning. Just as *Holzfällen* ends with the narrator's returning home, intent on starting work on the book we have just read, the extradiegetic narrator of *Auslöschung* returns us to the beginning at the moment that he reaches the end, forcing a renewed confrontation with Wolfsegg and its representation.

# Notes

[1] See the facsimile in Höller and Heidelberger-Leonard 106.

[2] One possible reason for Bernhard's decision is suggested by Hilde Spiel in an interview with Krista Fleischmann: "Und ich weiß, daß er einmal — das hat er mir erzählt — fast einen Flugzeugunfall hatte. Und da hab' ich gefragt, ja, wie war das denn? Sie mußten zurückfliegen, es war ein Motorschaden, er war mit jemandem andern. Und dann hat er gesagt, ja also, meine Begleiterin hat nur gebetet, und ich hab' nur darüber nachgedacht, ja, wie ist denn das letzte Buch jetzt, das ich veröffentlicht hab'? Ist das ein Buch, mit dem man aus dem Leben gehen kann? Das war sein einziger Gedanke." Fleischmann, *Erinnerung* 150.

[3] The semantic field "einsperren/absperren" *versus* "aufsperren" crops up frequently in connection with the libraries, and is echoed when Murau claims that Spadolini's silence about the true nature of his affair with Murau's mother is a case of "Einsperrung und Absperrung" (Aus 585), that is, yet another form of repression which it is Murau's task to lift.

[4] Numerous commentators have pointed out that Wolfsegg functions as a microcosm of Austrian history and society. See, for example, Höller and Part; Langer; Bodi, "Annihilating Austria"; Gößling, *"Eisenbergrichtung"* 10.

[5] See, for example, Mittermayer, *Thomas Bernhard* 111 and "Die Meinigen abschaffen" 125; Korte 96; Gößling, *"Eisenbergrichtung"* 16; Eyckeler 161.

[6] This statement is later relativized. Murau confesses that he had examined the photographs "um [sich] von der Furchtbarkeit mehr oder weniger abzulenken," then adds, "*diese* Methode war die beste, wie ich jetzt sah" (Aus 387, my italics). The key term, however, is "ablenken," betraying Murau's reluctance to "come to the point."

[7] Early structuralism stressed the analogy between narrative texts and the sentence: see, for example, Barthes, "Introduction." It would seem not only possible but highly apposite to link the structures of narrative enigma and postponement to Bernhard's sentence structure; the extensive use of subordinate clauses and extended adjectival phrases defers the end of the sentence, often to an extent that stretches the possibilities of German syntax to their probable limits. See, for example, the first sentence of *Die Billigesser*.

[8] See the first two chapters of White, *Content*.

[9] For an account of contemporary historical fiction (primarily in the Anglo-American tradition) see Hutcheon.

[10] See, for example, pp. 7, 72, 77, 97, 139, 212, 214, 334, 528, 611, 651.

[11] Bernhard's use of quotation and embedded perspectives has attracted extensive critical commentary, most critics agreeing that embedded perspectives problematize questions of representational authenticity. A dissenting reading of Bernhard can be found in Bernardi's article "Bernhards Stimme." He writes: "Nur durch die Rückkehr zur Mündlichkeit, d.h. zur tatsächlichen Anwesenheit des Erzählers und eine Stimme, die spricht, könnte die Sprache von der Lüge befreit werden, die der Schriftlichkeit innewohnt" (35). To interpret Bernhard in terms of an aesthetics of presence, however, would seem a foolhardy enterprise for two reasons. The first is that the structure of the texts actually *forbids* this; the second is that such an emphasis on the voice as a source of authentic meaning betrays a "phonocentrism" that would be a proverbial red rag to the deconstructionist bull.

[12] Cf. Marquardt, who discusses the conflicting portraits of Murau's parents given by Murau himself and Spadolini: "Spadolinis und Muraus Charakterisierung der Eltern spinnt einerseits den Erzählfaden weiter und bewirkt doch auf einer höheren Ebene die Aufhebung der Glaubwürdigkeit jeglicher Erzählung" (63). The same Spadolini episode forms the basis of Eyckeler's chapter on perspectivism in *Auslöschung*. He argues "daß jede urteilende Aussage über Sachverhalte irreduzibel von Stimmungen, Situationen, Wirkungsintentionen der Beteiligten usw. abhängig ist" (162), but his discussion draws largely on Murau's own reflections on perspectivism, and is divorced from any consideration of narrative structure.

[13] The metonymic links between Wolfsegg and the family are particularly evident at those points in the text where Wolfsegg refers not merely to the specific geographical place but also to the family and the ideology that it represents. Place and character are related in terms not of resemblance, but of contiguity.

[14] There are various hints of Wolfsegg's final dissolution throughout the text. Caecilia's marriage to the "Weinflaschenstöpselfabrikant" inaugurates a chain of usurpations. Spadolini usurps Murau's father, first in his affair with Murau's mother, and then symbolically by sleeping in the father's bed before the funeral; and the "Titiseetante," having brokered Caecilia's marriage in order to spite her sister-in-law (that is, Murau's mother), compounds the infamy by sleeping in the maternal bed.

[15] Sorg reads the refusal of history implied by Murau's "Erbverweigerung" as positive, but also sees it as an ambivalent act of violence that is opposed to the destructivity of the family and state (*Thomas Bernhard* 125–6). Korte reads the gift of Wolfsegg to the Israelitische Kultusgemeinde as a theatrical gesture that ironizes the illusion of denazification (99), but his discussion pays no attention to the problems raised by questions of narrative form.

# Conclusion

## The Form and Function of Narrative

A T A TIME when newspaper critics had begun to berate Bernhard for the alleged repetitiveness of his novels, Joachim Kaiser grudgingly acknowledged that Bernhard's prose works of the 1980s continued to compel attention: "die Bernhard-Novellen besitzen gewiß bis zum Überdruß ihren Ton, doch eine jede von ihnen bringt auch etwas prinzipiell Neues. Darum dürfen wir nach wie vor auf jede neue gespannt sein."

The analyses of Bernhard's major novels offered here corroborates Kaiser's diagnosis, for each of them evinces a different relationship between thematic concerns and formal issues. In the early fiction, Bernhard mobilizes techniques of framing and quotation, which differ considerably from novel to novel. The diary form of *Frost* represents the narrator's response to his meeting with the painter Strauch, and reproduces within its very structure the blurring of the boundaries between sanity and madness that had affected him while he was within Strauch's sphere of influence. In *Verstörung*, structures of problematic narrative transmission within the text create a sense of stasis which, in Bernhard's view, corresponds to the historical stasis that characterized the Second Austrian Republic. *Das Kalkwerk* uses complex forms of narrative embedding as a means of obfuscating the violence perpetrated upon the female victim by the main character, while the ironic teleological structuration of *Korrektur* functions as a formal analogue to Roithamer's ironized teleological thought.

The narrative form of Bernhard's late fiction is less varied than that of the four early novels. *Ja* is perhaps the exception, as the text's narrative form exists in a demonstrably contradictory relationship to the narrator's professed intentions in writing the book, resulting in the narrator's misogyny being exposed. From *Wittgensteins Neffe* onward, however, Bernhard's narrative strategies become more homogeneous, particularly in terms of time structure: writing on the time-level that we have called the discursive situation, the narrators of the late fiction recall a series of events which themselves serve as the pretext for further reminiscence. This tripartite division of time levels is common to *Der Untergeher*, *Holzfällen*, *Alte Meister*, and *Auslöschung*. But within each text this time-structure fulfills a different function. In *Der Untergeher*, it combines with the fluid relationship between story and discourse to subvert the detective-novel genre on which the text is ostensibly based. The dynamic form of *Holzfällen*, on the other hand, can be understood as a solution to the criticisms of stagnation and repression that are leveled at the characters within the text's represented world. In *Alte Meister*, the distinctions between textual levels are blurred to the extent that they provide a formal correlative to the techniques of fragmentation adopted by Reger in dealing with the burden of the historical and cultural heritage. Finally, the tripartite time structure of *Auslöschung* functions as the means by which Murau can come to terms with both his "Herkunftskomplex" and his "Zukunftskomplex."

On this reading, Bernhard's "Werkgeschichte" emerges as a series of overlappings: a fairly narrow range of thematic concerns recurs throughout his work, but the formal devices employed in order to address these concerns vary considerably. So, for example, the problems of the Habsburg legacy pervade the thematics of *Verstörung*, *Korrektur*, *Alte Meister*, and *Auslöschung*, yet all four texts are profoundly different in terms of narrative structure. The domination of women is common to *Das Kalkwerk* and *Ja*, yet the narrative strategies of the former are geared toward clearing the main character of blame, while in the latter they function as a critique of the narrator. The difficulties of constructing adequate biographical narratives forms a core problematic of *Ja*, *Wittgensteins Neffe*, and *Der Untergeher*, but the specific problems they raise necessitate widely divergent formal solutions.

## Austria and the "sozialpartnerschaftliche Ästhetik"

Despite the basically formal focus of this study, reference to Thomas Bernhard's vexed relationship with his homeland has been inevitable throughout. Many of the texts under discussion — and particularly those dealt with in the last three chapters — explicitly thematize questions of Austrian history and culture, and the narrative form of those texts has been examined as a response to such questions. In conclusion, I would like to relate Bernhard's narrative techniques more systematically to the history and politics of postwar Austria by considering the degree to which Bernhard's texts correspond to Robert Menasse's notion of the "sozialpartnerschaftliche Ästhetik."

Generally speaking, the writing of literary history is a problematic undertaking, for two reasons. First, the attempt to relate literature to the socio-historical or political circumstances of its production runs the risk of degenerating into a naive positivism, according to which literature is a mere "reflection" of the wider social sphere. This is literary history as the history of content. An equal but opposite pitfall, however, is to regard literature as a closed system, divorced from social and political reality and progressing purely through the evolution of new techniques. This is literary history as the history of form. Menasse's essay "Die sozialpartnerschaftliche Ästhetik" represents a sophisticated neo-Marxist attempt to transcend this dichotomy by relating the ideology underpinning the political life of the Second Austrian Republic to the ideology implied by the form of literary texts. It is arguably the most influential account of Austrian literary history since Claudio Magris's book *Der habsburgische Mythos in der österreichischen Literatur.*

The initial phenomenon to which Menasse draws attention is the paradoxical relationship between

> der außerordentlichen "Hochblüte" der österreichischen Literatur, ihrer überproportionalen Bedeutung im deutschen Sprachraum, und der gleichzeitigen politischen und ökonomischen Bedeutungslosigkeit Österreichs im Vergleich mit den modernen Industriemächten, aber auch mit seiner eigenen einstigen Größe. ( *Überbau* 17)

Menasse seeks the foundation of Austria's literary predominance in the peculiarities of its economic structure, and isolates the Social Partnership as the one factor that makes Austria unique among the capitalist democracies of Western Europe. The term "Social Partnership" refers to a committee constituted of the leaders of various interest groups (the unions, the chambers of trade and agriculture) and members of the government. They meet informally behind closed doors, and their task is to reach unanimity regarding the fundamental political, social and economic issues with which Austria has to deal. Elsewhere, Menasse compares the Social Partnership to a "Stammtisch": both are informal, nonregistered men's clubs, where political questions are discussed and agreement reached, the one significant difference being that any decision made by the Social Partnership automatically becomes Austrian law ( *Land ohne Eigenschaften* 97). Because the Social Partnership meets behind closed doors and is made up of unelected representatives, it is not subject to democratic control and is hence immune to the vagaries of electoral politics: no matter which government is in power, the decision-making process remains the same, which has led to considerable efficiency, homogeneity, and continuity ( *Überbau* 20).

The Social Partnership, writes Menasse,

> zielt auf eine konfliktminimierende Zusammenarbeit der Interessenorganisationen der Unternehmer und der Lohn- und Gehaltabhängigen, um das dem Klassencharakter der Gesellschaft innewohnende Kon-

fliktpotential zum "Klassenkampf am grünen Tisch" zu sublimieren
und auf dem Verhandlungsweg beizulegen. (19)

One consequence of this is that conflict is removed from public life:
compromise is not the result of a disagreement, but an *a priori* that effectively prevents disagreement. Decisions are made in private, and
overt party-political confrontation is obviated (25). Meanwhile, the
genuine cause of conflict within capitalist society, namely property, remains unaffected and is never discussed; social antagonisms are defused
by a political structure whose function is to create the illusion of harmony. This system, legitimized only because it is tolerated by the vast
majority of Austrian citizens, is "die konkrete bürgerliche Gegenutopie
zur 'klassenlosen Gesellschaft,' also das der bürgerlichen Gesellschaft
innewohnende Geschichtsziel" (19).

If the Social Partnership represents the "Geschichtsziel" of the
bourgeoisie, then it follows that the Second Republic can claim to have
"put an end to history": "[die Geschichte] scheint mit der Sozialpart-
nerschaft nicht nur an ihrem Ziel, an ihrem Ende angekommen zu sein,
sondern ist überhaupt, auch als Wissen von Geschichte und als histori-
sches Bewußtsein, verschwunden" (96). Once genuine historical
knowledge and consciousness have disappeared, history itself can be reduced to the visible and *commodifiable* cultural relics of the past, a process that was encouraged by the restorative tendencies in the years
immediately following the signing of the State Treaty in 1955 (40),
and by Austria's tendency to define itself as the guardian of its own past
cultural glories. This throws light on a topos that has cropped up
throughout this study, namely the notion of Austria as a museum. As
Menasse writes, "Österreich hat sich vor seiner Geschichte abgeschottet
und versucht dennoch von seiner Musealität zu leben" (*Land ohne Eigenschaften* 74). In literary texts, the "end of history" manifests itself in
narratives that imply dehistoricization or stagnation, and this is the first
major aspect of Menasse's "sozialpartnerschaftliche Ästhetik."

Menasse goes on to link the political structure of the Second Republic to Austria's centuries-old status as a center of political Catholicism.
He argues that countries that define themselves — even politically — in
terms of Catholicism differ from Protestant countries in the influence
exerted by ritualized confession on the forms of social discourse: "Im
Beichtverhältnis geht die Macht von dem, der etwas zu sagen hat, auf
den Zuhörenden über, der nun die Möglichkeit hat, Befehle auszuspre-
chen und die Absolution zu erteilen, also eine Harmonie herzustellen,
die ein Geschenk der Allmacht ist" (*Überbau* 29). This structure of
power, mediated by "Mitwisserschaft" or shared knowledge, also characterizes the social structures of postwar Austria:

Ist die Form der Ohrenbeichte und die regelmäßige Erfahrung mit ihr nun mitkonstitutiv für die Entwicklung des gesellschaftlichen Diskurses, so erhalten die Repräsentanten des gesellschaftlichen Widerspruchs, in dem Maß, wie sie gesellschaftliche Machtpositionen institutionell einnehmen und sich zu verständigen suchen, zunehmend über Mitwisserschaft vermittelte Macht, dadurch aber nur Macht miteinander. Diese Vermittlung scheint erlösende Wirkung auf die Konflikte des wirklichen Lebens zu haben und ist den realen Gegebenheiten gleichzeitig völlig entrückt: Widerprüche werden gleichsam transzendiert, in der Realität aber nicht angetastet. (29)

The second major aspect of Menasse's pronouncements on the aesthetics of postwar Austrian literature, then, is concept of the confessional, which manifests itself most prominently in the topos of the "Herr-Knecht-Verhältnis." The notion of a harmonious relationship between masters and men was a significant pillar of Habsburg ideology, serving to obscure the economic inequalities on which that relationship was based. It formed a classic topos of the literature of the "Habsburg Myth," and, as Menasse points out, has been repeatedly taken up, quoted, and applied to post-Habsburg situations by the novelists of the Second Republic (76–7). Like the confessional, the harmonious relationship between master and servant is based on "Mitwisserschaft" and the power that it conveys upon the listener. Rather than exhausting itself in a structure of command and execution, the master-servant relationship consists of a complex chain of "Befehl-Widerspruch-Geständnis-Mitwisserschaft-Verständnis" in a way which harmonizes social contradictions — but purely at the level of discourse (77). In other words, power relationships are maintained by creating the illusion of harmony, which is in turn attained by suppression of the material basis of power and fixation on the linguistic and ornamental trappings ("Allüren") thereof. Social systems, as exemplified in the master-servant relationship, thus become formalistic rituals, which are then precipitated in literary texts: "Bedeutsam ist also, *daß* einer sagt, und nicht *was* er sagt, nicht *was* einer gesteht, verleiht dem anderen Macht, sondern prinzipiell, *daß* er gesteht" (81).

Menasse's two main categories — the confessional situation and a dehistoricized sense of time — appear easily applicable to Bernhard's work, and Menasse himself exemplifies his thesis with reference to several novels. It should be noted, though, that the manuscript of "Die sozialpartnerschaftliche Ästhetik" was first written in 1981, and when the Sonderzahl-Verlag offered to publish it almost a decade later, Menasse deliberately did not update his examples (8). Although the essay first appeared in print in 1990, therefore, it includes no consideration of

Bernhard's later work, which allows ample scope for an extended discussion of Bernhard and the "sozialpartnerschaftliche Ästhetik."

## Master and Servant

In his analysis of the "confessional" situation in Bernhard's novels, Menasse points out that the exchange between the narrators and the characters they quote involves a constant verbal oscillation of power relationships. This has the effect of abolishing conflict, and ultimately results in the two main characters melting or collapsing into one. Language in Bernhard's texts is employed in order to pass judgment rather than to express opinions or reasoned valuations. Instead of being the result of a process of weighing up conflicting views, judgment becomes an *a priori* that removes the possibility of contradiction in advance: "was bleibt, ist die scheinbare Egalität derer, die ihre Geständnisse austauschen, die Identität der Widersetzlichkeiten, das Verschmelzen aller, die etwas sagen, in einer *herrschenden* Harmonie, und diese ist die entsetzlichste, so Bernhard" (84). In Bernhard's hypertrophic use of the verb "sagen" and the particle "so" ("so Karrer zu Oehler," to use Menasse's example), the confessional structure of his texts becomes so dominant that it takes precedence over what is actually said. The confessional *form* of the characters' speech makes them resemble each other far more than the *content* of what they say distinguishes them from each other, and this represents a formal analogue of the Social Partnership, which can only function "weil die, die in ihr verschiedene Standpunkte und Interessen vertreten, durch die ritualisierte Mitwisserschaft längst schon ununterscheidbar geworden sind" (85).

The "confessional" structure is clearly discernible in many of Bernhard's texts, with the situation in *Frost* corresponding most closely to Menasse's scheme. As we have seen, the novel dramatizes the narrator's loss of individual contours as he gradually succumbs to the world of Strauch, even to the extent of adopting the latter's linguistic habits. Furthermore, the trope of pan-signification and the tendency of Strauch's monologues to stress the equivalence — the "Gleich-Gültigkeit" — of opposite concepts can be seen as contributing to the same goal: everything is ultimately identical to everything else. Nevertheless, such a reading of the text is only half the equation. The confessional situation based on the harmonization of conflict may apply to the development of the relationship between Strauch and the narrator, but as my analysis shows, the conflict between their respective worldviews is re-installed in the very fabric of the text, which pits linear narrative against discursive stasis at both the micro- and macrotextual levels. This tendency of Bernhard's novels to install *and problematize* the "sozialpartnerschaftliche Ästhetik" at the same time becomes increasingly prominent as his work progresses.

*Verstörung* is the one text by Bernhard to which Menasse devotes considerable attention. The topos of master and servant, he claims, is incorporated within the novel not in the relationship between two characters, but in the monological language of the novel's main speaker, Saurau:

> In der Sprache des Fürsten sind alle Elemente des klassischen Herr-Knecht-Topos sprachlich aufgehoben: die Apodiktik der Macht, die sich im Geständnis auflöst, um sie zu erhalten; der Hang zum Widerspruch als Allüre, die die eigene Ohnmacht aber hinnimmt und sich daher in völliger Akzeptanz des Gegebenen auflöst; das Zusammenfließen der beiden Momente zu einem Kompromiß, zu einer Identität, der alles identisch wird. Bernhard gestaltet also die besondere Organisationsform des Herr-Knecht-Verhältnisses nicht mehr in einem Verhältnis von zwei Figuren, die diese Dialektik vorführen, wie noch die traditionell erzählende Literatur [. . .]. Wesentlich ist [. . .], daß beide Seiten des Verhältnisses, des Widerspruchs, in den Text zurückgenommen sind, deren Dialektik als *Monolog* gestaltet ist — so wie die beiden Seiten des Widerspruchs realiter ja längst verschmolzen sind und eine entsprechende gesellschaftlich allgemeinverbindliche Diskursform hervorgebracht haben, in der die Synthese immer schon erhalten ist. (*Überbau* 86–7)

This synthesis, argues Menasse, is not genuine identity: although for Saurau the interior and exterior worlds have become identical, this is experienced as a "Verstörungszustand." At the same time, however, the synthesis does not allow genuine contradiction because contradiction is always already absorbed in the monologic structure of the text (87).

It is difficult to disagree with this diagnosis of Saurau's predicament, but like many critics of *Verstörung*, Menasse seems to assume that the only significant speaker is Saurau, thereby ignoring those aspects of the text that would call his reading into question. As my discussion of *Verstörung* suggests, however, many of the verbal exchanges in the text actually dramatize the disintegration of the confessional relationship. "Alle Personen gestanden etwas" wrote Handke in his review of *Verstörung* (292). But the confessions no longer result in "Mitwisserschaft" and the harmonization of antagonisms because they are constantly blocked or diverted from their intended recipient. As we saw in chapter 1, for example, the narrator's confession to his father that he had always had great pleasure in coping with his own difficulties goes unheard (V 69). The doctor's confession about the difficult relationship between himself and his children is aimed at Frau Ebenhöh, but she falls asleep with the result that the only person to hear it is the narrator, much to his father's embarrassment (V 38–9). Likewise, Saurau's attempts to establish communication with his son fail to produce the intended effect (V 135, 166, 171): the harmonizing effect of the confessional structure is undermined.

Menasse points out that the one thing the Prince finds truly threatening is a radically "other" form of discourse as typified by his son's mode of speech, "eine Redeweise, die schmerzt, die abtötet" (*Überbau* 96). This betrays the unwillingness of Saurau's son to collude with a social discourse that serves to suppress conflict, and the same tendency can be witnessed in the narrator's letter, which attempts to elicit some response from his father concerning his mother's suicide and the current family situation (V 20–1). While at one level, then, the "sozialpartnerschaftliche Ästhetik" remains reasonably intact, the text is invaded by modes of discourse that threaten to destabilize the surface harmony and bring to light the conflicts that are simmering beneath. Although these may appear to be purely personal, Menasse's mode of reading stresses the fact that personal interaction is determined by forms of social discourse whose provenance is ultimately political, and so the generation conflicts of *Verstörung* take on a wider significance. The younger generation attempts to break out of discursive forms that prevent conflict from being aired and resolved openly. In *Verstörung*, the dominant discourse can still contain these impulses. This harmonizing function is fulfilled not only by the medical discourse of the doctor and the confessional monologue of the Prince, but also by Thomas Bernhard, who locates the dissenting voices either outside the time-frame of the novel (the narrator's letter), or outside its spatial confines (Saurau's son). In the very act of conforming to Menasse's categories, then, the text inscribes elements that destabilize them, which leads to a *Verstörung* — but not an invalidation — of the "sozialpartnerschaftliche Ästhetik."

In *Das Kalkwerk*, the structure of narrative transmission turns everybody into a "Mitwisser": Fro and Wieser acquire and disseminate knowledge about Konrad and his wife. Although their accounts of Konrad's marriage and the murder often diverge, the conflict that this implies retreats beneath the fact that both Fro and Wieser serve exactly the same function within the economy of the novel. Their role within the structure of "Mitwisserschaft" renders them effectively indistinguishable, and all they ultimately do is produce a discourse that leaves the genuine cause of conflict, namely the politics of gender, largely untouched. At the same time, Konrad's relationship with his wife is constituted as a classic "Herr-Knecht-Verhältnis," except that it collapses. We saw in chapter 2 that the power relations in the Konrads' marriage may appear to be reciprocal, but that the derived power that Frau Konrad gains by ordering her husband about in fact colludes with the structures of domination that oppress her, just as the derived power of the "Knecht" is precisely the means by which his subjugation is perpetuated. However, rather than producing harmony, the "Herr-Knecht-Verhältnis" in *Das Kalkwerk* exists in its dystopic transformation as eternal mutual torture whose only issue can be death. The capacity of this death to erupt into the surface of the text, disturb the discourse responsible for keeping it in check, and expose the contradictions of patriarchy, threatens once again to subvert the "sozialpartnerschaftliche Ästhetik."

The novels of Bernhard's late phase represent an attempt to break out of the "sozialpartnerschaftliche Ästhetik." This largely entails the abandonment of the confessional dyad that characterizes the earlier work: *Wittgensteins Neffe*, *Der Untergeher*, and *Holzfällen*, in particular, resist any attempt to read them in the light of Menasse's categories. Where the semblance of the confessional remains, it tends to dissolve, collapse, or fulfill a very different function from that of the earlier fiction. On first glance, for example, the central relationship in *Ja* appears to evince the "Form der Ohrenbeichte": the developing friendship between the narrator and the Persian woman involves confession and the power that is derived from "Mitwisserschaft." However, my reading of the text shows that the narrative form of *Ja* exposes the inability of the discourse to sublimate the patriarchal ideology that sanctions the exploitation and physical abuse of the "Perserin." The illusory reciprocity in the relationship between the narrator and the Persian is exposed as precisely that: an illusion.

In *Auslöschung*, the relationship between Murau and Gambetti bears many of the traits of the "Herr-Knecht-Verhältnis": "Mitwisserschaft," reciprocity through contradiction (Gambetti's laughter), and the capacity of discourse to harmonize conflict (the narrator's own laughter at his "Übertreibungskunst"). Furthermore, the relationship is characterized by the total absence of any genuine power, so Murau's tirades against Austria or Gambetti's desire "die Welt zu zersägen und in die Luft zu sprengen" (Aus 543) exist purely in discourse, and leave the real systems of power untouched. The Murau-Gambetti relationship, though, is not constitutive of the entire narrative situation in *Auslöschung*, being rather a localized device whose function has been largely fulfilled by the end of the first section. The second section of *Auslöschung* represents the moment when the production of discourse gives way to action: because Murau finds himself in the position of heir to the Wolfsegg estate, he is forced to confront directly the structures of domination and historical repression that he had previously merely derided. Thus *Auslöschung* dramatizes the failure of surface discourse to harmonize the social contradictions that erupt into the stable situation of "Mitwisserschaft."

The one exception to the dissolution of the "sozialpartnerschaftliche Ästhetik" in Bernhard's later work is *Alte Meister*. Superficially, the novel consists almost entirely of tirades against Austria, from the revered names of the Habsburg past (Stifter, Bruckner, Mahler) to the current lamentable state of Viennese public toilets. Predictably, *Alte Meister* caused considerable outrage, which culminated in Herbert Moritz, the Austrian Minister of Education, remarking: "In letzter Zeit wird [Bernhard] immer mehr zu einem Thema der Wissenschaft, wobei ich aber nicht mehr allein die Literaturwissenschaft meine" — implying, of course, psychiatry! Yet despite the ostensibly critical intention of *Alte Meister*, the confessional "Herr-Knecht-Verhältnis" is even more obviously apparent here than in the early work. Two recent studies have argued that the narrator Atzbacher and the museum attendant Irrsigler serve merely to reproduce the words of the central character Reger (Hens 139; Betz 74). Despite the embedded perspectives, then, the structure of the text is fundamentally monological, and all possibility of dissent or contradiction is precluded. The relationship between Reger and Irrsigler, moreover, revives the master-servant topos in its most unmediated form. Irrsigler, described by Reger as a "Dummkopf als Sprachrohr" (AM 33) comes from the provincial peasant class, and has become a member of the Viennese petty bourgeoisie. Reger is a "Privatgelehrter" who possesses not only his own private means but has also inherited his wife's fortune. Both thus represent class interests that are in fact antagonistic, but "das dem Klassencharakter der Gesellschaft innewohnende Konfliktpotential" (Menasse, *Überbau* 19) is sublimated by confession and the resultant "Mitwisserschaft" that gives Irrsigler the illusion of sharing the power that oppresses him. *Alte Meister* appears to be a critical text, but its confessional structure means that the criticisms it contains meet with approval from the other characters in a way that harmonizes the potential for social discord. Reger's multifaceted critique of Austria is purely symbolic; its *performative* function is ultimately to preserve the status quo rather than change it.

### Dehistoricization

Menasse's assertion that "[e]s gibt [. . .] in den Romanen [. . .] Bernhards grundsätzlich keine Konkretisierung des historischen Moments" (*Überbau* 96) is clearly a statement that could not have been made in the light of Bernhard's major novels of the 1980s. Like the notion of confessional character constellations, this aspect of the "sozialpartner-schaftliche Ästhetik" turns out to be applicable only in part to Bernhard's work.

The readings of *Frost* and *Verstörung* offered in chapter 1 stress that the structural capacity of the narrative syntagma is severely reduced in a way that diverts the reader's attention to the similarity between the various events. This narrative technique is the formal correlative of the "enthistorisierte Meta-Zeit" within which the action appears to take place: temporal relations are reduced to a series of more or less static moments: "Es kann keine Entwicklung geben, wo es keine Geschichte gibt. Die jähen Wechsel sind nur Wechsel von einem statischen Zustand in den anderen" (98). In *Frost* this phenomenon is partly due to the psychopathology of Strauch, whereas in *Verstörung* its historical relevance is foregrounded to a much greater degree: the stasis implied by the narrative form can be seen as symptomatic of the "Stillstand der Geschichte" of the Second Republic. Those studies that concentrate on the historical thematics of Bernhard's texts corroborate rather than contradict this view. The critical method adopted by Gößling (and, to a lesser extent, by Helms-Derfert) involves reading physical objects as symbols or traces of history, which is thereby reduced to a function of its spatial sedimentation. The entire historical process is simultaneously present in the concrete landscape.

*Das Kalkwerk* is an interesting case, because it highlights the negative aspects of the stasis implied by its narrative form. As O'Neill points out, the confusion of chronology in *Das Kalkwerk* results in a "picture of Konrad's life as essentially static rather than progressive, a portrait of a man always already on the brink of catastrophe" ("Endgame" 237). Just as the relationship between Konrad and his wife can be read as a dystopic transformation of the master-slave topos, so the eternal threat of catastrophe represents a dystopic inversion of "das der bürgerlichen Gesellschaft innewohnende Geschichtsziel" (Menasse, *Überbau* 19). Far from being a situation of harmonious stability, the end — or "end-game," as O'Neill puts it — is constantly on the brink of collapse. In its evocation of this instability, *Das Kalkwerk* once again both installs and negates the "sozialpartnerschaftliche Ästhetik."

Writing of *Korrektur*, Menasse states: "Die Zeiten ändern sich in Ermangelung allgemeiner Entwicklungen oft abrupt und ausschließlich privat, im ganzen bleibt alles beim alten" (*Überbau* 97). As we have seen, however, Bernhard's fiction from *Korrektur* onward repeatedly attempts to restore a sense of temporal progress. The analyses of textual dynamics in the section on *Korrektur* and in Parts Two and Three stress the role played by multiple time-levels, teleology, and hermeneutic sequences in both mediating between past and present within the narrative world, and guiding our reading of the texts through time. In both cases, the effect is to foreground the ineluctably temporal nature of narrative in terms of what it seeks to represent as well as how it is read. In *Wittgensteins Neffe* and *Der Untergeher*, narrative dynamics are conceived as an antidote to the compulsive repetition evinced by Paul Wittgenstein and Wertheimer, and in *Holzfällen* and *Auslöschung*, the narrative functions as a formal solution to the problems of cultural stagnation and political repression addressed at the level of explicit content. In other words, the form of the texts re-installs the genuinely historical consciousness that Menasse sees lacking in the literature typical of the "sozialpartnerschaftliche Ästhetik."

At the same time, however, texts such as *Der Untergeher* and *Holzfällen* mobilize the hermeneutic code only in order to problematize it: in the former text the projected discovery of Wertheimer's papers does not take place, while in the latter, the hermeneutic sequences are banal in the extreme. In both cases, the teleological expectations underpinning the entire narrative enterprise are foregrounded as a mere device that allows the story to "get told." The very technique that is supposed to restore a sense of temporal dynamics, then, is shown to be compromised to the extent that it can only now be deployed ironically. The trope of irony, traditionally defined, is the figure of speech according to which one means the opposite of what one says. On this reading, decoding irony involves substituting the "true" meaning of a given statement for the apparent meaning. But irony need not always function in this fashion; there is also the possibility of unstable irony that robs the reader of any fixed point for judgment by means of a perpetually self-undermining discourse.[1] This is what happens to the hermeneutic codes in Bernhard's late fiction: if one tries to assert that they genuinely do restore a historical sense to the texts, it can always be objected that they demonstrate the inadequacy of such attempts, and vice versa. Irony is uneasily double-edged. The effect of this is that Bernhard's attempts to break out of the "sozialpartnerschaftliche Ästhetik" are always liable to be re-enveloped by it, while any attempt to situate Bernhard within the "sozialpartnerschaftliche Ästhetik" will always come up against elements that resist such integration.

The tendency within Bernhard's texts to both install and subvert the formal features identified by Menasse as belonging to a specifically Austrian literary culture can be seen separately in Bernhard's last two published novels, *Alte Meister* and *Auslöschung*. As we saw in the discussion of the former text, Reger's "Zerlegungs- und Zersetzungsmechanismus" (AM 226) consists partly in his mentioning painters and writers arbitrarily with scant regard for the period in which they were working. He does this in order to subvert the historical continuity implied by the narrative ordering of the tradition museum. The formal analogue of this is the temporal unspecifiability of the discursive situation and the fragmentation of time levels. Paradoxically, however, this attempt to escape the tyranny of the Austrian cultural tradition results in precisely the kind of narrative stasis — the "enthistorisierte Meta-Zeit" — characteristic of the "sozialpartnerschaftliche Ästhetik." *Auslöschung*, on the other hand, is the one text of Bernhard's that seems truly to elude Menasse's categories. Its thematic emphasis on recent Austrian history, its complex manipulation of time structure, and the device of the narrative frame all contribute to this end, making sure that the text cannot be neutralized as an example of a harmonizing surface discourse. Ulrich Weinzierl is surely right when he claims that *Auslöschung* is Bernhard's "einziges *dezidiert politisches Buch*" (Weinzierl 192, my italics).

Menasse's study never spells out unequivocally whether the "sozialpartnerschaftliche Ästhetik" colludes with the Social Partnership itself, or whether it in fact possesses a critical capacity. Nevertheless, his discussions of Bernhard's novels occasionally suggest that even texts whose formal structures mirror the ideology of the Austrian social system can imply criticism of that system. When he writes, for example, of "das Verschmelzen aller, die etwas sagen, in einer *herrschenden* Harmonie, und diese ist die entsetzlichste, so Bernhard" (*Überbau* 84), Menasse is clearly implying that Bernhard's texts not only *reproduce* the ideology of the Social Partnership, but also somehow *pass judgment* on it. In the above discussion, I have attempted to work out in more detail the relationship between correspondence to and deviation from the "sozialpartnerschaftliche Ästhetik" in order to show how the form of the texts themselves might imply such value-judgments. It emerges that even in Bernhard's earliest major fiction, the "Herr-Knecht-Verhältnis" and the sense of temporal stasis cannot fully suppress that which would disrupt them: the absent son in *Verstörung* and the tension between linear and "spatial" form in *Frost* possess the potential to undermine the harmony of the surface discourse. In *Das Kalkwerk*, the structures that Menasse discusses are fully intact, but are presented in their dystopic inversion. In the later fiction, the master-servant dialectic slowly loses its capacity to structure the relationships between the main characters, while the "enthistorisierte Meta-Zeit" is repeatedly called into question by narrative techniques that stress the dynamic aspect of storytelling.

Were it not for the curious case of *Alte Meister*, in which a highly critical content is re-neutralized by the narrative form, it would be tempting to plot Bernhard's development in terms of his progressive emancipation from and problematization of the "sozialpartnerschaftliche Ästhetik." A totalizing narrative of this kind, however, might be less useful than a relational approach: each of Bernhard's texts is characterized by a different relationship between the elements that conform to the "sozialpartnerschaftliche Ästhetik" and the elements that subvert it or call it into question. The decision as to whether or not Bernhard was genuinely a socially critical author may ultimately depend on the mode of reading one adopts and on which aspect of his novels one wishes to emphasize.

This fundamental conflict within the novels themselves replicates the reciprocally ambivalent relationship between Bernhard and the Austrian cultural establishment. Bernhard's harvest of literary prizes demonstrates that the establishment paid official tribute to the significance of his achievement on numerous occasions. Bernhard had no qualms about accepting the honors offered to him by the very Austrian state whose political and intellectual life formed the subject of repeated derision in his books. Yet in the very act of accepting prizes, Bernhard would refuse to obey the conventions of prize-giving ceremonies. One of the most comical episodes in his entire body of work is the narration, in *Wittgensteins Neffe*, of the award of the Kleiner Österreichischer Staatspreis. His famous acceptance speech began, "es ist nichts zu loben, nichts zu verdammen, nichts anzuklagen, aber es ist vieles lächerlich; es ist alles lächerlich, wenn man an den *Tod* denkt" ("Rede" 7) and he complemented these existential comments with some critical remarks on Austria. As a result, Piffl-Perčevič, the minister presiding over the proceedings, shook his fists at Bernhard, shouted "Wir sind trotzdem stolze Österreicher!" and stormed out of the auditorium, slamming the glass doors behind him with such force that they shattered.

This incident betrays a desire, on the part of both Bernhard and the Austrian establishment, for mutual acceptance and mutual rejection at the same time. Official pronouncements by representatives of the Austrian government evince a similar split. As we have seen, Herbert Moritz suggested in 1985 that Bernhard was in need of psychiatric help, and this echoed Franz Vranitzky's earlier pronouncements that the function of Bernhard's play *Der Theatermacher* was "die eigene Verklemmung vom Leib zu schreiben." Similar sentiments were expressed in the aftermath of Bernhard's 1988 play *Heldenplatz*, with Helmut Zilk, one-time Arts Minister, suggesting that Bernhard's work was the projection of his own paranoia. Yet Moritz felt able, in 1992, to publish *Lehrjahre: Thomas Bernhard: Vom Journalisten zum Dichter*, a largely uncritical account of Bernhard's early journalistic articles. The current Austrian Chancellor, Viktor Klima, declared Bernhard to be "ohne Zweifel eine der ganz großen literarischen Persönlichkeiten in der zweiten Jahrhunderthälfte" (Qtd. in Steininger). Moritz's book and Klima's extravagant praise represent attempts to rehabilitate him and integrate him as part of "official" Austrian culture. The point to note is that this paradoxical mode of reception is effectively pre-programmed in the structure of the texts themselves.

Like the other theoretical concepts advanced throughout this study, the "sozialpartnerschaftliche Ästhetik" does not offer a set of categories that can be merely applied to Bernhard's texts, but rather a conceptual framework within which dialogue can take place. In order to facilitate such a dialogue, Bernhard's novels must be subjected to a formal analysis that allows a differentiated understanding of his narrative techniques. The reading of Bernhard's fiction offered here shows him to be a writer of considerable diversity, who was profoundly concerned with both the problems and the potential of storytelling. The self-confessed "Geschichtenzerstörer" emerges as a self-conscious "Geschichtenerzähler," for whom narrative — compromised as it may be — is nevertheless indispensable for any attempt to understand or come to terms with the individual life, the cultural past, and ultimately history itself.

# Notes

[1] Some particularly striking examples of this kind of irony are the works of Stephen Crane, the novels of Flaubert, and much of Thomas Mann.

# Bibliography

THIS BIBLIOGRAPHY lists all the texts referred to in the book, as well as other secondary and theoretical sources that I have found directly useful in the preparation of this study. It makes no claims to completeness. For full bibliographical information, the reader is directed to the sources listed under the first section below.

## Bibliographies

Dittmar, Jens, ed. *Thomas Bernhard Werkgeschichte*. Aktualisierte Neuausgabe. Frankfurt/Main: Suhrkamp, 1990.

Huntemann, Willi. "Kommentierte Bibliographie zu Thomas Bernhard." *Text+Kritik* 43. 3rd ed. (1991): 125–51.

Schindlecker, Eva. "Bibliographie zu Thomas Bernhards *Holzfällen*: Erreichbare Artikel aus Zeitungen und Zeitschriften, sowie Beiträge des Österreichischen Rundfunks." Huber and Schmidt-Dengler 40–59.

## Works by Thomas Bernhard

### Prose Works

Note: Works cited frequently are identified by the abbreviation preceding their bibliography entry. Where possible, references to Bernhard's works are to easily obtainable paperback editions. Dates in square brackets refer to the date (and publisher, if different) of the first edition.

[AM=] *Alte Meister: Komödie*. Frankfurt/Main: Suhrkamp, 1988 [1985].

*Amras*. Frankfurt/Main: Suhrkamp, 1988 [1964].

*Der Atem: Eine Entscheidung*. Munich: dtv, 1981 [Salzburg: Residenz, 1978].

[Aus=] *Auslöschung: Ein Zerfall*. Frankfurt/Main: Suhrkamp, 1988 [1986].

*Beton*. Frankfurt/Main: Suhrkamp, 1988 [1982].

*Die Billigesser*. Frankfurt/Main: Suhrkamp, 1988 [1980].

*Ereignisse*. Frankfurt/Main: Suhrkamp, 1994 [Berlin: Literarisches Colloquium, 1969].

*Erzählungen.* Frankfurt/Main: Suhrkamp, 1988.

[F=] *Frost.* Frankfurt/Main: Suhrkamp, 1972 [Frankfurt/Main: Insel, 1963].

*Gehen.* Frankfurt/Main: Suhrkamp, 1971.

[H=] *Holzfällen: Eine Erregung.* Frankfurt/Main: Suhrkamp, 1988 [1984].

*In der Höhe—Rettungsversuch, Unsinn.* Frankfurt/Main: Suhrkamp, 1990 [1989].

[It=] *Der Italiener.* Frankfurt/Main: Suhrkamp, 1989 [Salzburg: Residenz, 1971].

[Ja=] *Ja.* Frankfurt/Main: Suhrkamp, 1988 [1978].

[Kw=] *Das Kalkwerk.* Frankfurt/Main: Suhrkamp, 1973 [1970].

*Die Kälte: Eine Isolation.* Munich: dtv, 1984 [Salzburg: Residenz, 1981].

*Der Keller: Eine Entziehung.* Munich: dtv, 1979 [Salzburg: Residenz, 1976].

*Ein Kind.* Munich: dtv, 1985 [Salzburg: Residenz, 1982].

[Ko=] *Korrektur.* Frankfurt/Main: Suhrkamp, 1988 [1975].

*Der Kulterer: Eine Filmgeschichte.* Frankfurt/Main: Suhrkamp, 1973.

*Der Stimmenimitator.* Frankfurt/Main: Suhrkamp, 1987 [1978].

[Ug=] *Ungenach.* Frankfurt/Main: Suhrkamp, 1988 [1968].

[U=] *Der Untergeher.* Frankfurt/Main: Suhrkamp, 1988 [1983].

*Die Ursache: Eine Andeutung.* Munich: dtv, 1977 [Salzburg: Residenz, 1975].

[V=] *Verstörung.* Frankfurt/Main: Suhrkamp, 1988 [Frankfurt/Main: Insel, 1967].

*Watten: Ein Nachlaß.* Frankfurt/Main: Suhrkamp, 1988 [1969].

[WN=] *Wittgensteins Neffe: Eine Freundschaft.* Frankfurt/Main: Suhrkamp, 1987 [1982].

### Drama

*Claus Peymann kauft sich eine Hose und geht mit mir essen.* Frankfurt/Main: Suhrkamp, 1993.

*Der deutsche Mittagstisch.* Frankfurt/Main: Suhrkamp, 1988.

*Heldenplatz.* Frankfurt/Main: Suhrkamp, 1995 [1988].

*die rosen der einöde: fünf sätze für ballett, stimmen und orchester.* Frankfurt/Main: Fischer, 1959.

*Stücke 1.* Frankfurt/Main: Suhrkamp, 1988. (*Ein Fest für Boris* [1970], *Der Ignorant und der Wahnsinnige* [1972], *Die Jadggesellschaft* [1974], *Die Macht der Gewohnheit* [1974])

*Stücke 2.* Frankfurt/Main: Suhrkamp, 1988. (*Der Präsident* [1975], *Die Berühmten* [1976], *Minetti* [1977], *Immanuel Kant* [1978])

*Stücke 3.* Frankfurt/Main: Suhrkamp, 1988. (*Vor dem Ruhestand* [1979], *Der Weltverbesserer* [1979], *Über allen Gipfeln ist Ruh* [1981], *Am Ziel* [1981], *Der Schein trügt* [1983])

*Stücke 4.* Frankfurt/Main: Suhrkamp, 1988. (*Der Theatermacher* [1984], *Ritter, Dene, Voss* [1984], *Einfach Kompliziert* [1986], *Elisabeth II* [1987])

*Poetry*

*Gesammelte Gedichte.* ed. Volker Bohn. Frankfurt/Main: Suhrkamp, 1991.

*Periodical Publications*

". . .allerdings nur als Baß-Stimmführer." *Süddeutsche Zeitung* 3 Mar. 1987.

"Als Verwalter im Asyl: Fragment." *Merkur* 48 (1970): 1163–4.

"Der Berg: Ein Spiel fur Marionetten als Menschen oder Menschen als Marionetten." *Literatur und Kritik* 46 (1970): 330–52.

"Bernhard Minetti." *Theater Heute Sonderheft* (1975): 38–9.

"Der Briefträger." *Neunzehn deutsche Erzählungen.* Munich: Nymphenburger, 1963. 65–87.

"Beruhigung." *Merkur* 46 (1968): 721–6.

"Ebene." Walter Pichler, *111 Zeichnungen.* Salzburg: Residenz, 1973. 245–7. Rpt. in Dittmar, *Werkgeschichte* 149–51.

"Die Frau aus dem Gußwerk und der Mann mit dem Rucksack." *Almanach für Literatur und Theologie* 4 (1970): 23–4.

"Ein Frühling." *Spektrum des Geites 1964. Literaturkalender* Ebenhausen nr. Munich: Hartfrid Voss, 1963. 36. Rpt. in Dittmar, *Werkgeschichte* 59–60.

"[Erstes Leseerlebnis]." *Erste Lese-Erlebnisse.* Ed. Siegfried Unseld. Frankfurt/Main: Suhrkamp, 1975. 96.

"Goethe schtirbt." *Die Zeit* 19 Mar. 1982.

"Ein junger Schriftsteller." *Wort in der Zeit* 7 (1965): 56–9.

"Die Kleinbürger auf der Heuchelleiter." *Die Zeit* 17 Feb. 1978. Rpt. in Dittmar, *Werkgeschichte* 188–9.

"Mein glückliches Österreich." *Die Zeit* 11 Mar. 1988.

"Mit der Klarheit nimmt die Kälte zu." *Jahresring* 65–66 (1965): 243–245.

"Montaigne: Eine Erzählung in 22 Fortsetzungen." *Die Zeit* 8 Oct. 1982.

"Nie und mit nichts fertig werden." *Jahrbuch der Deutschen Akademie fur Sprache und Dichtung 1970.* Heidelberg: Lambert Schneider, 1971. 83–4.

"Politische Morgenandacht." *Wort in der Zeit* 8 (1966): 11–13.

"Rede." *Die Weltwoche* 22 Mar. 1968. Rpt. in Botond 7–8.

"Salzburg wartet auf ein Theaterstück." *Die Furche* 3 Dec. 1955.

"Der Schweinehüter." *Stimmen der Gegenwart 1956.* Ed. Hans Weigel. Vienna: Herold, 1956. 158–79.

"Unseld." *Der Verleger und seine Autoren: Siegfried Unseld zum sechzigsten Geburtstag.* Frankfurt/Main: Suhrkamp, 1984. 52–4. Rpt. in Dittmar, *Werkgeschichte* 285–6.

"Unsterblichkeit ist unmöglich: Landschaft der Kindheit." *Neues Forum* 169–70 (1968): 95–7.

"Vranitzky: Eine Erwiderung." *Die Presse* 13 Sept. 1985. Rpt. in Dittmar, *Werkgeschichte,* 295–7.

"Der Wahrheit und dem Tod auf der Spur." *Neues Forum* 173 (1968): 347–9.

"Eine Zeugenaussage." *Wort in der Zeit* 6 (1964): 38–43.

### Interviews

Fleischmann, Krista. *Thomas Bernhard—Eine Begegnung.* Vienna: Edition S, 1991.

Hofmann, Kurt. *Aus Gesprächen mit Thomas Bernhard.* Vienna: Löcker, 1988.

Müller, André. *André Müller im Gespräch mit Thomas Bernhard.* Weitra: Bibliothek der Provinz, 1992.

*Von einer Katastrophe in die andere: 13 Gespräche mit Thomas Bernhard.* Ed. Sepp Dreisinger. Weitra: Bibliothek der Provinz, 1992.

### Correspondence

Thomas Bernhard—Karl Ignaz Hennetmair. *Ein Briefwechsel 1965–1974.* Weitra: Bibliothek der Provinz, 1994.

### Secondary and Other Works

Adorno, Theodor W. *Philosophie der neuen Musik.* Frankfurt/Main: Suhrkamp, 1976.

Amann, Klaus. "Vorgeschichte: Kontinuitäten in der österreichischen Literatur von den dreißiger zu den fünfziger Jahren." *Literatur der Nachkriegszeit und der fünfziger Jahre in Österreich.* Ed. Friedrich Aspetsberger, Norbert Frei and Hubert Lengauer. Vienna: Österreichischer Bundesverlag, 1984. 46–58.

Bakhtin, Mikhail. *Rabelais and his World.* Trans. Hélène Iswolsky. Bloomington: Indiana UP, 1984.

Bal, Mieke. *Narratology: Introduction to the Theory of Narrative*. Toronto: University of Toronto Press, 1985.

Baranowski, Anne-Marie. "Antagonismes et polarités dans les romans de Thomas Bernhard *Beton* et *Auslöschung*." *Germanica* 10 (1992): 169–80.

Barry, Thomas F. "On Paralysis and Transcendence in Thomas Bernhard." *Modern Austrian Literature* 21.3–4 (1988): 187–200.

Barthes, Roland. "Introduction à l'analyse structurale des récits." *Communications* 8 (1966): 1–27.

———. *Mythologies*. Paris: Seuil, 1957.

———. *Le Plaisir du texte*. Paris: Seuil, 1973.

———. *S/Z*. Paris: Seuil, 1970.

Barthofer, Alfred. "Wittgenstein mit Maske: Dichtung und Wahrheit in Thomas Bernhards Roman *Korrektur*." *Österreich in Geschichte und Literatur* 23 (1979): 186–207.

Bartmann, Christoph. "Vom Scheitern der Studien: Das Schriftmotiv in Bernhards Romanen." *Text+Kritik* 43. 3rd ed. (1991): 22–9.

Bartsch, Kurt. "Die österreichische Gegenwartsliteratur." *Die Geschichte der deutschen Literatur*. Ed. Viktor Žmegač Vol. 3. Königstein/Ts: Athenäum, 1984. 697–825.

Bartsch, Kurt, Dietmar Goldschnigg, and Gerhard Melzer, eds. *In Sachen Thomas Bernhard*. Königstein/Ts: Athenäum, 1983.

Baudrier, Andrée-Jeanne. "Le thème du refuge dans trois romans allemands contemporains." *Espaces romanesques*. Ed. Michel Crouzet. Paris: Presses Universitaires de France, 1982. 59–69.

Benjamin, Walter. *Illuminationen: Ausgewählte Schriften I*. Selected by Siegfried Unseld. Frankfurt/Main: Suhrkamp, 1977.

———. "Der Erzähler: Bemerkungen zum Werk Nicolai Lesskows." *Illuminationen*. 385–410.

Bernardi, Eugenio. "Bernhards Stimme." Gebesmair and Pittertschatscher. 34–46.

Best, Alan, and Hans Wolfschütz, eds. *Modern Austrian Writing: Literature and Society after 1945*. London: Oswald Wolff; Ottowa: Barnes & Noble, 1980.

Betz, Uwe. *Polyphone Räume und karnevalisiertes Erbe: Analysen des Werks Thomas Bernhards auf der Basis Bachtinscher Theoreme*. Würzburg: Ergon, 1997.

Bjorklund, Beth. "Friedericke Mayröcker." *Austrian Fiction Writers after 1914*. Ed. James Hardin and Donald G Daviau. Vol. 85 of *Dictionary of Literary Biography*. Detroit: Gale Research, 1989. 247–51.

Bodi, Leslie. "Österreich in der Fremde—Fremde in Österreich: Zur Identitäts- und Differenzerfahrung in Thomas Bernhards *Auslöschung. Ein Zerfall.*" *Begegnung mit dem "Fremden": Akten des VIII Internationalen Germanisten-Kongresses Tokyo 1990.* Ed. Yoshinori Schichiji. Vol. 10. Munich: Iudicium, 1991. 120–5.

———. "Annihilating Austria: Thomas Bernhard's *Auslöschung: Ein Zerfall.*" *The Modern German Historical Novel: Paradigms, Problems, Perspectives.* Ed. David Roberts and Philip Thomson. New York: Berg, 1991. 201–16.

Bohnert, Karin. *Ein Modell der Entfremdung: Eine Interpretation des Romans "Das Kalkwerk" von Thomas Bernhard.* Wien: Verband der wissenschaftlichen Gesellschaft Österreichs, 1976.

Botond, Anneliese, ed. *Über Thomas Bernhard.* Suhrkamp: Frankfurt/Main, 1970.

Bronfen, Elisabeth. *Over Her Dead Body: Death, Femininity and the Aesthetic.* Manchester: Manchester UP, 1992.

Bronsen, David. "Autobiographien der siebziger Jahre: Berühmte Schriftsteller befragen ihre Vergangenheit." *Deutsche Literatur in der Bundesrepublik seit 1965.* Ed. Paul Michael Lützeler and Egon Schwarz. Königshausen/Ts: Athenäum, 1980. 202–14.

Brooks, Peter. *Reading for the Plot: Design and Intention in Narrative.* Cambridge, Mass.: Harvard UP, 1984.

Bürger, Christa. "Schreiben als Lebensnotwendigkeit: Zu den autobiographischen Fragmenten Thomas Bernhards." *Sehnsuchtsangst.* Ed. Alexander von Bormann. Amsterdam: Rodopi, 1987. 43–64.

Bürger, Peter. *Theorie der Avantgarde.* Frankfurt/Main: Suhrkamp, 1974.

Bushell, Anthony, ed. *Austria 1945–1955: Studies in Political and Cultural Re-emergence.* Cardiff: University of Wales Press, 1996.

Butzer, Günter. *Fehlende Trauer: Verfahren epischen Erinnerns in der deutschsprachigen Gegenwartsliteratur.* Munich: Fink, 1998.

Chambers, Ross. *Story and Situation: Narrative Seduction and the Power of Fiction.* Manchester: Manchester UP, 1984.

Chatman, Seymour. *Story and Discourse: Narrative Structure in Fiction and Film.* Ithaca: Cornell UP, 1978.

Cohan, Steven, and Linda M. Shires. *Telling Stories: A Theoretical Analysis of Narrative Fiction.* London: Routledge, 1988.

Culler, Jonathan. *On Deconstruction: Theory and Criticism after Structuralism.* London: Routledge and Kegan Paul, 1983.

———. *The Pursuit of Signs: Semiotics, Literature, Deconstruction.* London: Routledge and Kegan Paul, 1982.

———. *Structuralist Poetics: Structuralism, Linguistics and the Study of Literature*. London: Routledge and Kegan Paul, 1975.

Damerau, Burghard. *Selbstbehauptungen und Grenzen: Zu Thomas Bernhard*. Würzburg: Königshausen und Neumann, 1996.

de Lauretis, Teresa. "The Violence of Rhetoric: Considerations on Representation and Gender." *The Violence of Representation: Literature and the History of Violence*. Ed. Nancy Armstrong and Leonard Tennenhouse. London: Routledge, 1989. 239–58.

Dinnerstein, Dorothy. *The Mermaid and the Minotaur: Sexual Arrangements and Human Malaise*. New York: Harper, 1976.

Dittberner, Hugo, "Die heimliche Apologie der Macht: Kritisches zu Thomas Bernhards *Verstörung*." *Text+Kritik* 43. 2nd ed. (1982 ): 46–53.

———. "Der Dichter wird Kolorist: Thomas Bernhards Epochensprung." *Text+Kritik* 43. 3rd ed. (1991): 11–21.

Dittmar, Jens. "Thomas Bernhard als Journalist beim *Demokratischen Volksblatt*." Jurgensen, *Annäherungen* 15–35.

———. "Der skandalöse Bernhard: Dokumentation eines öffentlichen Ärgernisses." *Text+Kritik* 43. 2nd ed. (1982): 73–84.

Donahue, William J. "Zu Thomas Bernhards *Die Ursache: Eine Andeutung*." *Modern Austrian Literature* 21.3–4 (1988): 89–105.

Donnenberg, Joseph. "Zeitkritik bei Thomas Bernhard." *Zeit- und Gesellschaftskritik in der österreichischen Literatur des 19. und 20. Jahrhunderts*. Ed. Institut für Österreichkunde. Wien: Ferdinand Hirt, 1973. 115–43.

———. "Gehirnfähigkeit der Unfähigkeit der Natur." *Thomas Bernhard und Österreich: Studien zu Werk und Wirkung 1970–1989*. Stuttgart: Heinz, 1997. 25–52.

Dowden, Stephen D. *Understanding Thomas Bernhard*. Columbia, SC: University of South Carolina Press, 1991.

Dreissinger, Sepp, ed. *Thomas Bernhard: Portraits, Bilder, Texte*. Weitra: Bibliothek der Provinz, 1991.

Dusini, Arno. "Die Gehörschrift: Zu Thomas Bernhards Prosa." *Zeitschrift für studentische Forschung Sonderband Literatur: Österreichische Moderne* 1 (1986): 71–81.

Eagleton, Terry. *Literary Theory: An Introduction*. Oxford: Blackwell, 1983.

Endres, Ria. *Am Ende angekommen: Dargestellt am wahnhaften Dunkel der Männerporträts des Thomas Bernhard*. Frankfurt/Main: Fischer, 1980.

———. "Das Dunkel ist nicht finster genug." Jurgensen, *Annäherungen* 9–14.

Eyckeler, Franz. *Reflexionspoesie: Sprachskepsis, Rhetorik und Poetik in der Prosa Thomas Bernhards*. Berlin: Erich Schmidt, 1995.

Falke, Eberhard. "Abschreiben: Eine Auflehnung." *Der Spiegel* 3 Nov. 1986. Rpt. in Höller and Heidelberger-Leonard 70–4.

Fetz, Gerald A. "Kafka and Bernhard: Reflections on Affinity and Influence." *Modern Austrian Literature* 21.3–4 (1988): 217–41.

Fialik, Maria. *Der Charismatiker: Thomas Bernhard und die Freunde von einst.* Wien: Locker, 1992.

Finnern, Volker. *Der Mythos des Alleinseins: Die Texte Thomas Bernhards.* Frankfurt/Main: Lang, 1987.

Fleischmann, Krista. *Thomas Bernhard — Eine Erinnerung: Interviews zur Person.* Vienna: Edition S, 1992.

Forster, E. M. *Aspects of the Novel.* Ed. Oliver Stallybrass. Harmondsworth: Penguin, 1987.

Foucault, Michel. *Les Mots et les choses.* Paris: Gallimard, 1966.

Freud, Sigmund. *Jenseits des Lustprinzips.* 1920. *Studienausgabe.* Frankfurt/M: Fischer, 1989. Vol.3. *Psychologie des Unbewußten.* 213–72.

———. "Erinnern, Wiederholen, Durcharbeiten." 1914. *Studienausgabe.* Frankfurt/M: Fischer, 1989. Vol. 11. *Schriften zur Behandlungstechnik.* 205–15.

Friedrich, Otto. *Glenn Gould: A Life and Variations.* London: Elm Tree, 1990.

Fueß, Renate. *Nicht fragen: Zum Double-bind in Interaktionsformen und Werkstruktur bei Thomas Bernhard.* Frankfurt/Main: Lang, 1983.

Gamper, Herbert. "'Der hellsichtigste aller Narren': Der Künstler Gould als 'Gould' in Thomas Bernhards Figurengarten." *du: Zeitschrift für Kultur* 4 Apr. 1990: 68–71.

Gebesmair, Franz, and Alfred Pittertschatscher, eds. *Bernhard-Tage Ohlsdorf 1994.* Weitra: Bibliothek der Provinz, 1995.

Gehle, Holger. "Maria: Ein Versuch: Überlegungen zur Chiffrierungen Ingeborg Bachmanns im Werk Thomas Bernhards." Höller and Heidelberger-Leonard 159–80.

Genette, Gérard. "Discours du récit." *Figures III.* Paris: Seuil, 1972. 65–282.

Glaser, Horst Albert. "Die Krankheit zum Tode oder der Wille zum Leben: Überlegungen zu Thomas Bernhards Autobiographie." *Sehnsuchtsangst.* Ed. Alexander von Bormann. Amsterdam: Rodopi, 1987. 65–73.

Gleber, Anke. "*Auslöschung, Gehen*: Thomas Bernhards Poetik der Destruktion und Reiteration." *Modern Austrian Literature* 24 (1991): 85–97.

Görner, Rüdiger. "Gespiegelte Widerholungen: Zu einem Kunstgriff Thomas Bernhards." Schmidt-Dengler, Stevens and Wagner 111–25.

Gößling, Andreas. *Thomas Bernhards frühe Prosakunst: Entfaltung und Zerfall seines ästhetischen Verfahrens in den Romanen "Frost" — "Verstörung" — "Korrektur."* Berlin: de Gruyter, 1987.

———. *Die "Eisenbergrichtung": Versuch über Thomas Bernhards "Auslöschung."* Münster: Kleinheinrich, 1988.

Greiner, Ulrich. *Der Tod des Nachsommers: Aufsätze, Porträts, Kritiken zur österreichischen Gegenwartsliteratur.* Munich and Vienna: Hanser, 1979.

Greiner-Kemptner, Ulrike. *Subjekt und Fragment: Textpraxis in der (Post-) Moderne: Aphoristische Strukturen in Texten von Peter Handke, Botho Strauß, Jürgen Becker, Thomas Bernhard, Wolfgang Hildesheimer, Felix Ph. Ingold und André V. Heiz.* Stuttgart: Heinz, 1990.

Gross, Helmut. "Biographischer Hintergrund von Thomas Bernhards Wahrheitsrigorismus." *Text+Kritik* 43. 3rd ed. (1991): 112–21.

Häller, Heinz. "Glückliches Österreich: Österreich als Thema bei Thomas Bernhard." *Zeitschrift für studentische Forschung Sonderband Literatur: Österreichische Moderne.* 1 (1986): 83–111.

Hamburger, Käte. *Die Logik der Dichtung.* 3rd ed. Munich: dtv, 1987.

Handke, Peter. "Als ich *Verstörung* von Thomas Bernhard las." *Prosa Gedichte Theaterstücke Hörspiel Aufsätze.* Frankfurt/Main: Suhrkamp, 1969. 292–7.

Haslinger, Adolf. "Mütze, Mantel, Wetterfleck: Kleiderthematik und poetisches Verfahren bei Thomas Bernhard." Gebesmair and Pittertschatscher 17–33.

Heidelberger-Leonard, Irene. "Auschwitz als Pflichtfach für Schriftsteller." Höller and Heidelberger-Leonard 181–96.

Helms-Derfert, Hermann. *Die Last der Geschichte: Interpretationen zur Prosa von Thomas Bernhard.* Cologne: Böhlau, 1997.

Hennetmair, Karl Ignaz. *Aus dem "versiegelten" Tagebuch: Weihnacht mit Thomas Bernhard.* Weitra: Bibliothek der Provinz, 1992.

Hens, Gregor. *Thomas Bernhards Trilogie der Künste: "Der Untergeher," "Holzfällen," "Alte Meister."* Rochester NY: Camden House, 1999.

Herzog, Andreas. "Thomas Bernhards Poetik der prosaischen Musik." Höller and Heidelberger-Leonard 132–47.

———. "Vom Studenten der Beobachtung zum Meister der Theatralisierung: Bernhard I bis III." Gebesmair and Pittertschatscher 99–124.

Hirte, Chris. "Eine verhängnisvolle Erbschaft." Höller and Heidelberger-Leonard 86–8.

Hoell, Joachim. *Der "literarische Realitätenvermittler": Die "Liegenschaften" in Thomas Bernhards Roman "Auslöschung."* Berlin: Van Bremen, 1995.

Hoesterey, Ingeborg. "Visual Art as Narrative Structure: Thomas Bernhard's *Alte Meister.*" *Modern Austrian Literature* 21.3–4 (1988): 117–22.

Höller, Hans. "*Auslöschung* als Comédie humaine der österreichischen Geschichte." Gebesmair and Pittertschatscher 58–73.

———. "'Es darf nichts Ganzes geben', und 'In meinen Büchern ist alles künstlich': Eine Rekonstruktion des Gesellschaftsbilds von Thomas Bernhard aus der Form seiner Sprache." Jurgensen, *Annäherungen* 45–63.

———. *Kritik einer literarischen Form: Versuch über Thomas Bernhard.* Stuttgart: Heinz, 1979.

———. "Menschen, Geschichte(n), Orte und Landschaften." Höller and Heidelberger-Leonard 217–34.

——— "Rekonstruktion des Romans im Spektrum der Zeitungsrezensionen." Höller and Heidelbergerer-Leonard 53–69.

———. *Thomas Bernhard.* Reinbek bei Hamburg: Rowohlt, 1993.

Höller, Hans, and Erich Hinterholzer. "Poetik eines Schauplatzes: Texte und Photos zu Wolfsegg." Höller and Heidelberger-Leonard 235–50.

Höller, Hans, and Irene Heidelberger-Leonard, eds. *Antiautobiografie: Zu Thomas Bernhards "Auslöschung."* Frankfurt/Main: Suhrkamp, 1995.

Höller, Hans, and Matthias Part. "*Auslöschung* als Antiautobiografie: Perspektiven der Forschung." Höller and Heidelberger-Leonard 97–115.

Hornung, Alfred. "Fantasies of the Autobiographical Self: Thomas Bernhard, Raymond Federman, Samuel Beckett." *Journal of Beckett Studies* 11/12 (1989): 91–107.

Huber, Martin. "Glenn Steinway, Steinway Glenn nur für Bach: Zum Spiel mit Elementen der Schopenhauerschen Musikphilosophie in Thomas Bernhards Roman *Der Untergeher.*" *"Was wir aufschreiben, ist der Tod": Thomas-Bernhard-Symposium in Bonn 1995.* Ed. Karin Hempel-Hoos and Michael Serrer. Bonn: Bouvier, 1998. 56–68.

———. *Thomas Bernhards philosophisches Lachprogramm: Zur Schopenhauer-Aufnahme im Werk von Thomas Bernhard.* Wien: WUV-Universitätsverlag, 1992.

Huguet, Louis. *Thomas Bernhard ou le silence du Sphinx.* Cahiers de l'université de Perpignan 11. Perpignan: Presses universitaires de Perpignan, 1991.

Huntemann, Willi. *Artistik und Rollenspiel: Das System Thomas Bernhard.* Würzburg: Königshausen und Neumann, 1990.

———. "'Treue zum Scheitern': Bernhard, Beckett und die Postmoderne." *Text+Kritik* 43. 3rd ed. (1991): 42–74.

———. "Vita Thomas Bernhard." *Text+Kritik* 43. 3rd ed. (1991): 122–4.

Hutcheon, Linda. *A Poetics of Postmodernism: History, Theory, Fiction.* London: Routledge, 1988.

Ingen, Ferdinand van. "Denk-Übungen: Zum Prosawerk Thomas Bernhards." *Amsterdamer Beiträge zur neueren Germanistik* 14 (1982): 37–86.

———. "Thomas Bernhards *Holzfällen* oder die Kunst der Invektive." *Literatur und politische Aktualität.* Ed. Ferdinand van Ingen and Elrud Ibsch. Amsterdam: Rodopi, 1993. 257–82.

Jahraus, Oliver. *Die Wiederholung als werkkonstitutives Prinzip im Oeuvre Thomas Bernhards.* Frankfurt/Main: Lang, 1991.

———. *Das "monomanische" Werk: Eine strukturale Werkanalyse des Oeuvres von Thomas Bernhard.* Frankfurt/Main: Lang, 1992.

James, Henry. *The Critical Muse: Selected Literary Criticism.* Ed. and intr. Robert Gard. Harmondsworth: Penguin, 1987.

Jameson, Fredric. *Marxism and Form: Twentieth-Century Dialectical Theories of Literature.* Princeton: Princeton UP, 1971.

———. *The Political Unconscious: Narrative as a Socially Symbolic Act.* London: Routledge, 1989.

———. *Postmodernism; or, The Cultural Logic of Late Capitalism.* London: Verso, 1991.

———. *The Prison-House of Language: A Critical Account of Structuralism and Russian Formalism.* Princeton: Princeton UP, 1972.

Jaworska, Weronika. "Thomas Bernhards Helden als Selbstmörder." *Filologia Germanska* 20 (1995): 3–11.

Jelavich, Barbara. *Austria: Empire and Republic 1800–1986.* Cambridge: Cambridge UP, 1987.

Johnson, Lonnie R. "Interpreting the Anschluß." W. Wright 265–93.

Jokostra, Peter. "Experiment mit dem Wahnsinn: Eine Krankengeschichte als Roman." *Christ und Welt* 3 Apr. 1964.

Jooß, Erich. *Aspekte der Beziehungslosigkeit: Zum Werk von Thomas Bernhard.* Selb: Notos, 1976.

Jurdzinski, Gerald. *Leiden an der "Natur": Thomas Bernhards metaphysische Weltdeutung im Spiegel der Philosophie Schopenhauers.* Frankfurt/Main: Lang, 1984.

Jurgensen, Manfred, ed. *Bernhard: Annäherungen.* Bern: Francke, 1981.

———. "Das Bild Österreichs in den Werken Ingeborg Bachmanns, Thomas Bernhards und Peter Handkes." *Für und wider eine österreichische Literatur.* Ed. Kurt Bartsch, Dietmar Goldschnigg and Gerhard Melzer. Königstein/Ts: Athenäum, 1982. 152–74.

———. "Konjunktivisches Erzählen: Das fiktionale Ich auf der Flucht vor sich selbst: Thomas Bernhard, *Ja.*" *Erzählformen des fiktionalen Ich: Beiträge zum deutschen Gegenwartsroman.* Bern: Franke, 1980. 28–57.

————. "Die Sprachpartituren des Thomas Bernhard." Jurgensen, *Annähe-rungen* 99–122

————. *Thomas Bernhard: Der Kegel im Wald oder die Geometrie der Vernei-nung.* Bern: Lang, 1981.

Kaiser, Alfons. "'Ein Meister': Thomas Bernhards Autobiographie und die Tradi-tion des Bildungsromans." *Modern Austrian Literature* 29.1 (1996): 67–91.

Kaiser, Joachim. "Keiner spielte so gut wie Glenn." *Süddeutsche Zeitung* 9 Nov. 1983.

Kawin, Bruce. *Telling it Again and Again: Repetition in Literature and Film.* Ithaca: Cornell UP, 1972.

Kermode, Frank. *The Sense of an Ending: Studies in the Theory of Fiction.* London: Oxford UP, 1967.

Klug, Christian. "Interaktion und Identität: Zum Motiv der Willensschwäche in Thomas Bernhards *Auslöschung.*" *Modern Austrian Literarture* 23.3–4 (1990): 17–37.

————. "Thomas Bernhards Arbeiten fur das Salzburger *Demokratische Volks-blatt* 1952–1954." *Modern Austrian Literature* 21.3–4 (1988): 135–72.

Knight, Robert. "Narrative in Post-war Austrian Historiography." Bushell 11–36.

Kohlenbach, Margarete. *Das Ende der Vollkommenheit: Zum Verständnis von Thomas Bernhards "Korrektur."* Tübingen: Narr, 1986.

Kohlhage, Monike. *Das Phänomen der Krankheit im Werk von Thomas Bern-hard.* Herzogenrath: Murken-Altrogge, 1987.

König, Josef. *"Nichts als ein Totenmaskenball": Studien zum Verständnis der ästhetischen Intentionen im Werk Thomas Bernhards.* Frankfurt/Main: Lang, 1983.

————."Schöpfung und Vernichtung: Über die Kopf-Metapher in Thomas Bernhards Roman *Das Kalkwerk.*" *Sprache im technischen Zeitalter* 17 (1977): 231–41.

Köpnick, Lutz. "Goldberg und die Folgen: Zur Gewalt der Musik bei Tho-mas Bernhard." *Sprachkunst* 23 (1992): 267–90.

Korte, Hermann. "Dramaturgie der Übertreibungskunst: Thomas Bernhards Roman *Auslöschung. Ein Zerfall.*" *Text+Kritik* 43. 3rd ed. (1991): 88–103.

Kreuzwieser, Markus. "Schauplatz — Textplatz: Eine literarische Wande-rung." Gebesmair and Pittertschatscher 203–47.

Kucher, Gabriele. *Thomas Mann und Heimito von Doderer: Mythos und Ge-schichte: Auflösung als Zusammenfassung im modernen Roman.* Nurem-berg: Carl, 1980 [1981].

Kuhn, Gudrun. *"Ein philosophisch-musikalisch geschulter Sänger": Musikästhe-tische Überlegungen zur Prosa Thomas Bernhards.* Würzburg: Königshausen und Neumann, 1996.

Lachinger, Johann. "Paradoxer Anti-Bildungsroman." *Neues Volksblatt* [Linz] 12 Dec. 1986. Rpt. in Höller and Heidelberger-Leonard 92–3.

Langer, Renate. "Die Schwierigkeit, mit Wolfsegg fertig zu werden: Thomas Bernhards *Auslöschung* im Kontext der österreichischen Schloßromane nach 1945." Höller and Heidelberger-Leonard 197–214.

Leventhal, Robert. "The Rhetoric of Anarcho-Nihlilistic Murder: Thomas Bernhard's *Das Kalkwerk.*" *Modern Austrian Literature* 21.3–4 (1988): 19–38.

Lichtmann, Tamás ed. *Nicht aus, in, über, von Österreich.* Frankfurt/Main: Lang, 1995.

Lindenmayr, Heinrich. *Totalität und Beschränkung: Eine Untersuchung zu Thomas Bernhards Roman "Das Kalkwerk."* Königsstein/Ts: Athenäum, 1982.

Löffler, Sigrid. "'Öfter jemanden umbringen'." *Profil* 3 Sep. 1984. 60–4.

Long, Jonathan. "Veracity, Mendacity, Absurdity: Form and its Function in Thomas Bernhard's *Der Stimmenimitator.*" *Forum for Modern Language Studies* 32 (1996): 343–53.

———. "Resisting Bernhard: Women and Violence in *Das Kalkwerk, Ja* and *Auslöschung.*" *Seminar* 37:1 (February 2001): 33–52.

Ludewig, Alexandra. *Großvaterland: Thomas Bernhards Schriftstellergenese dargestellt anhand seiner (Auto-)Biographie.* Bern: Lang, 1999.

Maclean, Marie. *Narrative as Performance: The Baudelairean Experiment.* London: Routledge, 1988.

Magris, Claudio. *Der habsburgische Mythos in der österreichischen Literatur.* Salzburg: Otto Müller, 1966.

Mahler-Bungers, Annegret. "Die Antiautobiographie: Thomas Bernhard als 'Antiauto-biograph'?" *Über sich selber reden: Zur Psychoanalyse autobiographischen Schreibens.* Freiburger literaturpsychologische Gespräche 11. Ed. Johannes Cremerius. Würzburg: Königshausen und Neumann, 1992. 121–33.

Maleta, Gerda. *Seteais: Tage mit Thomas Bernhard.* Weitra: Bibliothek der Provinz, 1992.

Mann, Thomas. *Buddenbrooks.* 1901. *Gesammelte Werke in dreizehn Bänden.* Vol.1. Frankfurt/Main: Fischer, 1990.

Mariacher, Barbara. "Die Beziehung zwischen den Gegensätzen: Zu Thomas Bernhards Roman *Auslöschung. Ein Zerfall.*" Lichtmann 241–52.

———. *"Umspringbilder": Erzählen—Beobachten—Erinnern. Überlegungen zur späten Prosa Thomas Bernhards.* Frankfurt/Main: Lang, 1999.

Markolin, Caroline. *Die Großväter sind die Lehrer: Johannes Freumbichler und sein Enkel Thomas Bernhard.* Salzburg: Otto Müller, 1988.

Marquardt, Eva. *Gegenrichtung: Entwicklungstendenzen in der Erzählprosa Thomas Bernhards.* Tübingen: Niemeyer, 1990.

Mauch, Gudrun B. "Thomas Bernhards Roman *Korrektur*: Die Spannung zwischen dem erzählenden und dem erlebenden Erzähler." *Österreich in Geschichte und Literatur* 23 (1979): 207–219.

———. "Thomas Bernhards Roman *Korrektur*: Zum autobiographisch fundierten Pessimismus Thomas Bernhards." *Amsterdamer Beiträge zur neueren Germanistik* 14 (1982): 87–106.

McLintock, D. R. "Tense and Narrative Perspective in Two Works of Thomas Bernhard." *Oxford German Studies* 11 (1980): 1–26.

Meister, Christoph: *Ein Roman und sein Schauplatz: Die Logik des erzählten Raums bei Thomas Bernhard*. Bern: Lang, 1989.

Melzer, Gerhard. "Augen zu, Mund auf: Kindheit im Werk Thomas Bernhards." *Lesen und Schreiben. Literatur—Kritik—Germanistik. Festschrift für Manfred Jurgensen*. Ed. Volker Wolf. Tübingen: Francke, 1995. 150–9.

Menasse, Robert. *Das Land ohne Eigenschaften: Essay zur österreichischen Identität*. Frankfurt/Main: Suhrkamp, 1995.

———. *Überbau und Underground: Essays zum österreichischen Geist*. Frankfurt/Main: Suhrkamp, 1997.

Merchant, Carolyn. *The Death of Nature: Women, Ecology and the Scientific Revolution*. San Francisco: Harper and Row, 1990.

Meyerhofer, Nicholas J. *Thomas Bernhard*. Berlin: Colloquium, 1985.

Mitchell, Michael. "Restoration or Renewal? Csokor, the Austrian PEN Club and the Re-establishment of Literary Life in Austria, 1945–55." Bushell 54–83.

Mitchell, W. J. T., ed. *On Narrative*. Chicago: University of Chicago Press, 1981.

Mittermayer, Manfred. *Ich werden: Versuch einer Thomas-Bernhard-Lektüre*. Stuttgart: Heinz, 1988.

———. "'Die Meinigen abschaffen': Das Existenzgefüge des Franz-Josef Murau." Höller and Heidelberger-Leonard 116–31.

———. "Strauch im Winter: Thomas Bernhards *Frost* als Inszenierung eines Ichzerfalls." *Modern Austrian Literature* 21.3–4 (1988): 1–18.

———. *Thomas Bernhard*. Stuttgart: Metzler, 1995.

Mixner, Manfred. "Vom Leben zum Tode: Die Einleitung des Negationsprozesses im Frühwerk von Thomas Bernhard." Jurgensen, *Annäherungen* 65–97.

———. "'Wie das Gehirn plötzlich nur mehr Maschine ist . . .': Der Roman *Frost* von Thomas Bernhard." Bartsch, Goldschnigg and Melzer, 42–68.

Monk, Ray. *Ludwig Wittgenstein: The Duty of Genius*. London: Vintage, 1991.

Montaigne, Michel de. "De l'experience." *Oeuvres complètes*. Ed. Albert Thibaudet and Maurice Rat. Gallimard: Paris, 1962. 1041–97.

Moritz, Herbert. *Lehrjahre: Thomas Bernhard—vom Journalisten zum Dichter*. Weitra: Bibliothek der Provinz, 1992.

Neumann, Bernd. "Die Vermessung des Bernhard-Massifs." *Text+Kontext* 14.2 (1986): 169–75.

Neumeister, Sebastian. *Der Dichter als Dandy: Kafka, Baudelaire, Thomas Bernhard*. Munich: Fink, 1973.

Nickel, Eckhard. *Flaneur: Die Ermöglichung der Lebenskunst im Spätwerk Thomas Bernhards*. Heidelberg: Manutius, 1997.

Niekerk, Carl. "Der Umgang mit dem Untergang: Projektion als erzählerisches Prinzip in Thomas Bernhards *Untergeher*." *Monatshefte* 85 (1993): 464–77.

Obad, Vlado. "Die Kunst, die weh tut: Bernhards Auseinandersetzung mit dem Faschismus." *Zagreber germanistische Beiträge*. Beiheft 2 (1994): 27–36.

Obermayer, August. "Der Locus terribilis in Thomas Bernhards Prosa." Jurgensen, *Annäherungen* 215–29.

Olson, Michael P. "Misogynist Exposed? The Sister's Role in Thomas Bernhard's *Beton* and *Der Untergeher*." *New German Review* 3 (1987): 30–40.

———. "Playing it Safe: Historicising Thomas Bernhard's Jews." *Modern Austrian Literature* 27.3–4 (1994): 37–49.

———. "Thomas Bernhard, Glenn Gould and the Art of Fugue: Contrapuntal Variations in *Der Untergeher*." *Modern Austrian Literature* 24 (1991): 73–83.

O'Neill, Patrick. "Endgame Variations: Narrative and Noise in Thomas Bernhard's *Das Kalkwerk*." *Hinter dem schwarzen Vorhang: Die Katastrophe und die epische Tradition: Festschrift für Anthony Riley*. Ed. Friedrich Gaede, Patrick O'Neill and Ulrich Scheck. Tübingen: Francke, 1994. 231–41.

———. *Fictions of Discourse: Reading Narrative Theory*. Toronto: Toronto UP, 1994.

Pail, Gerhard. "Perspektivität in Thomas Bernhards *Holzfällen*." *Modern Austrian Literature* 21.3–4 (1988): 51–68.

Parth, Thomas. *"Verwickelte Hierarchien": Die Wege des Erzählens in den Jugenderinnerungen Thomas Bernhards*. Bern: Francke, 1995.

Pelinka, Anton. "Perception of the Anschluß after 1945." W. Wright 223–36.

Perloff, Marjorie. *Wittgensteins Ladder: Poetic Language and the Strangeness of the Ordinary*. Chicago: University of Chicgo Press, 1996.

Petersen, Jürgen H. "Beschreibung einer sinnentleerten Welt: Erzähltthematik und Erzählverfahren in Thomas Bernhards Romanen." Jurgensen, *Annäherungen* 143–76.

———. *Der deutsche Roman der Moderne: Grundlegung—Typologie—Entwicklung*. Stuttgart: Metzler, 1991.

Petrasch, Ingrid. *Die Konstitution der Wirklichkeit in der Prosa Thomas Bernhards: Sinnbildlichkeit und groteske Überzeichnung.* Frankfurt/Main: Lang, 1987.

Pfabigan, Alfred. *Thomas Bernhard: Ein österreichisches Weltexperiment.* Vienna: Zsolnay, 1999.

Pfaff, Peter, and Gerhard vom Hofe. *Das Elend des Polyphem: Zum Thema der Subjektivität bei Thomas Bernhard, Wolfgang Koeppen und Botho Strauß.* Königstein/Ts: Athenäum, 1980.

Plow, Geoffrey. "The Affliction of Prose: Thomas Bernhard's Critique of Self-Expression in *Korrektur, Ja,* and *Der Stimmenimitator.*" *German Life and Letters* 44.2 (1991): 133–42.

Prince, Gerald. *Narratology: The Form and Functioning of Narrative.* Berlin: Mouton, 1983.

Pütz, Herbert. "Einige textlinguistische Bemerkungen zu *Beton,*" *Text + Kontext* 14.2 (1986): 211–36.

Ransmayr, Christoph. *Die Schrecken des Eises und der Finsternis.* Frankfurt/Main: Fischer, 1987.

Rath, Helmut. "Thomas Bernhard und Carl Schmitt." *Text+Kritik* 43. 3rd ed. (1991): 30–41.

Reich-Ranicki, Marcel. "Der Sieg vor dem Abgrund." *Frankfurter Allgemeine Zeitung* 5 Feb. 1982.

Reid, Ian. *Narrative Exchanges.* London: Routledge, 1992.

Reiter, Andrea. "'Die Bachmann hab' ich sehr gern mögen, die war halt eine gescheite Frau. Eine seltsame Verbindung, nicht?' Women in Thomas Bernhard's Prose Writings." *From High Priests to Desecrators.* Ed. Ricarda Schmidt and Moray McGowan. Sheffield: Sheffield Academic Press, 1993. 155–73.

———. "Thomas Bernhard's Musical Prose." *Literature on the Threshold: The German Novel in the 1980s.* Ed. Arthur Williams, Stuart Parkes and Rowland Smith. New York: Berg, 1990. 187–207.

Riemer, Willi. "Thomas Bernhard's Glenn Gould." *Österreich aus amerikanischer Sicht: Das Österreichbild im amerikanischen Schulunterricht* 7 (1992): 28–39.

Rietra, Madeleine. "Zur Poetik von Thomas Bernhards Roman *Korrektur.*" Bartsch, Goldschnigg and Melzer 107–23.

Rimmon-Kenan, Shlomith, ed. *Discourse in Psychoanalysis and Literature.* London: Methuen, 1987.

———. "Narration as Repetition: The Case of Günter Grass's *Cat and Mouse.*" Rimmon-Kenan, *Discourse* 176–87.

———. *Narrative Fiction: Contemporary Poetics.* London: Methuen, 1983.

Roberts, David. "Korrektur der Korrektur? Zu Thomas Bernhards Lebenskunstwerk *Korrektur*." Jurgensen, *Annäherungen* 199–213.

Roberts, David, and Philip Thomson, eds. *The Modern German Historical Novel: Paradigms, Problems, Perspectives*. New York: Berg, 1991.

Rossbacher, Karl Heinz. "Thomas Bernhard: *Das Kalkwerk*." *Deutsche Romane des 20. Jahrhunderts*. Ed. Paul Michael Lützeler. Königsstein T/s: Athenäum, 1983. 372–387.

Rushdie, Salman. *Midnight's Children*. 1981. London: Vintage, 1993.

Ryu, Eun-Hee. *Auflösung und Auslöschung: Genese von Thomas Bernhards Prosa im Hinblick auf die Studie*. Frankfurt/Main: Lang, 1998.

Sagmo, Ivar. "'Denn wir alle sind in der Künstlichkeit aufgewachsen, in dem heillosen Zustand der Künstlichkeit [. . .]': Zu Thomas Bernhards Prosabände *Holzfällen* und *Alte Meister*." *Text+Kontext* 14.2 (1986): 238–52.

Saunders, Barbara. *Contemporary German Autobiography: Literary Approaches to the Problem of Identity*. London: Institute of Germanic Studies, 1985.

Schafroth, Heinz F. "Hauptwerk—oder doch nicht?" *Frankfurter Rundschau* 4 Oct. 1986. Rpt. in Höller and Heidelberger-Leonard 75–7.

Scheitler, Irmgard. "Musik als Thema und Struktur in deutscher Gegenwartsprosa." *Euphorion* 92.1 (1998): 79–102.

Schindlecker, Eva, "*Holzfällen. Eine Erregung*: Dokumentation eines österreichischen Literaturskandals." Huber and Schmidt Dengler 13–39.

Schlichtmann, Silke. *Das Erzählprinzip "Auslöschung": Zum Umgang mit der Geschichte in Thomas Bernhards Roman "Auslöschung. Ein Zerfall."* Frankfurt/Main: Lang, 1996.

Schmied, Wieland. "Der Lyriker wird Romancier: Zur Erinnerung an Thomas Bernhard." Dreissinger 320–1.

Schmidt-Dengler, Wendelin. *Bruchlinien: Vorlesungen zur österreichischen Literatur 1945 bis 1990*. Salzburg: Residenz, 1995.

———. "Der Tod als Naturwissenschaft neben dem Leben, Leben." Botond 34–41.

———. *Der Übertreibungskünstler: Studien zu Thomas Bernhard*. Vienna: Sonderzahl, 1989.

———. "Zurück zum Text: Vorschläge für die Lektüre von Thomas Bernhards *Frost*." Schmidt-Dengler, Stevens and Wagner 201–220.

———. Schmidt-Dengler, Wendelin, Adrian Stevens and Fred Wagner, eds. *Thomas Bernhard: Beiträge zur Fiktion der Postmoderne*. Frankfurt/Main: Lang, 1997.

Schultheiss, Helga. "Wie überleben? Alles weglachen!" *Nürnberger Zeitung* 22 Nov. 1986. Rpt. in Höller and Heidelberger-Leonard 79–85.

Sebald, W. G. "'Wo die Dunkelheit den Strick zuzieht': Zu Thomas Bernhard." *Die Beschreibung des Unglücks: Zur österreichischen Literatur von Stifter bis Handke.* Salzburg: Residenz, 1985. 103–14.

Sharp, Francis Michael. "Thomas Bernhard: Literary Cryogenics or Art on Ice." *Modern Austrian Literature* 21.3–4 (1988): 201–16.

Sorg, Bernhard. *Thomas Bernhard.* 2nd ed. Munich: Beck, 1992.

———. "Die Zeichen des Zerfalls: Zu Thomas Bernhards *Auslöschung* und *Heldenplatz.*" *Text + Kritik* 43. 3rd ed. (1991): 75–87.

Stanzel, Franz. *Theorie des Erzählens.* 5th ed. Göttingen: Vandenhoeck und Ruprecht, 1991.

Steinert, Hajo. *Das Schreiben über den Tod: Von Thomas Bernhards "Verstörung" zur Erzählprosa der siebziger Jahre.* Frankfurt/Main: Lang, 1984.

Steininger, Gerhard. "Guter toter Dichter. Thomas Bernhard und die Politiker: Grobe Keiler auf grobe Klötze." *Salzburger Nachrichten* 6 Feb. 1999.

Steinmann, Siegfried. "Bernhard und Peymann—müssen sie ernst genommen werden? Realität und Fiktion zweier Störenfriede." *Text+Kritik* 43. 3rd ed. (1991): 104–11.

Tabah, Mireille. "Dämonisierung und Verklärung: Frauenbilder in *Auslöschung.*" Höller and Heidelberger-Leonard 148–58.

———. "Die Methode Misogynie in *Auslöschung.*" *Thomas Bernhard: Die Zurichtung des Menschen.* Ed. by Alexander Honold and Markus Joch. Würzburg, Königshausen und Neumann, 1999. 77–82.

Tanner, Laura. *Intimate Violence: Reading Rape and Torture in Twentieth-Century Fiction.* Bloomington: Indiana UP, 1993.

Theisen, Bianca. "Comitragedies: Thomas Bernhard's Marionette Theater." *Modern Language Notes* 111 (1996): 533–59.

Thomas, Chantal: *Thomas Bernhard.* Paris: Seuil, 1990.

Thorpe, Kathleen. "Der Guckkasten des eigenen Kopfes: Anmerkungen zum Theaterbegriff in *Frost.*" Jurgensen, *Annäherungen* 177–98.

———. "Reading the Photographs in Thomas Bernhard's *Auslöschung.*" *Modern Austrian Literature* 21.3–4 (1988): 39–50.

Tismar, Jens. "Thomas Bernhards Erzählerfiguren." Botond 68–77.

Todorov, Tzvetan. *Introduction à la littérature fantastique.* Paris: Seuil, 1970.

———. *Poétique de la prose, suivi de Nouvelles recherches sur le récit.* Paris: Seuil, 1978.

———. "Typologie du roman policier." *Poétique de la Prose* 9–19.

Toolan, Michael J. *Narrative: A Critical Linguistic Introduction.* London: Routledge, 1988.

Töteberg, Michael. "Höhenflüge im Flachgau: Drei Anläufe, dreimal abgestürzt: die Vorgeschichte des Autors Thomas Bernhard." *Text+Kritik* 43. 3rd ed. (1991): 3–10.

Treichel, Hans-Ulrich. *Auslöschungsverfahren: Exemplarische Untersuchungen zur Literatur und Poetik der Moderne.* Munich: Fink, 1995.

Tschapke, Reinhard. *Hölle und Zurück: Das Initiationsthema in den Jugenderinnerungen Thomas Bernhards.* Hildesheim: Olms, 1984.

Tunner, Erika. "Scheitern mit Vorbedacht." Jurgensen, *Annäherungen* 231–41.

———. "La dance de mort dans *La Plâtrière* et *Perturbation*." *Thomas Bernhard.* Ed. Hervé Lenormand and Werner Wögerbauer. Nantes: Arcane 17, 1987. 193–200.

Vellustig, Robert. "Thomas Bernhard und *Wittgensteins Neffe*: Die Bewegung des Hinundher." *Modern Austrian Literature* 23.3–4 (1990): 39–52.

———. "Thomas Bernhards Gesprächs-Kunst." Schmidt-Dengler, Stevens and Wagner 25–46.

Vogel, Juliane. "Die Gebetbücher der Philosophen: Lektüren in den Romanen Thomas Bernhards." *Modern Austrian Literature* 21.3–4 (1988): 173–86.

Vogl, Walter. "Durch und durch verkommen, tief verrottet." *Basler Zeitung* 12 Sep. 1986. Rpt. in Höller and Heidelberger-Leonard 89–91.

Weinzierl, Ulrich. "Bernhard als Erzieher: Thomas Bernhards *Auslöschung*." *Spätmoderne und Postmoderne.* Ed. Paul Michael Lützeler. Frankfurt/Main: Fischer, 1991. 186–96.

Weiss, Gernot. *Auslöschung der Philosophie: Philosophiekritik bei Thomas Bernhard.* Würzburg: Königshausen und Neumann, 1993.

Wolfschütz, Hans. "Thomas Bernhard: The Mask of Death." Best and Wolfschütz 214–35.

Wright, Elisabeth. *Psychoanalytic Criticism: Theory in Practice.* London: Routledge, 1987.

———. "Transmission in Psychoanalysis and Literature: Whose Text is it Anyway?" Rimmon-Kenan, *Discourse* 90–103.

Wright, William, ed. *Austria 1938–1988: Anschluss and Fifty Years.* Riverside: Ariadne, 1995.

Zeyringer, Klaus. *Innerlichkeit und Öffentlichkeit: Österreichische Literatur der 80er Jahre.* Tübingen: Francke, 1992.

Zuckmayer, Karl. "Ein Sinnbild der großen Kälte." Botond 81–8.

# Index